§sas. | SAS Publishing

SAS® for Monte Carlo Studies
A Guide for Quantitative Researchers

Xitao Fan

Ákos Felsővályi

Stephen A. Sivo

Sean C. Keenan

The Power to Know.

The correct bibliographic citation for this manual is as follows: Fan, Xitao, Ákos Felsővályi, Stephen A. Sivo, and Sean C. Keenan. 2002. *SAS® for Monte Carlo Studies: A Guide for Quantitative Researchers*. Cary, NC: SAS Institute Inc.

SAS® for Monte Carlo Studies: A Guide for Quantitative Researchers

SAS Publishing provides a complete selection of books and electronic products to help customers use SAS software to its fullest potential. For more information about our e-books, e-learning products, CDs, and hardcopy books, visit the SAS Publishing Web site at **www.sas.com/pubs** or call 1-800-727-3228.

Table of Contents

Acknowledgments

Putting all the pieces together for this project has taken more than what we originally expected. During the process, it has been our pleasure to work with the patient and supportive members of the Books by Users program. We are especially grateful for two members of BBU who have made our project possible. From the very beginning of the project, Julie Platt has given us great encouragement and support, as well as her understanding and patience, even at a time when our project appeared to be faltering. Efficient, helpful, and pleasant, John West has kept us on the right path in the later stage of the project, and finally guided us to bring the project to fruition.

We are very thankful for the technical reviewers who have provided us with constructive comments and have pointed out our errors. Our gratitude goes to Jim Ashton, Brent Cohen, Michael Forno, Phil Gibbs, Sunil Panikkath, Mike Patetta, Jim Seabolt, Paul Terrill, and Victor Willson, for their time and effort in scrutinizing our draft chapters. We, of course, take full responsibility for any errors that remain.

Chapter **1** Introduction

1.1 Introduction

As the title of this book clearly indicates, the purpose of this book is to provide a practical guide for using the SAS System to conduct Monte Carlo simulation studies to solve many practical problems encountered in different disciplines. The book is intended for quantitative researchers from a variety of disciplines (e.g., education, psychology, sociology, political science, business and finance, marketing research) who use the SAS System as their major tool for data analysis and quantitative research. With this audience in mind, we assume that the reader is familiar with SAS and can read and understand SAS code.

Although a variety of quantitative techniques will be used and discussed as examples of conducting Monte Carlo simulation through the use of the SAS System, quantitative techniques per se are not intended to be the focus of this book. It is assumed that readers have a good grasp of the relevant quantitative techniques discussed in an example such that their focus will not be on the quantitative techniques, but on how the quantitative techniques can be implemented in a simulation situation.

Many of the quantitative techniques used as examples in this book are those that investigate linear relationships among variables. Linear relationships are the focus of many widely used quantitative techniques in a variety of disciplines, such as education, psychology, sociology, business and finance, agriculture, etc. One important characteristic of these techniques is that they are all fundamentally based on the least-squares principle, which minimizes the sum of residual squares. Some examples of these widely used quantitative methods are regression analysis, univariate and multivariate analysis of variance, discriminant analysis, canonical correlation analysis, and covariance structure analysis (i.e., structural equation modeling).

Before we begin our detailed discussion about how to use the SAS System to conduct Monte Carlo studies, we would like to take some time to discuss briefly a few more general but relevant topics. More specifically, we want to discuss the following:

- ❑ What is a Monte Carlo study?

- ❑ Why are Monte Carlo studies often necessary?

- ❑ What are some typical situations where Monte Carlo simulation is needed?

- ❑ Why use the SAS System for conducting Monte Carlo studies?

1.2 What Is a Monte Carlo Study?

What is a Monte Carlo study? According to Webster's dictionary, Monte Carlo relates to or involves "the use of random sampling techniques and often the use of computer simulation to obtain approximate solutions to mathematical or physical problems especially in terms of a range of values each of which has a calculated probability of being the solution" (Merriam-Webster, Inc., 1994, pp. 754-755). This definition provides a concise and accurate description for Monte Carlo studies. For those who are not familiar with Monte Carlo studies, a simple example below will give you a good sense of what a Monte Carlo study is.

1.2.1 Simulating the Rolling of a Die Twice

Suppose that we are interested in knowing what the chances are of obtaining two as the sum from rolling a die twice (assuming a fair die, of course). There are basically three ways of obtaining an answer to our question. The first is to do it the hard way, and you literally roll a die twice tens of thousands of times so that you could reasonably estimate the chances of obtaining two as the sum of rolling a die twice.

Another way of estimating the chance for this event (i.e., obtaining two as the sum from rolling a fair die twice) is to rely on theoretical probability theory. If you do that, you will reason as follows: to obtain a sum of two from rolling a fair die twice necessarily means you obtain one in each roll. The probability of obtaining one from rolling the die once is 1/6 (0.167). The probability of obtaining one from another rolling of the same die is also 1/6. Because each roll of the die is independent of another, according to probability theory, the joint probability of obtaining one from both rolls is the product of two—that is, $0.167 \times 0.167 \approx 0.028$. In other words, the chances of obtaining the sum of two from rolling a fair die twice should be slightly less than 3 out of 100, a not very likely event. In the same vein, the chances of obtaining the sum of 12 from rolling a fair die twice can also be calculated to be about 0.028. Although it is relatively easy to calculate the theoretical probability of obtaining two as the sum from rolling a fair die twice, it is more cumbersome to figure out the probability of obtaining, say, seven as the sum from rolling the die twice, because you have to consider multiple events (6+1, 5+2, 4+3, 3+4, 2+5, 1+6) that will sum up to be seven. Because each of these six events has the probability of 0.028 to occur, the probability of obtaining the sum of seven from rolling a die twice is $6 \times 0.028 = 0.168$.

Instead of relying on actually rolling a die tens of thousands of times, or on probability theory, we can also take an empirical approach to obtain the answer to the question without actually rolling a die. This approach entails a Monte Carlo simulation (MCS) in which the outcomes of rolling a die twice are *simulated*, rather than actually rolling a die twice. This approach is only possible with a computer and some appropriate software, such as SAS. The following (Program 1.1) is an annotated SAS program that conducts an MCS to simulate the chances of obtaining a certain sum from rolling a die twice.

Program 1.1 *Simulating the Rolling of a Die Twice*

```
                         *** simulate the rolling of a die twice and the distribution;
                         *** of the sum of the two outcomes;

DATA DIE(KEEP=SUM) OUTCOMES(KEEP=OUTCOME);
    DO ROLL=1 TO 10000;                      *** roll the two die 10,000 times.;
        OUTCOME1=1+INT(6*RANUNI(123));       *** outcome from rolling the first die;
        OUTCOME2=1+INT(6*RANUNI(123));       *** outcome from rolling the second die;
        SUM=OUTCOME1+OUTCOME2;               *** sum up the two outcomes.;
        OUTPUT DIE;                        *** save the sum.;
        OUTCOME=OUTCOME1; OUTPUT OUTCOMES; *** save the first outcome.;
        OUTCOME=OUTCOME2; OUTPUT OUTCOMES; *** save the second outcome.;
    END;
RUN;

PROC FREQ DATA=DIE;          *** obtain the distribution of the sum.;
    TABLE SUM;
RUN;

PROC FREQ DATA=OUTCOMES;     *** check the uniformity of the outcomes.;
    TABLE OUTCOME;
RUN;
```

Output 1.1a presents part of the results (the sum of rolling a die twice) obtained from executing the program above. Notice that the chances of obtaining two as the sum from rolling a die twice (2.99%) is very close to what was calculated according to probability theory (0.028). In the same vein, the probability of obtaining the sum of 7 is almost identical to that based on probability theory (16.85% from MCS versus 0.168 based on probability theory).

Output 1.1b presents the estimated chances of obtaining an outcome from rolling a die once. Note that the chances of obtaining 1 though 6 are basically equal from each roll of the die, as theoretically expected if the die is fair.

Output 1.1a
Chances of
Obtaining a
Sum from
Rolling a
Die Twice

SUM	Frequency	Percent	Cumulative Frequency	Cumulative Percent
2	299	2.99	299	2.99
3	534	5.34	833	8.33
4	811	8.11	1644	16.44
5	1177	11.77	2821	28.21
6	1374	13.74	4195	41.95
7	1685	16.85	5880	58.50
8	1361	13.61	7241	72.41
9	1083	10.83	8324	83.24
10	852	8.52	9176	91.76
11	540	5.40	9716	97.10
12	284	2.84	10000	100.00

Output 1.1b
Chances of
Obtaining
an Outcome
from Rolling
a Die Once

OUTCOME	Frequency	Percent	Cumulative Frequency	Cumulative Percent
1	3298	16.49	3298	16.49
2	3367	16.84	6665	33.33
3	3362	16.81	10027	50.14
4	3372	16.86	13399	67.00
5	3341	16.71	16740	83.70
6	3260	16.30	20000	100.00

Some readers may have some trouble understanding all the elements in the program presented in Program 1.1. We elaborate on the details of the program in later sections. The basic idea of this program is to use a computer to simulate the process of rolling a die twice, and then sum up the outcomes of the two rolls. After 10,000 replications (each consisting of rolling a die twice), we obtain 10,000 sums, each of which is based on rolling a die twice. By using the SAS FREQ procedure, we obtain the percentage associated with each sum (2 through 12), and this percentage represents the chance of obtaining a specific sum from rolling a die twice.

As implied from the above, Monte Carlo simulation offers researchers an alternative to the theoretical approach. There are many situations where the theoretical approach is difficult to implement, much less to find an exact solution. An empirical alternative like the one above is possible because of technological developments in the area of computing. As a matter of fact, with computing power becoming increasingly cheap and with powerful computers more widely available than ever, this computing-intensive approach is becoming more popular with quantitative researchers. In a nutshell, MCS simulates the sampling process from a defined population repeatedly by using a computer instead of actually drawing multiple samples (i.e., in this context, actually rolling dice) to estimate the sampling distributions of the events of interest. As we will discuss momentarily, this approach can be applied to a variety of situations in different disciplines.

1.3 Why Is Monte Carlo Simulation Often Necessary?

After going over the example provided in the previous section, some readers may ask the question: Why is MCS needed or necessary? After all, we already have probability theory which allows us to figure out the chances of any outcome as the sum from rolling a dice twice, and using probability theory is relatively efficient, obviously more so than writing the SAS program presented in Program 1.1. For the situation discussed above, it is true that using probability theory will be more efficient than using the MCS approach to provide the answer to our question. But please keep in mind that the example provided in Program 1.1 is for illustration purposes only, and there are many situations where MCS is needed, or where MCS is the only viable approach to providing analytic solutions to some quantitative research questions.

Although statistical theories are efficient, the validity of any statistical theory is typically contingent upon some theoretical assumptions. When the assumptions of a theory are met by the data that we have in hand, the statistical theory provides us with valid and efficient estimates of sampling distribution characteristics for a statistic of our interest. On the other hand, when the assumptions of a theory are violated in the data that we have, the validity of the estimates about certain sampling distribution characteristics based on the theory is often compromised and uncertain; consequently, we are often at a loss about how much we can trust the theoretical estimates, or about how erroneous our conclusion might be if we blindly rely on the theory, even if some crucial assumptions of the theory have been violated. It is in these kind of analytic situations that MCS becomes very useful to quantitative researchers, because this approach relies on *empirical* estimation of sampling distribution characteristics, rather than on *theoretical* expectations of those characteristics. With a large number of replications, the empirical results should asymptotically approach the theoretical results, and this can be demonstrated when the theoretical results can be obtained.

In addition to the situations discussed above in which the assumptions of statistical theories may not be met by the data we have at hand, and where consequently, MCS becomes an empirical alternative to theoretical approach, there are some other situations where statistical theories are either so weak that they can not be fully relied upon, or statistical theories simply do not exist. In these situations, MCS may be the only viable approach to providing answers to a variety of questions quantitative researchers may have.

Such situations abound. For example, the distributional characteristics of sample means are well known (e.g., unbiased, with mean equal to μ and standard deviation equal to $\sigma/\sqrt{N}$). But how about the distributional characteristics of sample medians? Is a sample median an unbiased estimate? What is the expected standard deviation of a distribution of sample medians? Does the central limit theorem, which is so important for the distribution of sample means, apply to the distribution of sample medians? These and other similar questions may not be answered from statistical theory, because it is an area where theory is weak or nonexistent. As a result, these questions may need to be answered empirically by conducting MCS, and the distributional characteristics of sample medians can be examined empirically, rather than theoretically based on statistical theory.

1.4 What Are Some Typical Situations Where a Monte Carlo Study is Needed?

As the brief discussion in the previous section indicates, for quantitative researchers in a variety of disciplines, there are two typical situations in which MCS may be called for: when theoretical assumptions of a statistical theory may not hold; and when statistical theory is either weak or nonexistent. In this section, we will discuss some typical situations in which MCS becomes relevant or necessary.

1.4.1 Assessing the Consequences of Assumption Violations

As is well known, statistical techniques can generally be classified into two broad categories: parametric and non-parametric. Most popular statistical techniques belong to the category of parametric statistics. A common characteristic for all parametric statistics is that there are certain assumptions about the distribution of the data. If the assumptions are violated, the validity of the results derived from applying these techniques may be in question. However, statistical theory itself does not usually provide any indication about what, if any, the consequences are, and how serious the consequences will be. If a quantitative researcher wonders about these questions, MCS becomes, in many situations, the only viable approach to obtaining answers to these questions.

For example, for the very popular statistical technique of analysis of variance (ANOVA), which is designed to test the hypothesis of equal means on the dependent variable from two or more groups, a fundamental assumption for the validity of the probability statement from ANOVA is that the groups involved come from populations with equal population variances on the variable of interest (homogeneity of variance assumption). What happens if, in reality, the populations that the groups are from do not have equal population variances on the variable of interest? To what extent is the probability statement from ANOVA invalid? How robust is the ANOVA technique in relation to the violation of this equal variance assumption?

To answer these and other similar questions, we may want to design a MC study in which we intentionally manipulate the variances of different population groups, draw samples from these populations, and apply ANOVA to test the hypothesis that the groups have equal means. Over repeated replications, we will be able to derive an empirical distribution of any sample statistic of our interest. Based on these distributions, we will be able to provide some answers to the questions that cannot be addressed by the statistical theory. Researchers have long used MCS to examine these issues related to ANOVA. (For a very early review, see Glass, Peckham, & Sanders 1972.)

For many popular statistical techniques, data normality is an important assumption. For example, for regression analysis, which is used in almost all disciplines, the tests for regression model parameters, both for the overall regression model fitted to the sample data and for the individual regression coefficients, it is assumed that the data are normally distributed. What are the consequences if the data are not normally distributed as assumed? How extreme should the non-normality condition be before we discount the regression analysis results as invalid? These are only a few of the potential questions quantitative researchers may ask. As discussed before, the answers to these questions may be provided by MCS, because statistical theory only stipulates what the condition should be, and it does not provide a clear indication of what the reality would be if the conditions were not met by the data.

1.4.2 Determining the Sampling Distribution of a Statistic That Has No Theoretical Distribution

In some situations, due to the complexity of a particular statistic, a theoretical sampling distribution of the statistic may not be available. In such situations, if one is interested in understanding how the statistic will vary from sample to sample, i.e., the sampling distribution of the statistic, MCS becomes one viable and realistic approach to obtaining such information.

For example, discriminant analysis and canonical correlation analysis are two multivariate statistical techniques widely used in different disciplines. In both of these techniques, there are (discriminant and canonical) function coefficients which are analogous to regression coefficients in regression analysis, and also, there are (discriminant and canonical) structure coefficients which are the correlations between the measured variables and the (discriminant and canonical) functions. Because of the complexity of these statistics, theoretical distributions are not available for these coefficients (both function and structure coefficients). In the case of discriminant or canonical correlation analysis, there has been a lot of debate about which type of coefficients, function or structure, is more stable across samples (Stevens 1996). Because theoretical sampling distributions are not available for these two type of coefficients, it is not possible to answer the question from any theoretical perspective. Faced with this lack of theoretical sampling distributions, Thompson (1991) conducted a Monte Carlo study in which the sampling distributions of these two types of coefficients were empirically generated, and based on these empirical sampling distributions, this issue was empirically investigated.

The same situation exists for exploratory factor analysis, a popular statistical technique widely used in psychometrics and in social and behavioral science research in general. In factor analysis, factor pattern coefficients play an important role. Unfortunately, the theoretical sampling distributions of factor pattern coefficients are not available. The lack of theoretical sampling distributions for factor pattern coefficients makes it difficult to assess the importance of a variable in relation to a factor. In practice, such assessment often relies on half guess work and half common sense. It is often suggested that factor pattern coefficients smaller than 0.30 be discounted. Ideally, such an assessment should be made by taking into consideration the sampling variability of the factor pattern coefficient. If one wants to get some idea about the sampling variability of such factor pattern coefficients, in the absence of the theoretical sampling distribution, MCS becomes probably the only viable approach. Quantitative researchers have utilized MCS to investigate this issue in factor analysis. (For examples, see Stevens 1996, pp. 370-371.)

In the past two decades, covariance structure analysis, more commonly known as structural equation modeling (SEM), has become a popular analytic tool for quantitative researchers. In SEM analysis, a group of descriptive model fit indices have been developed to supplement the model fit information provided by the χ^2 test, or to compensate for the widely perceived limitations of the χ^2 test in SEM, that is, it is heavily influenced by the sample size used in testing the model fit (Fan & Wang, 1998). These descriptive fit indices, however, have unknown theoretical sampling distributions, so it is not clear how these fit indices will vary from sample to sample. Again, MCS becomes the primary tool for providing the information about the variability of these fit indices, and many researchers have used this approach in their research (e.g., Fan, Thompson, & Wang 1999; Fan & Wang 1998; Marsh, Balla, & Hau 1996).

1.5 Why Use the SAS System for Conducting Monte Carlo Studies?

As discussed above, Monte Carlo simulation has been an important research area for quantitative researchers in a variety of disciplines. Because MCS is computation-intensive, it is obvious that MCS research typically requires programming capabilities. Furthermore, because many MC studies involve some type of statistical techniques and/or mathematical functions, statistical/mathematical capabilities are also essential. The SAS System has the combination of a powerful variety of built-in statistical procedures (e.g., in SAS/STAT and SAS/ETS software), mathematical functions, and the versatile programming capabilities (in base SAS, the SAS Macro Facility, and SAS/IML software). This combination makes the SAS System ideal for conducting Monte Carlo simulation research, especially research related to statistical techniques. Such a combination of built-in statistical procedures and versatile programming capabilities makes it much more convenient for MCS researchers to get their job done. Without such a combination of statistical capabilities and programming capabilities within the same system, an MCS researcher may have to deal with different systems, and consequently worry about the interface among different systems.

For example, some MCS researchers use the Fortran language for programming their Monte Carlo simulations. Because there are no built-in statistical procedures, any statistical analysis will either have to be programmed by the researchers themselves (a formidable task if one is dealing with a complicated quantitative technique), or some other system has to be used for the purpose (e.g., IMSL: International Mathematical & Statistical Libraries, a package of mathematical routines). In the latter case, the interface between different programs in the programming process may become cumbersome and difficult.

By relying on the SAS System for statistical simulation, almost all statistical procedures are already built in, and statistical analysis results are easily obtained either through the built-in statistical procedures, or through programming using the powerful interactive matrix language (PROC IML) under the SAS System. In either case, both the statistical computation and programming are highly integrated within the same system, which considerably simplifies the tasks of Monte Carlo researchers. In addition, the SAS System offers great flexibility in data generation, data transformation, obtaining and saving simulation results, etc. The completeness and the flexibility of the SAS System have convinced us that currently no other system makes Monte Carlo research, especially research involving statistical techniques, easier and more efficient than the SAS System does.

1.6 About the Organization of This Book

This book has nine chapters. The first two chapters provide an overview of the Monte Carlo research process. Starting with the third chapter, we lead the readers through a step-by-step process of conducting a Monte Carlo simulation. The third chapter discusses data generation by using different random number generators that are available in base SAS. This chapter lays the foundation for Chapter 4, which focuses on generating multiple variables that are correlated and that have different population characteristics (e.g., variables that deviate from the theoretical normal distribution to different degrees). As a matter of fact, data generation is so crucial that it is no exaggeration to say that the success of Monte Carlo simulation research hinges on the correct data generation process.

Once readers understand the data generation process in Monte Carlo simulation research, the next chapter, Chapter 5, discusses an important programming aspect of a Monte Carlo study: automation of the simulation process. Because a Monte Carlo study usually involves a large number (e.g., thousands, or hundreds of thousands) of replications (i.e., repeatedly drawing samples from a specified statistical population, and obtaining and analyzing the sample statistic of interest), unless the process can be automated through programming, MCS would be almost impossible to do in practice. Chapter 5 provides a detailed practical guide for automating the MCS process in SAS.

Chapter 6 and Chapter 7 present some Monte Carlo simulation examples involving both univariate and multivariate statistical techniques widely used by researchers in different fields. The examples in these two chapters integrate what has been discussed up to Chapter 5. Quantitative researchers who are interested in conducting Monte Carlo simulation involving statistical techniques will find these two chapters very useful and practical. For each of the examples used, a problem is presented, and the rationale for conducting a Monte Carlo simulation study is provided. Then, the SAS program and explanatory comments are presented step by step. Finally, some selected results of the simulation are presented. Thus, each example provides a complete examination of a Monte Carlo study.

In Chapter 8, our focus shifts a little, and we discuss Monte Carlo simulation examples related to the financial industry. As the examples in this chapter clearly indicate, the issues addressed by Monte Carlo simulation tend to be quite different from those in Chapters 6 and 7. For this reason, we present these examples from the financial industry in this separate chapter. Lastly, Chapter 9 provides discussion about implementing a Monte Carlo simulation study using techniques that involve SAS/ETS software. Examples related to time series analysis are presented in Chapter 9 as well.

Combined, the chapters in this book provide a systematic and practical guide to conducting Monte Carlo simulation studies in SAS. In our presentation of the examples, if a quantitative technique is involved, the quantitative technique per se is not our focus; instead, we focus more on the programming aspects of the Monte Carlo study, and the quantitative technique is presented as an example. Because of this, we provide little elaboration on the mathematical or statistical aspects of the quantitative techniques used as examples, and we assume that readers who are interested in the quantitative techniques will consult other relevant sources.

1.7 References

Fan, X., B. Thompson, and L. Wang. 1999. "The Effects of Sample Size, Estimation Methods, and Model Specification on SEM Fit Indices." *Structural Equation Modeling: A Multidisciplinary Journal* 6:56-83.

Fan, X., and L. Wang. 1998. "Effects of Potential Confounding Factors on Fit Indices and Parameter Estimates for True and Misspecified SEM Models." *Educational and Psychological Measurement* 58:699-733.

Glass, G. V., P. D. Peckham, and J. R. Sanders. 1972. "Consequences of Failure to Meet Assumptions Underlying the Fixed-Effects Analysis of Variance and Covariance." *Review of Educational Research* 42:237-288.

Marsh, H. W., J. R. Balla, and K. T. Hau. 1996. "An Evaluation of Incremental Fit Indices: A Clarification of Mathematical and Empirical Properties." In *Advanced Structural Equation Modeling: Issues and Techniques,* ed. G. A. Marcoulides and R. E. Schumacker, 315-353. Mahwah, NJ: Lawrence Erlbaum Associates.

Merriam-Webster, Inc. 1994. *Merriam-Webster's Collegiate Dictionary.* 10th ed. Springfield, MA: Merriam-Webster, Inc.

Stevens, J. 1996. *Applied Multivariate Statistics for the Social Sciences.* 3d ed. Mahwah, NJ: Lawrence Erlbaum Associates.

Thompson, B. 1991. "Invariance of Multivariate Results: A Monte Carlo Study of Canonical Function and Structure Coefficients." *Journal of Experimental Education* 59:367-382.

Chapter 2 Basic Procedures for Monte Carlo Simulation

2.1 Introduction

In Chapter 1 we provided an introduction to this book in which we discussed what a Monte Carlo (MC) study is and what some of its major characteristics are. In this chapter, we continue our discussion started in Chapter 1, and we will discuss the basic procedures or steps needed to successfully implement an MC study. In a very general sense, the following are the basic steps necessary for an MC study:

- ❑ Ask questions that can be examined through a Monte Carlo study.

- ❑ Design a Monte Carlo study to provide answers to the questions.

- ❑ Generate data.

- ❑ Implement the quantitative technique.

- ❑ Obtain and accumulate the statistic of interest from each replication.

- ❑ Analyze the accumulated statistic of interest.

- ❑ Draw conclusions based on the empirical results.

In this chapter, we will provide some discussion related to each of the above steps. To facilitate our discussion, we will use one simple SAS MC example to illustrate each step listed above.

2.2 Asking Questions Suitable for a Monte Carlo Study

It may be obvious, but unless you ask the right question(s), it may not be possible or necessary to conduct an MC study in the first place. As discussed in Chapter 1, an MC study is essentially concerned about how a statistic of interest may vary from sample to sample. In other words, an MC study is about obtaining the sampling distribution of a statistic of interest by repeatedly drawing random samples from a specified population. In this sense, the questions suitable for an MC study are typically related to some aspects of the sampling distribution of a statistic.

For example, you may be interested in comparing the distribution of a sample median versus that of a sample mean, or you may be interested in knowing how the variability of a sample correlation coefficient is influenced by the sample size, or you are interested in something related to more sophisticated statistical techniques, such as how data non-normality affects the sampling distribution of regression coefficients in regression analysis. In short, questions related to sampling distributions of a statistic of interest are generally suitable for an MC study, especially when such questions do not have trustworthy theoretical answers because 1) the theoretical assumptions for the statistical theory are violated; 2) the theory about the statistic of interest is weak; or 3) no theory exists about the statistic of interest. Our examples in later chapters will illustrate a variety of questions that are suitable for an MC study. In this chapter, we will use a simple example to illustrate the steps in a typical MC study.

Correlation between two variables is the statistic of interest in many applications. For example, an educator may be interested in the relationship between time spent on school work at home and academic achievement in school; an industrial psychologist may be interested in the relationship between mechanical aptitude and job performance; a stock analyst may be interested in the strength of the relationship between a company's price/sale (P/S) ratio and the company's stock performance.

As an example of an MC study in this chapter, we are interested in the question: How high should a correlation coefficient be before we feel comfortable that the observed correlation coefficient is unlikely to have occurred by chance (i.e., the observed value of a sample correlation coefficient is not the result of sampling error)? In other words, although two variables may not be correlated (population correlation coefficient $\rho=0$), that does not mean that for every sample, the sample correlation coefficient between the two variables will always be zero. As a matter of fact, almost none of the samples will have a correlation coefficient of zero because of sampling variability of the statistic: in some samples, the sample correlation coefficient may be positive; in some other samples, it may be negative. Some samples may have sample correlation coefficients substantially different from zero, while others have correlation coefficients very close to zero, or even zero itself. (This occurrence, however, will be rare.) In the long run, however, the average of the sample correlation coefficients should be zero or very close to zero.

The situation described above means that, from a particular sample, we may obtain a correlation coefficient quite different from zero even if there is absolutely no relationship between the two variables of interest. A natural question to ask is: How high should a sample correlation coefficient be before we conclude that the sample coefficient represents some degree of *real* relationship between the two variables, not just the occurrence due to sampling error? Let's suppose that the statistical theory about the correlation coefficient between two variables were not well developed, or that we simply do not trust the validity of the theory that much. We therefore want to adopt an empirical approach to provide some answers to our question.

Because we are interested in the variability of sample correlation coefficients when the true population correlation coefficient is zero, our question is easily translated into a question about the sampling distribution of the correlation coefficient when the null hypothesis is true, i.e., when the true population correlation coefficient is zero. Because we want some *empirical* answers to our question, not theoretical answers, it is a question suitable for an MC study. In this chapter, we will use SAS to implement an MC study to obtain answers to this question.

2.3 Designing a Monte Carlo Study

Once we have identified the question(s) suitable for an MC study, we need to figure out how we can answer our questions by designing an appropriate MC study. To do this, we have to consider the major factor(s) that may affect the variability of sample correlation coefficients. The variability of sample correlation coefficients is affected by sample size. To see the influence of sample size on the statistics of interest (the sample correlation coefficient, in this case), let us consider a simpler and more intuitive case.

Assume that in a moderately large university of 20,000 students, the true population ratio of male vs. female student numbers is 1, that is, 50% of students are male and 50% are female. However, if we get a random sample of students, the percentages of male vs. female students will almost certainly differ from 50/50. If we get another random sample, it will almost certainly differ from both 50/50 (the population ratio) and from whatever ratio we obtained from the first sample. Now the question is, how much can the sample ratio vary just by chance, or simply due to sampling error?

The answer to this question will not be known unless we take sample size into consideration. If we draw a random sample of ten students, it is possible to have a sample with just five male and five female students (proportion = 0.5), which actually reflects the population proportions, but it is also possible to have 10 male and zero female students. From another sample of ten students, we may get one male and nine female students. So under the condition of sample size ten (n=10), the proportion of male students may vary from 1 to 0, quite far from 0.5. But if we draw a *random* sample of 100 students (n=100), we are much *less* likely to have 90 male and 10 female students. In other words, although it may not be too surprising to have a sample male student proportion of 0.9 when the sample size is 10, it is very *unlikely* that we will have a sample male student proportion of 0.9 or 0.1 when the sample size is 100. This simple and intuitive example contains what is scientifically true: the variability of a sample statistic is inversely affected by sample size: the larger the sample size, the smaller the variability of the sample statistic.

2.3.1 Simulating Pearson Correlation Coefficient Distributions

Now let us come back to our correlation coefficient example. We want to know how much the sample correlation coefficient can vary when the null hypothesis is true (the population correlation coefficient between two variables is zero). In order to have some understanding about the issue, we have to take sample size into consideration. So sample size becomes a prominent factor in our MC study design.

Although there may be other factors we can consider, e.g., whether data are normally distributed or not, or the degree of data non-normality, for the time being and to avoid unnecessarily complicating the matter, we only want to consider sample size in our MC study design.

After deciding that only sample size will be considered as a factor in our MC study about the distribution of sample correlation coefficients, next we need to consider what sample size conditions we are willing to simulate. In this illustrative example, we make a somewhat arbitrary decision that we are going to simulate sample size conditions of n=10, 20, 40, and 100. Of course, if we are not concerned about the time it takes for the computer to get the job done, we can add as many sample size conditions as we want.

Once the question about sample size conditions is settled, we need to consider another important issue: Under each sample size condition, how many random samples are we going to draw from a specified statistical population that represents the null hypothesis (i.e., the true population correlation coefficient is zero between the two variables)? The decision must be made carefully so that reasonably accurate answers to our question can be obtained. Because we are trying to obtain the sampling distributions of correlation coefficients under the true null hypothesis, the number of samples drawn under a particular sample size condition will greatly influence the accuracy of the simulated sampling distribution of correlation coefficients. If too few samples are drawn under each sample size condition, our answers might be too crude to be useful. For our illustrative example, let's assume that, after our review of previous studies in this area, we decide that 2,000 samples is the minimum number we can live with, and that a sampling distribution of correlation coefficients based on 2,000 random samples for a particular sample size condition should be accurate enough for our illustrative purpose.

We have now figured out all the important design characteristics for our MC study of sampling distributions of correlation coefficients, as follows:

- ❑ Four sample size conditions: 10, 20, 50, and 100.

- ❑ Under each sample size condition, 2,000 random samples will be drawn from the statistical population under which there is zero correlation between two variables, i.e., the statistical population represents the true null hypothesis (population $\rho=0$).

Given our design, there will be $4 \times 2000 = 8000$ random samples to be drawn from the specified statistical population under the true null hypothesis. This design is implemented in the annotated Program 2.1. Although we provide more details later about Program 2.1, you can probably see that the number of samples under each sample size condition is 2,000 (SAS macro variable NO_SMPL=2000), and there are four sample size conditions (SAS macro variable SMPLSIZE=10, 20, 50, 100).

Program 2.1 *Simulating Pearson Correlation Coefficient Distributions*

```
LIBNAME CORR 'C:\CORR_EG';
%LET NO_SMPL=2000;                         *** macro variable for # of random samples;
                                           *** under each sample size condition;

%MACRO CORR_RDM;
%DO A = 1 %TO 4;                           *** specify four sample size conditions;
   %IF &A=1 %THEN %DO; %LET SMPLSIZE=10;   %END;
   %IF &A=2 %THEN %DO; %LET SMPLSIZE=20;   %END;
   %IF &A=3 %THEN %DO; %LET SMPLSIZE=50;   %END;
   %IF &A=4 %THEN %DO; %LET SMPLSIZE=100; %END;

%DO B=1 %TO &NO_SMPL;                      *** # of samples for each sample size condition;

DATA DAT;             *** generate two uncorrelated random variables;
   DO I=1 TO &SMPLSIZE;
     X=RANNOR(0);
     Y=RANNOR(0);
     OUTPUT;
   END;
                      *** use PROC CORR to get Pearson r, results as SAS data set PEARSON;
PROC CORR DATA=DAT NOPRINT OUTP=PEARSON;
   VAR X Y;
RUN;
               *** collect Pearson r from each sample, add sample size condition;
               *** accumulate Pearson r from samples by appending the Pearson r from a
                   sample to a SAS System file COR_RDM;

DATA PEARSON; SET PEARSON;
   SMPLSIZE=&SMPLSIZE;
   IF _NAME_='X';
   CORR=Y;
   KEEP CORR SMPLSIZE;
PROC APPEND BASE=CORR.COR_RDM;
%END;
%END;
%MEND CORR_RDM;
%CORR_RDM;
RUN; QUIT;
                      *** obtain descriptive statistics on the Pearson r's;
                      *** under each of the four sample size conditions;
DATA A; SET CORR.COR_RDM;
PROC SORT; BY SMPLSIZE;
PROC MEANS; BY SMPLSIZE;
   VAR CORR;
TITLE1 'DESCRIPTIVE STATS FOR PEARSON RS BETWEEN TWO RANDOM VARIABLES';
TITLE2 'FOR FOUR DIFFERENT SAMPLE SIZE CONDITIONS';
TITLE3 '*************************************************************';
RUN; QUIT;
                           * obtain bar graphs to show the
                           distribution characteristics of
                           Pearson rs under true null hypothesis
                           for each of the four sample size
                           conditions ;

DATA A; SET CORR.COR_RDM;
PROC SORT; BY SMPLSIZE;

AXIS1 LABEL=(HEIGHT=1.0 FONT=TRIPLEX) ORDER=(0 TO 20 BY 5)
      VALUE=(HEIGHT=1.0 FONT=TRIPLEX) MINOR=NONE;
AXIS2 LABEL=(HEIGHT=1.0 FONT=TRIPLEX) VALUE=(HEIGHT=1.0 FONT=TRIPLEX)
      MINOR=NONE;
PATTERN COLOR=BLACK VALUE=X2;
```

```
PROC GCHART DATA=A; BY SMPLSIZE;  * use PROC GCHART for nicer graphs;
  VBAR CORR/ TYPE=PERCENT
           MIDPOINTS= -.9 TO .9 BY .05
           RAXIS=AXIS1 MAXIS=AXIS2
           WIDTH=1
           SPACE=1;
RUN; QUIT;
```

2.4 Generating Sample Data

Once the MC study design has been worked out, the next step is to generate sample data to be used in the MC study. It is worth pointing out that data generation is probably the most important step in any MC study. This is so because MC study results are based on the data generated in the process. If the data generated in the process are not what you think they should be, the validity of the MC study results will obviously be in serious question. From this perspective, the importance of data generation in an MC study can never be overemphasized.

Depending on the complexity of an MC study, the process of data generation can involve three major steps, as follows:

1. Generate data from a distribution with known characteristics.

2. Transform the data so that the data have desired shapes.

3. Transform the data so that the simulated variables can be considered as samples randomly drawn from a population with a known inter-variable relationship pattern.

2.4.1 Generating Data from a Distribution with Known Characteristics

This first step is really what we need for our illustrative example of simulating the distribution of correlation coefficients under the true null hypothesis of zero population correlation between two variables. For our purposes, we need to generate two variables not related to each other. We choose to generate two independent *normally distributed* random variables. Because the two variables are random and independent, they are not related to each other. In other words, the value of one variable will be totally unrelated to the value of the other variable. We can use the SAS random normal variable generator RANNOR to accomplish this. The two variables generated by the program are called X and Y in the program. Because X and Y are generated as independent random samples from a normal distribution, we know the underlying distributions for X and Y have a mean of 0 and a standard deviation of 1. In statistical terms, both X and Y are random variables from population distributed as $N(0,1)$. The details about the SAS data generator will be discussed in Chapter 3.

Program 2.1 presented the SAS code for data generation for our problem through the use of base SAS. In some examples in later chapters, the IML procedure (PROC IML) of SAS/IML (Interactive Matrix Language) will be used for the same purpose. Either way, the same thing can be accomplished: two independent random variables are generated from the normal distribution [$N(0,1)$] for specified sample size conditions (SMPLSIZE).

2.4.2 Transforming Data to Desired Shapes

In many situations, sample data generated in the previous step need to be transformed to simulate particular population characteristics. There are two major purposes for which it is necessary to transform an individual variable: 1) to transform the data so that the data can be considered as a random sample from a population with a *specified mean and standard deviation*; 2) to transform the data so that the data can be considered as a random sample from a population with *specified shapes* (e.g., specified population skewness and kurtosis). The first transformation is simply a linear transformation that does not change the shape of the data. That is, if originally it is normally distributed, it remains normally distributed after the transformation. For any variable X, such a linear transformation can easily be achieved by the formula

$$X_{new} = X * SD_{new} + Mean_{new} \tag{2.1}$$

where X_{new} is the transformed variable, SD_{new} is the desired new standard deviation, and $Mean_{new}$ is the desired new mean. The new variable X_{new} has exactly the same distribution shape as X in terms of skewness and kurtosis.

The second kind of transformation changes the shape of the distribution—for example, in terms of skewness and/or kurtosis. This kind of transformation is often necessary in statistical simulation to investigate the effect of non-normality on certain statistics of interest. This transformation is more complicated, and the necessary details for such a transformation will be discussed in Chapter 4. In our illustrative example in Program 2.1, there is no need to perform either of the two transformations. The SAS programming examples for these transformations will be presented in later chapters.

2.4.3 Transforming Data to Simulate a Specified Population Inter-variable Relationship Pattern

The two transformations discussed in the previous section involve only one variable at a time. In many situations, multiple variables are used in analyses, and the multiple variables are supposed to be correlated to specified degrees. In such situations, procedures are needed to transform the independent variables (such X and Y in Program 2.1) into correlated variables with specified correlation pattern. This transformation will be discussed in Chapter 4, where multivariate data generation is covered. Obviously, for our illustrative example of correlation coefficient distribution under the true null hypothesis of no relationship between the two variables, we want to keep the two variables (X and Y) independent, so there is no need to implement this transformation.

2.5 Implementing the Statistical Technique in Question

Although some MC studies do not involve statistical techniques, in many MC studies, some type(s) of statistical techniques are involved. For example, the illustrative MC study example in Chapter 1 (simulating the sum of throwing a dice twice) involves only simple frequency counts. On the other hand, in the example presented in Program 2.1, the Pearson product-moment correlation coefficient needs to be computed for each of the 8,000 samples. There are, of course, different ways to implement the statistical computation of the Pearson correlation coefficient. One can either program the statistical computation by using either the IML procedure (PROC IML) or base SAS, or one can use SAS procedures. In Program 2.1, we chose to use the SAS CORR procedure (PROC CORR) to do the computation, which minimizes the programming demand for the task. As readers can see, the SAS code for this step is very straightforward.

2.6 Obtaining and Accumulating the Statistic of Interest

Once the statistical technique is implemented and the statistic of interest is computed, the statistic of interest *from each random sample* must be obtained, and it must be accumulated across samples. In our example in Program 2.1, we need to obtain each of the 8,000 correlation coefficients (2,000 under each of the four sample size conditions) and to accumulate them for later analyses. Again, this can be accomplished in different ways. In Program 2.1, we used PROC CORR for computing Pearson r, so the computed Pearson r is contained in the PROC CORR output. To obtain the Pearson r from each sample, we request SAS to output the results of PROC CORR to a SAS data set named PEARSON (OUTP=PEARSON). Because the PEARSON data set contains more than just the Pearson r that we are interested in, we need to do a little programming to keep only what we want to obtain, and discard the rest. In order to do that, we need to understand what the PEARSON data set contains.

The contents of the temporary PEARSON data set can be displayed by running a simple PROC PRINT DATA=PEARSON step. The following is the output of the temporary SAS data set PEARSON for a small (n=4) hypothetical data set.

OBS	_TYPE_	_NAME_	X	Y
1	MEAN		1.50000	2.75000
2	STD		0.57735	0.50000
3	N		4.00000	4.00000
4	CORR	X	1.00000	**0.57735**
5	CORR	Y	0.57735	1.00000

In this temporary SAS data set, the Pearson r, which is highlighted above, is the only thing we are interested in keeping at this time. Although the sample size N is also relevant, it can be obtained somewhere else. A few commands in Program 2.1 accomplish the goal of discarding everything else from the temporary PEARSON data set except the Pearson r. Sample size information is added to the data. So now, the temporary PEARSON data set only contains two variables: CORR for the sample Pearson correlation coefficient, and SMPLSIZE for the sample size condition.

After obtaining the statistic of interest from a sample, that statistic should be stored somewhere so that SAS will go on to draw another sample and repeat the whole process again. In the example in Program 2.1, this is achieved by appending the Pearson correlation coefficient from each sample, together with the information about sample size (SMPLSIZE), to a permanent SAS data set (COR_RDM) on the hard disk in the directory "C:\CORR_EG", as indicated by the LIBNAME statement at the beginning of the SAS program in Program 2.1. Once this information is stored in the permanent SAS data set (COR_RDM), the SAS program repeats the process for the remaining 7,999 samples until all 8,000 Pearson correlation coefficients from all the 8,000 samples have been accumulated.

2.7 Analyzing the Accumulated Statistic of Interest

By the time the statistic of interest from all the samples has been obtained and accumulated, the simulation process of the MC study is complete. Depending on the nature of the question(s) in a particular MC study, data analysis after the simulation may be simple or complicated. In our illustrative example in Chapter 1 (Program 1.1), the analyses are simple and straightforward frequency counts, proportions, and cumulative proportions. In some MC studies, the analyses of the data accumulated from an MC simulation can be quite complicated. As a matter of fact, data analyses in an MC study are no different from data analyses in many other research situations.

In our illustrative example in Program 2.1, the data analyses involve obtaining the descriptive statistics of the Pearson r sample distributions under the four sample size conditions. Output 2.1 presents this basic descriptive information. In addition, the Pearson r sample distributions are presented in bar graphs that graphically illustrate the distributions of the Pearson r's under the true null hypothesis for the four sample size conditions (Figure 2.1). Of course, other types of analyses can be conducted on the data, but to keep our presentation simple, we do only two here.

Output 2.1
Descriptive
Statistics for
Pearson r
Sample
Distributions

```
----------------------------------SMPLSIZE=10----------------------------
      N            Mean         Std Dev        Minimum        Maximum
-------------------------------------------------------------------------
     2000      -0.0079822      0.3400933     -0.9171933      0.8923352


----------------------------------SMPLSIZE=20----------------------------
      N            Mean         Std Dev        Minimum        Maximum
-------------------------------------------------------------------------
     2000      -0.0063981      0.2293055     -0.7653282      0.7339653


----------------------------------SMPLSIZE=50----------------------------
      N            Mean         Std Dev        Minimum        Maximum
-------------------------------------------------------------------------
     2000       0.0026309      0.1418088     -0.4412904      0.4752965


---------------------------------SMPLSIZE=100----------------------------
      N            Mean         Std Dev        Minimum        Maximum
-------------------------------------------------------------------------
     2000      -0.0022238      0.1036991     -0.4455782      0.4067127
```

Figure 2.1   *Empirical Distributions of Sample Correlation Coefficients under the True Null Hypothesis of $\rho=0$*

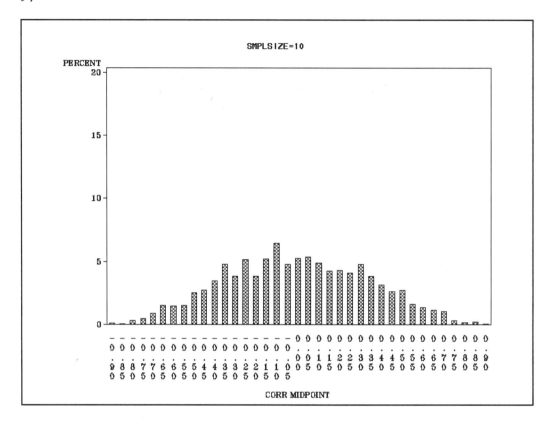

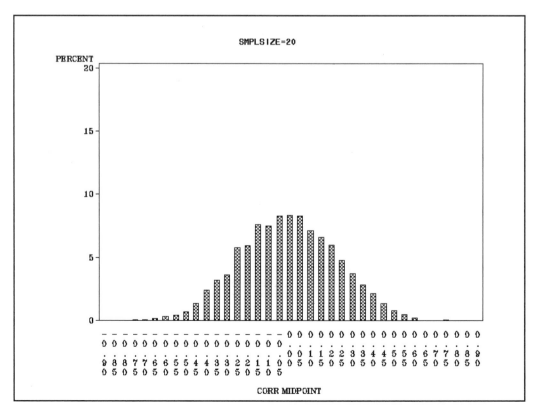

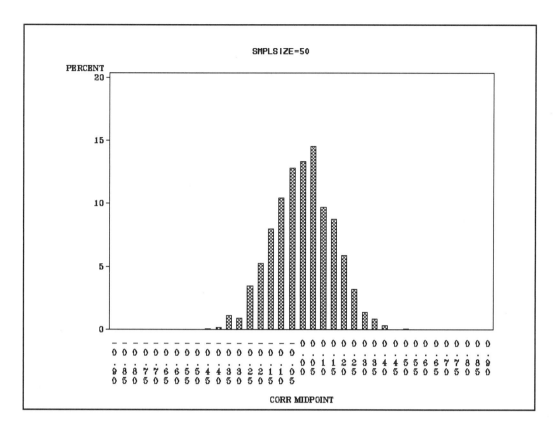

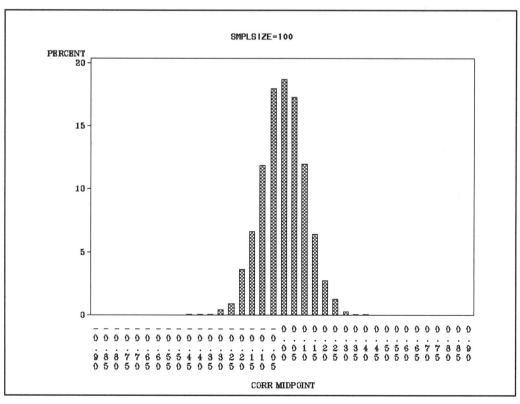

2.8 Drawing Conclusions Based on the MC Study Results

We conducted our MC study for the purpose of answering our questions about the distributional characteristics of the statistic of interest to determine what factors may affect such distributional characteristics. The data analyses conducted in the previous step should be conducive to providing answers to the question(s) that motivated the MC study in the first place. To illustrate this last step in the MC study, let us go back to our original question: How high should a correlation coefficient be before we feel comfortable that the observed correlation coefficient is unlikely to have occurred by chance (i.e., the observed value of the sample correlation coefficient is the result of sampling error)? To answer this question, we conducted an MC study to obtain the sampling distributions of Pearson r's under the true null hypothesis (population correlation $\rho=0$). We wanted to see how high a sample correlation coefficient could be just by sampling chance alone when the two variables have no relationship at all. Because the variability of the sample correlation coefficient is affected by sample size, we considered four sample size conditions in our MC study.

Output 2.1 presented the descriptive statistics for the correlation coefficients under the four sample size conditions (N=10, 25, 50, 100). Two observations are noted from Output 2.1. First, the means of the correlation coefficients under each of the four sample size conditions are very close to zero. This makes perfect sense, because the two variables are *independent* random variables not related to each other. As a result, although sample correlation coefficients may vary within certain ranges, the mean of the sample correlation coefficients should converge on the population coefficient ($\rho=0$). Second, the standard deviation of the sampling distribution of the correlation coefficient is larger when the sample size is smaller, and it decreases with an increase in sample size. This indicates that when the sample size is small, there is more variability in the sample correlation coefficients than there is when the sample size is large. The same phenomenon is reflected by the range (range = maximum - minimum).

Figure 2.1 presents a graphic illustration of the distribution of sample correlation coefficients for the four sample size conditions under the true null hypothesis ($\rho=0$). These four graphs make it very obvious that even when the population correlation coefficient is zero, we may observe substantial *sample* correlation coefficients. For example, for a random sample of 10 observations, the sample correlation coefficient can easily be as high (low) as ±0.50. But when the sample size increases to 100, it becomes highly unlikely that one could obtain a sample correlation coefficient close to ±0.50 just by chance. Based on the simulation results presented in Figure 2.1, we can make probability statements about obtaining an outcome under a sample size condition. For example, we can say that if the population correlation coefficient is 0 ($\rho=0$), for a sample of 10 observations (N=10), the probability of getting a sample r ≥ 0.50 in absolute value is higher than 0.05. That is,

$$p \text{ (getting } r \geq 0.50 \text{ or } r \leq -0.50 \mid \rho=0) > 0.05$$

Obviously, if an outcome could have occurred by chance with considerable probability, this outcome would not be considered trustworthy. In other words, if you have obtained a correlation of ±0.50 from a sample of 10, this would not give you much confidence that there is indeed a relationship between the two variables under your consideration. In statistical terms, you would not feel comfortable in rejecting the null hypothesis that there is no correlation between the two variables, because the statistical evidence is not strong enough.

2.9 Summary

In this chapter, we navigated conceptually through the major steps in a typical Monte Carlo study, such as study design considerations, the data generation process, obtaining and accumulating the statistic of interest, etc. These steps are common for Monte Carlo studies in general. Among these major steps, data generation warrants special attention, because the validity of the Monte Carlo study's results hinges on this step. In Chapters 3 and 4, we provide some mathematical and procedural details for the data generation process.

Chapter 3 Generating Univariate Random Numbers in SAS

3.1 Introduction

Simulation is the representation of the behavior of a physical or abstract system by the behavior of another system (Ralston 1976). Simulation is applied when the experiment with or the observation of the original system is dangerous (e.g., an epidemic or a nuclear reaction), impossible (global warming, meteor impact), expensive (optimal shape of a new vehicle), or when we want to study the effect of many different conditions on the system (effect of a new policy), etc. It is also utilized when the original system is too complicated to be investigated with exact analytic tools and the simulation can simplify the problem. The computer-based simulation can be deterministic or stochastic. In the latter case, which is also called Monte Carlo simulation, at least one variable of the system behaves by chance. Thus, we generate many sets of random numbers obeying certain a priori distributions and examine the results of our model.

The heart of every Monte Carlo simulation is the random number generator. And the heart of the various random number generators is the *uniform random number generator*, because the random numbers of a certain distribution can be derived from uniformly distributed random numbers (Rubinstein 1981). The concept of randomness is a mysterious one, because no events in nature are truly random. We may not know all their influencing factors, and thus they just appear random to our limited knowledge. Similarly, our computer-generated random numbers are called pseudo or quasi-random numbers, because they are constructed by some deterministic algorithm and they only "appear" random. However, if they satisfy the randomness required by our problem, we can utilize them.

Generating a random number in SAS requires a simple function or subroutine call in a DATA step (or in PROC IML), as shown here. Variable *R* in the following two examples holds a uniform random number.

```
DATA …;                              DATA …;
    …;                                   …;
    R = RANUNI(123);                     SEED = 123;
    …;                                   CALL RANUNI(SEED,R);
    RUN;                                 …;
                                         RUN;
```

In this chapter, we will discuss many aspects of generating univariate random numbers. We will introduce and review RANUNI, the uniform random number generator of the SAS System. Then, we will test certain measures of uniformity and randomness. Most random number generators can be invoked as functions or as CALL routines, and their differences will be examined later in this chapter, along with the use of the seed value. A table will describe all random number generator functions available in SAS for reference purposes.

This chapter will also present several examples for creating random samples with various characteristics. Finally, the RANTBL function will be discussed separately for its practical importance in generating random numbers of any distribution.

3.2 RANUNI, the Uniform Random Number Generator

The RANUNI function (and the identical UNIFORM) returns uniform random numbers utilizing the most widely used generator, the congruential generator, which originates from D.H. Lehmer (Lehmer 1951). This generator produces random numbers by using the following recursive formula, where R_i is the *i*th random number, *a* is the multiplier, and *c* is the increment:

$$R_{i+1} = (aR_i + c) \ (\mathrm{mod} \ m) \ i = 0, 1, 2, \ldots \tag{3.1}$$

The formula can be written in the SAS statement

```
R = MOD(A*R+C,M);
```
(3.2)

The stream of random numbers (R_i) is started and controlled by the first random number (R_0), which is called the *seed*. The generator produces uniform random numbers in (0,*m*), but its SAS implementation returns them transformed into (0,1) by dividing them by *m*. Since the actual random numbers returned by RANUNI and the seed along with its subsequent values are the same irrespective of that transformation, the terms *seed* and *random numbers* are used interchangeably in this chapter.

The above constants in the SAS System are $a = 397,204,094$, $m = 2^{31}-1$ (which is a prime), and $c = 0$. Due to (3.1), the seed (or R_0) value must be an integer satisfying $1 \le R_0 \le m-1$ (m-1=2147483646.) In this special case, when $c = 0$, the generator is called a *multiplicative congruential generator*. (If we wish to calculate the random numbers with these constants substituted into (3.2), we will not obtain the random numbers generated by SAS software, because the calculations require extended precision beyond the standard double precision.) This type of generator has been extensively tested and found to be a reliable one (Clark & Woodward 1992; Fishman & Moore 1982; Killam 1987). The period of this generator, i.e., the number of elements produced before it begins repeating the elements, is $m = 2^{31}-2$. The program below gives the length of the period to be $2^{31}-2$.

```
DATA _NULL_;
    R0=RANUNI(123);
    DO I=2 TO 2**31-1;
        IF RANUNI(123)=R0
            THEN DO; PUT 'End of period at element #' i;
                STOP;
            END;
    END;
    RUN;
```

A great deal of attention and care have been given to the statistical tests of the random number generators. However, there is no single definition of randomness or a single statistical test for it. We should extensively test a generator before accepting it. The most widely applied tests are the chi-square, Kolmogorov-Smirnov, Cramer-von Mises, serial, run, gap, poker, permutation, serial correlation, and maximum tests (Knuth 1982; Rubinstein 1981). RANUNI must satisfy two requirements: *uniformity* and *randomness*.

3.3 Uniformity (the EQUIDST Macro)

Uniformity means that the random numbers fill the unit interval uniformly. It can easily be tested by the equidistribution or frequency test. One such test is described by the EQUIDST macro (Program 3.1). It tests uniformity by dividing (0,1) into 2, 3,...n subintervals of equal length:

2-subinterval division: $(0, \frac{1}{2}), (\frac{1}{2}, 1)$

3-subinterval division: $(0, \frac{1}{3}), (\frac{1}{3}, \frac{2}{3}), (\frac{2}{3}, 1)$

...

n-subinterval division: $(0, \frac{1}{n}), (\frac{1}{n}, \frac{2}{n}),... (\frac{n-1}{n}, 1)$

The macro tallies the frequencies in these subintervals and calculates the goodness-of-fit test for the uniform distribution. If the random numbers uniformly fill (0,1), the subintervals of any number of divisions would get about the same number of random numbers. Thus, most of the divisions will result in a non-significant chi-square value, i.e., the null hypothesis (the random numbers are from a uniform distribution) can be kept. Output 3.1 shows the results when we generate one million random numbers and divide (0,1) into 2,3,...,100 subintervals with the following macro call:

```
%EQUIDST(NRANNUM=1000000,HNSINT=100,SEED=123)
```

RANUNI really generates uniform random numbers, because only 9 out of 99 divisions have significant chi-square values at the 0.05 level. If we choose the 0.01 level, then none of the divisions reject the uniformity. The SERIAL macro (published in Felsővályi 1994) provides another type of uniformity test for RANUNI, where we test whether the random numbers defined as vectors in the *n*-dimensional space fill the unit hypercube uniformly.

Program 3.1 *The EQUIDST Macro*

```
/*******************************************************/
/* Macro EQUIDST executes an equidistribution test to  */
/* check the uniform distribution of random numbers    */
/* generated by RANUNI.                                */
/*                                                     */
/* Parameters:                                         */
/* NRANNUM # of random numbers to be generated.        */
/* HNSINT  highest number of subintervals. The macro   */
/*         calculates the chi-square test for          */
/*         2,3,...,HNSINT divisions of equal subintervals */
/*         of (0,1).                                   */
/* SEED    Seed of RANUNI function.                    */
/*******************************************************/
%MACRO EQUIDST(NRANNUM=,HNSINT=,SEED=0);
  DATA WORK(KEEP=SINTERV X);

        /* generate the requested number of random numbers.*/

        LENGTH SINTERV X 3;
        DO I=1 TO &NRANNUM;
          R=RANUNI(&SEED);

            /* determine the interval number (variable 'X') into */
            /* which the random number falls. Do this for each   */
            /* division (2-subinterval, 3-subinterval,...        */
            /* divisions).                                       */

            DO SINTERV=2 TO &HNSINT;
                X=1+INT(SINTERV*R);
                OUTPUT;
            END;
        END;
        RUN;

  /* determine the frequency of each subinterval by division.  */

  PROC FREQ DATA=WORK;
      TABLE SINTERV*X/LIST OUT=WORK(KEEP=SINTERV COUNT) NOPRINT;
      RUN;

  /* calculate the chi-square test for each division. */
```

```
DATA WORK(KEEP=PVALUE);
     SET WORK;
     BY SINTERV;
     RETAIN EXPFREQ CHISQ;

     /* a division starts. */

     IF FIRST.SINTERV THEN DO; EXPFREQ=&NRANNUM/SINTERV;
                               CHISQ=0;
                               END;
     CHISQ=CHISQ+(COUNT-EXPFREQ)**2/EXPFREQ;

     /* the last interval of the division is read. */
     /* determine the p-value of the test.         */

     IF LAST.SINTERV THEN DO; PVALUE=1-PROBCHI(CHISQ,SINTERV-1);
                              OUTPUT;
                              END;
PROC FORMAT;
   VALUE SIGNIF 0.0000-0.0001='P<0.0001'
                0.0001-0.001 ='P<0.001'
                0.001 -0.01  ='P<0.01'
                0.01  -0.05  ='P<0.05'
                0.05  -0.10  ='P<0.10'
                0.10  -0.15  ='P<0.15'
                0.15  -1     ='P>0.15';

PROC FREQ DATA=WORK;    *** summarize the results;
   TABLE PVALUE;
   FORMAT PVALUE SIGNIF.;
   TITLE1 "Results of the Uniformity Test";
   TITLE2 "-----------------------------";
   TITLE3 "# of Random Numbers: &NRANNUM";
   TITLE4 "Subintervals Tested: 2 to &HNSINT";
RUN;
```

Output 3.1
Uniformity
Test of
RANUNI

```
                    Results of the Uniformity Test
                    -----------------------------
                    # of Random Numbers: 1000000
                    Subintervals Tested: 2 to 100

                                       Cumulative  Cumulative
         PVALUE   Frequency   Percent   Frequency    Percent
         -----------------------------------------------------
         P<0.05        9         9.1          9         9.1
         P<0.10        5         5.1         14        14.1
         P<0.15        8         8.1         22        22.2
         P>0.15       77        77.8         99       100.0
```

3.4 Randomness (the CORRTEST Macro)

Randomness is an elusive concept, and it cannot be measured by a single test. It posseses many facets, and we should examine as many of them as possible. The CORRTEST macro (Program 3.2) executes one of the many tests of randomness, the correlation test, which examines the correlation between the ith and the $(i+j)$th random numbers. The hypothesis is that if the numbers generated by RANUNI are random, the correlation between the ith and the $(i+j)$th numbers is not significant for any j. The macro calculates these correlation coefficients for $j=1, 2,\ldots, n$ at once (the value of n in the macro is specified by the HLAG parameter). Output 3.2a shows the results when we generate one million uniform random numbers and calculate the correlations of up to 100 lags with the following statements:

```
DATA SAMPLE(KEEP=X);
    DO I=1 TO 1000000;
        X=RANUNI(123);
        OUTPUT;
    END;
    RUN;
%CORRTEST(DATA=SAMPLE,HLAG=100,VAR=X)
```

RANUNI satisfies the randomness as required by the correlation test, because only 10 out of 100 have significantly high correlation coefficients at the 0.05 level. If we choose the 0.01 level, then only one is significantly high. The correlation test delivers similar results when we examine the other random number generator functions available in SAS. For example, if we test the RANGAM function with the following code,

```
DATA SAMPLE(KEEP=X);
    DO I=1 TO 1000000;
        X=RANGAM(123,2);
        OUTPUT;
    END;
    RUN;
%CORRTEST(DATA=SAMPLE,HLAG=100,VAR=X)
```

we obtain that only 2 out of 100 correlation coefficients have p-values less than 0.05, and none are less than 0.01 (see Output 3.2b).

Program 3.2 *The CORRTEST Macro*

```
/***************************************************************/
/*                                                           */
/*  The CORRTEST macro executes the correlation test of randomness.  */
/*                                                           */
/*  Parameters:                                              */
/*  DATA    the name of the table containing a random variable. */
/*  VAR     the name of the random variable.                 */
/*  HLAG    the highest lag of correlation to be calculated. */
/*          The macro calculates the correlation coefficients */
/*          between subsequent random values with lags of 1, 2, */
/*          3, ... &HLAG. One correlation coefficient is     */
/*          calculated for each lag.                         */
/*                                                           */
/*  Notes                                                    */
/*  1. The macro assumes that there is no missing value in the */
/*     input table and it has at least HLAG number of rows.  */
/*  2. The name of the random variable must not start with   */
/*     'lag'.                                                 */
/*                                                           */
/***************************************************************/

%MACRO CORRTEST(DATA=,HLAG=,VAR=);

   /* Create a new table that has the original random value in */
   /* column named 'lag0' and one column for each lag specified.*/
   /* For example                                             */
   /*                                                         */
   /* Original                                                */
   /*  Table          New Table                               */
   /*                                                         */
   /*   X       LAG0 LAG1 LAG2 LAG3                           */
   /*   -       ---- ---- ---- ----                           */
   /*   1        1    2    3    4                             */
   /*   2        2    3    4    5                             */
   /*   3        3    4    5    6                             */
   /*   4        4    5    6    .                             */
   /*   5        5    6    .    .                             */
   /*   6        6    .    .    .                             */

   DATA WORK(KEEP=LAG0-LAG&HLAG);
        SET &DATA NOBS=NOBS END=END;
        ARRAY LAGARRAY(*) LAG0-LAG&HLAG;
        RETAIN LAG0-LAG&HLAG;
        IF _N_<=&HLAG THEN LAGARRAY(_N_+1)=&VAR;
                    ELSE DO; DO I=1 TO &HLAG;
                                 LAGARRAY(I)=LAGARRAY(I+1);
                             END;
                             LAGARRAY(&HLAG+1)=&VAR;
                             OUTPUT;
                         END;
```

```
         IF END THEN DO; CALL SYMPUT('N',
                        COMPRESS(PUT(NOBS,BEST10.)));
                   DO J=0 TO &HLAG-2;
                       DO I=1 TO &HLAG-J;
                           LAGARRAY(I)=LAGARRAY(I+1);
                       END;
                       LAGARRAY(&HLAG-J+1)=.;
                       OUTPUT;
                   END;
               END;
         END;
      RUN;
/* calculate the correlation coefficients for each lag and   */
/* save them.                                                 */

PROC CORR DATA=WORK OUTP=WORK(WHERE=(_TYPE_='CORR')) NOPRINT;
      VAR LAG0;
      WITH LAG1-LAG&HLAG;

/* calculate the p-value for each correlation coefficient    */
/* (because PROC CORR does not save it along with the        */
/* correlation coefficient).                                 */

DATA WORK(KEEP=PVALUE);
      SET WORK;
      RETAIN N &N;
      CORR=LAG0;
      N=N-1;                 *** Number of values - degrees of freedom.;
      IF ABS(CORR)=1 THEN PVALUE=0;
                  ELSE PVALUE=2*(1-PROBT(ABS(CORR/
                      SQRT(1-(CORR*CORR))*SQRT(N-2)),N-2));
      OUTPUT;
      RUN;
PROC FORMAT;
      VALUE SIGNIF 0.0000-0.0001='P<0.0001'
                   0.0001-0.001 ='P<0.001'
                   0.001 -0.01  ='P<0.01'
                   0.01  -0.05  ='P<0.05'
                   0.05  -0.10  ='P<0.10'
                   0.10  -0.15  ='P<0.15'
                   0.15  -1     ='P>0.15';

/* summarize the results */

PROC FREQ DATA=WORK;
      TABLE PVALUE;
      FORMAT PVALUE SIGNIF.;
      TITLE1 "Results of the Correlation Test";
      TITLE2 "----------------------------";
      TITLE3 "# of Random Numbers: &N";
      TITLE4 "Lags Tested: 1 to &HORDER";
   RUN;
%MEND;
```

Output 3.2a
Correlation Test
of RANUNI

```
                      Result of the Correlation Test
                      ------------------------------
                     # of Random Numbers: 1000000
                        Lags Tested: 1 to 100

                                          Cumulative  Cumulative
            PVALUE      Frequency   Percent  Frequency    Percent
            ---------------------------------------------------------
            P<0.01          1        1.0        1          1.0
            P<0.05          9        9.0       10         10.0
            P<0.10          5        5.0       15         15.0
            P<0.15          3        3.0       18         18.0
            P>0.15         82       82.0      100        100.0
```

Output 3.2b
Correlation Test
of RANGAM

```
                      Result of the Correlation Test
                      ------------------------------
                     # of Random Numbers: 1000000
                        Lags Tested: 1 to 100

                                          Cumulative  Cumulative
            PVALUE      Frequency   Percent  Frequency    Percent
            ---------------------------------------------------------
            P<0.05          2        2.0        2          2.0
            P<0.10          2        2.0        4          4.0
            P<0.15          7        7.0       11         11.0
            P<0.15         89       89.0      100        100.0
```

Examining the correlation coefficients and their p-values using the CORRTEST macro, the curious mind might ask: What is the distribution of these p-values? The SAS System is a great tool for conducting experimental mathematics, and we can easily answer that question by using the table WORK, which was created by the CORRTEST macro, as shown in the program below.

```
DATA SAMPLE(KEEP=X);
    DO I=1 TO 500000;

        /* this time, we carry out the test on  */
        /* normally distributed random numbers. */

        X=RANNOR(123);
        OUTPUT;
    END;
    RUN;
%CORRTEST(DATA=SAMPLE,HLAG=1000,VAR=X)
PROC CHART DATA=WORK;
    VBAR PVALUE / LEVELS=10;
    LABEL PVALUE="p-values of the Correlation Test";
    RUN;
```

The answer is given using RANNOR in Output 3.2c: uniform distribution. If the generated numbers are close to a random sequence, then as the number of replicated correlation coefficients increases, the distribution in Output 3.2c should smoothen, and our results should more closely approximate the theoretical results — a uniformity of frequency.

Output 3.2c
The p-values of the Correlation Test Distribute Uniformly

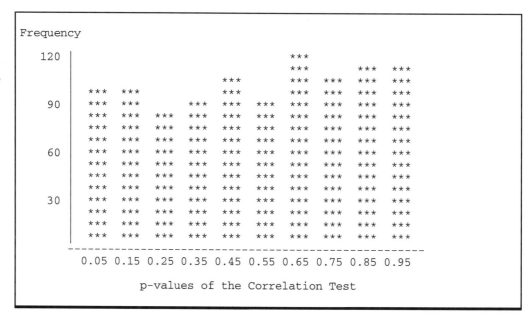

3.5 Generating Random Numbers with Functions versus CALL Routines

The stream of the random numbers is determined by the so-called seed value, or R_0 in (3.1). *Seed* is always the first parameter of each random number generator function or CALL routine, and $seed = 0, \pm 1, \pm 2, \ldots, \pm (2^{31} - 2)$.

The actual starting number of the stream depends on the seed value specified by the user according to the rule given here.

If seed is	R₀, the starting number of the stream, is set to the	and the streams of the random numbers at repeated executions are
≤ 0	time since midnight	different
> 0	seed value specified by the user	the same

The precision of the time since midnight (in the case of *seed*≤0) depends on the operating system. For example, Windows returns it in units of milliseconds. If the seed is specified as a fraction or as a value greater than $2^{31}- 2$, SAS issues an error message. You can specify a *seed* $\leq -(2^{31} -2)$, but it may return a degenerated stream, so it must be avoided.

Since the random numbers are calculated by a recursive formula, the first number determines all subsequent random numbers. A benefit to using a specific seed value is that the results can be replicated by using the same seed again. The debugging of your code becomes easier, and others can check your work by replicating it (see section 5.4 for more about the use of the seed value). Once a random number generator is started, SAS maintains only one stream of numbers, regardless of the number of references made to it. The code on the right hand side of Program 3.3 returns only one stream of random numbers, even though the RANUNI function is referenced twice with two different seeds. The random numbers in variables RUNI1 and RUNI2 correspond to the first invocation of RANUNI with seed=123 specified. The second invocation with seed=456 does not start a new stream of numbers (Output 3.3).

Program 3.3 *Seed Value – Example 1*

```
DATA TEMP1(DROP=I);                DATA TEMP2(DROP=I);
    DO I=1 TO 10;                      DO I=1 TO 5;
        RUNI=RANUNI(123);                 RUNI1=RANUNI(123);
        SEED=RUNI*(2**31-1);              /* The second seed (456) has no*/
        OUTPUT;                           /* effect, because the stream has */
    END;                                  /* already started with seed=123.*/
    RUN;                                  RUNI2=RANUNI(456);
PROC PRINT DATA=TEMP1;                     OUTPUT;
    RUN;                              END;
                                      RUN;
                                  PROC PRINT DATA=TEMP2;
                                      RUN;
```

Output 3.3 *The Function Produces Only One Stream of Numbers*

OBS	RUNI	SEED	OBS	RUNI1	RUNI2
1	0.75040	1611463328	1	0.75040	0.32091
2	0.32091	689153326	2	0.17839	0.90603
3	0.17839	383088854	3	0.35712	0.22111
4	0.90603	1945691870	4	0.78644	0.39808
5	0.35712	766903084	5	0.12467	0.18769
6	0.22111	474838741			
7	0.78644	1688863383			
8	0.39808	854874385			
9	0.12467	267716529			
10	0.18769	403052287			

The seed value starts the recursive algorithm of (3.1), and at each execution the seed gets re-calculated. The new value is stored internally in the function hidden from the user, and its value transformed into (0,1) is returned by RANUNI as the next random number. If we multiply this random number by the period (i.e., $m=2^{31}-1$) of (3.1), we obtain that hidden seed. (See the variable SEED in the left-hand side of Program 3.3 — it will be discussed below).

If we utilize the RANUNI CALL routine instead of the RANUNI function, it returns not only the next random number, but this re-calculated seed value as well. We then have the ability to alter this seed value and to thus alter the stream of the random numbers.

Program 3.4 illustrates many important facts about RANUNI and the two forms of invocation: function and CALL. These facts apply equally to all random number generator functions available in SAS. The random number returned by the CALL routine is always its last parameter.

Program 3.4 *Seed Value – Example 2*

```
DATA TEMP3(DROP=I);
     RETAIN SEED1 123 SEED2 123 SEED3 123 SEED4 456;
     DO I=1 TO 10;
         RUNI1=RANUNI(SEED1);
         CALL RANUNI(SEED2,RUNI2);
         CALL RANUNI(SEED3,RUNI3);
         CALL RANUNI(SEED4,RUNI4);
         /* Change the first and third seed values */
         /* for observations #6 and onward.        */
         IF I=5 THEN DO; SEED1=456;
                         SEED3=456;
                    END;
         OUTPUT;
     END;
     RUN;
PROC PRINT DATA=TEMP3;
     RUN;
```

- The random number returned by RANUNI is the same as the seed value irrespective of the transformation into (0,1). Compare the variables SEED in Output 3.3 and SEED2 in Output 3.4.

- In the function, the stream of numbers is determined by the first seed value, and it is not altered regardless of the change in the seed variable. See the SEED1 values, and compare RUNI1 to RUNI2 in Output 3.4.

- Either a function and a CALL routine together, or any number of CALL routines, produce independent streams of random numbers. Variables RUNI1 and RUNI2 in Output 3.3 are from one stream, but variables RUNI1 – RUNI4 in Output 3.4 are from four independent streams.

- In the CALL routine form, we can change the seed value and it causes the stream to be re-started with the new value. See variable RUNI3 in Output 3.4 and compare its values starting with observation #6 to the values of variable RUNI4 starting with observation #1.

- The seed value for a function can be specified either as a scalar or as a variable. The seed value of a CALL routine must always be specified as a variable.

Output 3.4
Altering the Stream by Changing the Seed

OBS	SEED1	SEED2	SEED3	SEED4	RUNI1	RUNI2	RUNI3	RUNI4
1	123	1611463328	1611463328	736440516	0.75040	0.75040	0.75040	0.34293
2	123	689153326	689153326	774069794	0.32091	0.32091	0.32091	0.36045
3	123	383088854	383088854	686944750	0.17839	0.17839	0.17839	0.31988
4	123	1945691870	1945691870	613712798	0.90603	0.90603	0.90603	0.28578
5	456	766903084	456	538536300	0.35712	0.35712	0.35712	0.25078
6	456	474838741	736440516	2127021321	0.22111	0.22111	0.34293	0.99047
7	456	1688863383	774069794	1285275311	0.78644	0.78644	0.36045	0.59850
8	456	854874385	686944750	969429106	0.39808	0.39808	0.31988	0.45143
9	456	267716529	613712798	1516286558	0.12467	0.12467	0.28578	0.70608
10	456	403052287	538536300	760955526	0.18769	0.18769	0.25078	0.35435

As we mentioned earlier, if SEED=0 is specified, the streams of random numbers are different at each execution of the code. Program 3.5 generates three random numbers inside a macro with SEED=0 specified. The two successive executions result in two different streams of random numbers, because internally, SAS starts the RANUNI function with different seed values. Output 3.5 shows the different random numbers and also the differing seed values.

Program 3.5 *Streams with SEED=0*

```
%MACRO SEED0;
 DATA TEMP4(DROP=I);
      SEED=0;
      DO I=1 TO 3;
         CALL RANUNI(SEED,RUNI);
         OUTPUT;
      END;
      RUN;
 PROC PRINT DATA=TEMP4;
      RUN;
%MEND;
TITLE 'First Macro Call';
%SEED0
TITLE 'Second Macro Call';
%SEED0
RUN;
```

Output 3.5
Different Streams of Random Numbers with SEED=0

```
                  First Macro Call
            OBS       SEED       RANUI
            1      21287539    0.00991
            2    1972737807    0.91863
            3     790022720    0.36788


                 Second Macro Call
            OBS       SEED      RANUNI

            1     156935322    0.07308
            2     972755748    0.45297
            3    2060025218    0.95927
```

3.6 Generating Seed Values (the SEEDGEN Macro)

Since the random numbers are the result of the recursive deterministic algorithm of (3.1), they can be thought of as a huge chain of all integers between 1 and 2^{31}-1 with their "random" sequence fixed. When we invoke a random number generator function, i.e., start a stream of random numbers, we merely point to one number in this gigantic sequence and take out a segment of numbers (e.g., 100,000 of them) starting at that number. If we need more than one stream, we may select overlapping streams, even though the chain is more than two billion numbers long. To ensure non-overlapping streams, the starting numbers of the streams must be far apart. More precisely, they must be separated by at least the length of the desired streams. The SEEDGEN macro of Program 3.6 provides seed values that produce non-overlapping streams of random numbers. (See also Clark & Woodward 1992.) Output 3.6 shows 10 seed values that would produce 10 non-overlapping streams of one million random numbers each. The length of the streams should be set sufficiently large by considering all streams that are to be generated by our program. For example, if we need to generate 100,000 uniform and 100,000 normal random numbers, the length should be set to at least 300,000, because the creation of one normal random number requires two random uniform numbers (see Section 3.7).

Program 3.6 The SEEDGEN Macro

```
/*********************************************************/
/* Macro SEEDGEN generates seed values to produce       */
/* non-overlapping streams of random numbers.           */
/*                                                       */
/* Parameters                                            */
/* FSSED    first seed                                   */
/* LSTREAM  the length of the non-overlapping streams    */
/* NSEEDS   the number of seed values requested          */
/*                                                       */
/* Note                                                  */
/* 1. Each paramater must be a positive integer less     */
/*    than 2**31-1.                                       */
/* 2. The macro may generate a smaller number of seeds, if */
/*    LSTREAM*NSEEDS>2**31-1.                             */
/*                                                       */
/*********************************************************/
%MACRO SEEDGEN(FSEED=,LSTREAM=,NSEEDS=);
   DATA TEMP(KEEP=SEED);
        RETAIN SEED &FSEED;
        OUTPUT;
        DO I=1 TO MIN((&NSEEDS-1)*&LSTREAM,2**31-1) BY &LSTREAM;
           DO J=1 TO &LSTREAM;
              CALL RANUNI(SEED,X);
           END;
           OUTPUT;
        END;
        RUN;
   PROC PRINT DATA=TEMP;
        TITLE "List of &NSEEDS Seed Values";
        TITLE2 "Apart by &LSTREAM Numbers";
        RUN;
   %MEND;
```

Output 3.6
Seed Values
Generated by the
SEEDGEN Macro

```
            List of 10 Seed Values
           Apart by 1000000 Numbers

            OBS           SEED

             1             123
             2         587760465
             3         127671937
             4        1323234103
             5         619707514
             6        1330454004
             7        1307130277
             8         294729579
             9         689565084
            10         491301990
```

3.7 List of All Random Number Generators Available in SAS

Most generators in SAS can be utilized as functions or as CALL routines. The general syntax is

Form	SAS Code	Description	
function	$r=name(seed,p_i)$;	*r*:	SAS variable holding the random number.
		name:	one of the generators as given in Table 3.1.
		seed:	a scalar or a SAS variable (in case of the function) or a SAS variable (in case of the CALL routine) holding the starting value of the generator.
CALL	call $name(seed,p_i,r)$;	p_i:	one or more parameters described in Table 3.1.

Table 3.1 describes all generators available in SAS. The first column gives the function reference. The uniform random generator can be referred to by two names: RANUNI and UNIFORM. Table 3.2 provides examples for some special uses of these functions.

Table 3.1 *Random Number Generator Functions Available in SAS*

SAS Function[1]	Distribution	Function Parameters	Probability Density Function[2]
RANBIN(*seed,n,p*)	Binomial	*seed:* See section 3.5 for seed values *n:* number of independent trials, *n*=1, 2, 3… *p:* probability of success, 0≤p≤1	$\begin{cases} \dbinom{n}{m} p^m (1-p)^{n-m} & 0 \le m \le n \\ 0 & elsewhere \end{cases}$
RANCAU(*seed*)	Cauchy	*seed:* See section 3.5 for seed values	$\dfrac{1}{\pi}\left(\dfrac{\lambda}{\lambda^2 + (x-\theta)^2} \right)$ where -∞<θ<∞ and θ is the location parameter (0), λ>0 and λ is the scale parameter (1)
RANEXP(*seed*)	Exponential	*seed:* See section 3.5 for seed values	$\begin{cases} 0 & x < 0 \\ \dfrac{1}{\lambda} e^{\left(-\frac{x}{\lambda}\right)} & x \ge 0 \end{cases}$ where λ>0 and λ is the scale parameter (1)
RANGAM(*seed,a*)	Gamma	*seed:* See section 3.5 for seed values *a:* shape, a>0	$\begin{cases} 0 & x < 0 \\ \dfrac{1}{\lambda^a \Gamma(a)} x^{a-1} e^{-\frac{x}{\lambda}} & x \ge 0 \end{cases}$ where λ>0 and λ is the scale parameter (1)
RANNOR(*seed*) or NORMAL(*seed*)[3]	Normal	*seed:* See section 3.5 for seed values	$\dfrac{1}{\lambda\sqrt{2\pi}} e^{-\frac{(x-\theta)^2}{2\lambda^2}}$ where -∞<θ<∞ and θ is the location parameter (0), λ>0 and λ is the scale parameter (1)
RANPOI(*seed,m*)	Poisson	*seed:* See section 3.5 for seed values *m:* mean, m>0	$\begin{cases} 0 & n < 0 \\ e^{-m} \dfrac{m^n}{n!} & n \ge 0 \end{cases}$

[1] When the function is utilized as a CALL routine, there is one extra parameter that is always the last one and which holds the random number returned by the generator. For example, r=RANBIN(*seed,n,p*); becomes CALL RANBIN(*seed,n,p,r*);
[2] The number in parentheses indicates the value of the parameter assumed in SAS.
[3] Functions RANNOR and NORMAL are identical. Function NORMAL cannot be utilized as a CALL routine.

Table 3.1 *Random Number Generator Functions Available in SAS (continued)*

RANTBL(*seed*,p_1,p_2, ...p_n)	Defined by a probability mass function	*seed:* See section 3.5 for seed values p_i: probabilities, $p_i>0$ and $$\sum_{i=1}^{n} p_i = 1$$	$$\sum_{j=1}^{i} p_j \quad i=1,2,\ldots n$$
RANTRI(*seed*,*h*)	Triangular	*seed:* See section 3.5 for seed values *h:* hypotenuse, $0 \leq h \leq 1$	$$\begin{cases} \dfrac{2}{(r-l)(h-l)}(x-l) & l \leq x \leq h \\[2ex] \dfrac{2}{(r-l)(h-r)}(x-r) & h \leq x \leq r \\[2ex] 0 & elsewhere \end{cases}$$ $-\infty < l < \infty$ and l is the left endpoint of the interval (*0*), $l < r < \infty$ and r is the right endpoint of the interval (*1*)
RANUNI(*seed*) or UNIFORM(*seed*)[4]	Uniform	*seed:* See section 3.5 for seed values	$$\begin{cases} \dfrac{1}{r-l} & l \leq x \leq r \\[2ex] 0 & elsewhere \end{cases}$$ $-\infty < l < \infty$ and l is the left endpoint of the interval (0), $l < r < \infty$ and r is the right endpoint of the interval (*1*)

Table 3.2 Special Use of Some Random Number Generator Functions

SAS Code	Returns variates with distribution of
`x=theta+lambda*rancau(seed);`	Cauchy with given location (*theta*) and scale (*lambda*) parameters.
`x=ranexp(seed)/lambda;`	Exponential with given scale (*lambda*) parameter.
`x=floor(-ranexp(seed)/log(1-p));`	Geometric: $p(1-p)^n$ where $0 \leq p \leq 1$, $n = 0, 1, 2,\ldots$
`x=lambda*rangam(seed,a);`	Gamma with given shape (*a*) and scale (*lambda*) parameters. If *lambda*=2 and 2*a* is an integer, chi-square with degrees of freedom of 2*a*. If *a*=1,2,..., Erlang (i.e., the sum of *a* independent exponential variates whose means are *lambda*).

`y1=rangam(seed,a);`
 `y2=rangam(seed,b);`
 `x=y1/(y1+y2);`
	Beta:
	 $\dfrac{1}{B(a,b)} x^{a-1}(1-x)^{b-1}$ where $1 \leq a \leq \infty$ and $1 \leq b \leq \infty$

`x=theta+lambda*rannor(seed);`	Normal with given location (*theta*) and scale (*lambda*) parameters.

---

[4] Functions RANUNI and UNIFORM are identical. Function UNIFORM cannot be utilized as a CALL routine.

All random number generator functions are based on RANUNI, because all distributions can be obtained from a uniform distribution according to a theorem of probability theory. The transformations from uniform to other distributions are carried out by the inverse transform method, the Box-Müller transformation, and the acceptance-rejection procedure applied to the uniform variates generated by RANUNI. Internally, SAS generates only uniform random numbers with RANUNI and transforms them to the desired distribution. For example, if u_1, u_2 and u_3 are from a uniform distribution, then n in formula (3.3) follows the standard normal distribution

$$n = \sqrt{-2\ln u_1}\,\cos(2u_2\pi), \tag{3.3}$$

and e calculated with formula (3.4) will be from an exponential distribution with a scale of one

$$e = -\ln(u_3). \tag{3.4}$$

The fact that there is only one real generator is demonstrated by Program 3.7.

Program 3.7 *Demonstration of One Generator*

```
DATA TEMP5(DROP=I);                    DATA TEMP6(DROP=I);
    DO I=1 TO 12;                          DO I=1 TO 3;
        RUNI=RANUNI(123);                     RUNI=RANUNI(123);
        OUTPUT;                               RNOR=RANNOR(456);
    END;                                      REXP=RANEXP(789);
    RUN;                                      OUTPUT;
PROC PRINT DATA=TEMP5;                     END;
    RUN;                                   RUN;
                                       PROC PRINT DATA=TEMP6;
                                           RUN;
```

Output 3.7
Many
Distributions
but Only One
Generator

OBS	RUNI		OBS	RUNI	RNOR	REXP
1	0.75040		1	0.75040	0.65572	0.09868
2	0.32091		2	0.35712	0.39428	0.92110
3	0.17839		3	0.12467	0.29958	0.82994
4	0.90603					
5	0.35712					
6	0.22111					
7	0.78644					
8	0.39808					
9	0.12467					
10	0.18769					
11	0.77618					
12	0.43607					

See the values of RUNI on the right hand side of Output 3.7: they are the first, fifth and ninth values of the left hand side. It seems that three numbers are skipped for each observation in file TEMP5. Indeed, SAS takes two uniform random numbers to return one normal random number, and another uniform random number to return an exponential random number.

Program 3.8 generates these same normal and exponential random numbers by taking those *skipped* uniform random numbers and transforming them according to formulae (3.3) and (3.4). The random numbers generated by our program in Output 3.8 are identical to the ones returned by the RANNOR and RANEXP functions in Output 3.7.

Program 3.8 *Uniform Random Numbers for Different Distributions*

```
DATA TEMP7(DROP=I);
     DO I=1 TO 3;
         RUNI=RANUNI(123);

         /* take the next three random numbers. */

         U1=RANUNI(123);
         U2=RANUNI(123);
         U3=RANUNI(123);

         /* 2*arsin(1) is used to obtain the value of pi. */

         RNOR=SQRT(-2*LOG(U1))*COS(4*ARSIN(1)*U2);
         REXP=-LOG(U3);
         OUTPUT;
     END;
     RUN;
PROC PRINT DATA=TEMP7;
     RUN;
```

Output 3.8
Uniform Random
Numbers Are
Used for Random
Numbers of
Different
Distributions

OBS	RUNI	U1	U2	U3	RNOR	REXP
1	0.75040	0.32091	0.17839	0.90603	0.65572	0.09868
2	0.35712	0.22111	0.78644	0.39808	0.39428	0.92110
3	0.12467	0.18769	0.77618	0.43607	0.29958	0.82994

Figure 3.1 is a comparative chart showing the execution times of the generators with certain parameters. The measured quantities depend highly on several hardware/software factors, so they are shown only for general guidance.

As expected, RANUNI takes the least amount of time. As seen before, RANNOR takes two uniform random numbers and transforms them, so it takes a little more than two times that of RANUNI. Similarly, the execution of RANEXP takes a little longer than that of RANUNI. Figure 3.1 plots the execution time of the generators when referenced as functions. When we switch to the CALL routines, the execution time increases by about 10% on average.

Figure 3.1 *Benchmarking the Random Number Generators*

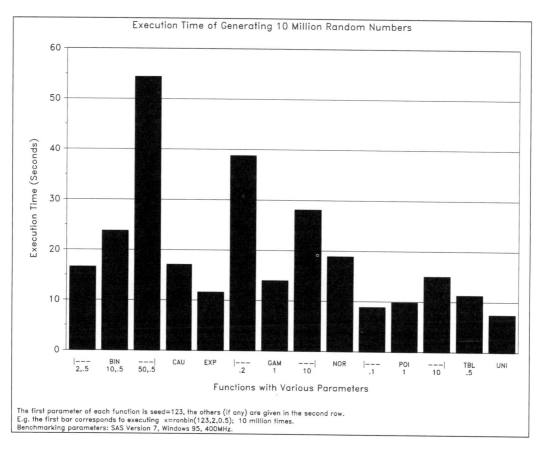

3.8 Examples for Normal and Lognormal Distributions

3.8.1 Random Sample of Population Height (Normal Distribution)

One of the first variables that comes to mind when discussing normal distribution is height. In this example, we will generate a random population of 50,000 adults with height measurement. Height is normally distributed in the U.S. adult population (18-74 years) with a mean of 69.12 inches and a standard deviation of 2.85 inches for men; and 63.68 and 2.68 for women (Brainard & Burmaster 1992). The following statement generates a random height value for men.

```
HEIGHT=69.12+2.85*RANNOR(123);
```

Program 3.9 generates 50,000 random, gender-dependent height values. The ratio of women to men in the U.S. adult population is 50.96 to 49.04 (U.S. Bureau of the Census 1998). The program first randomly chooses the gender code and then calculates the random height using the gender-dependent formula. The results in Output 3.9 indicate that the random sample of height in the female population is normally distributed with the requested parameters (see the normality test and the Q-Q plot). The male random population possesses identical characteristics (not shown here).

The logarithm of weight is also normally distributed, and it is highly correlated with height. In Chapter 4, we will demonstrate how to generate multivariate random variables with a given degree of correlation.

Program 3.9 Generation of Random Height Values

```
DATA RNDPOP;
    DO I=1 TO 50000;
        IF RANUNI(123)<0.5096
            THEN DO; GENDER='F';
                    HEIGHT=63.68+2.68*RANNOR(123);
                END;
            ELSE DO; GENDER='M';
                    HEIGHT=69.12+2.85*RANNOR(123);
                END;
        OUTPUT;
    END;
    RUN;

/*check the distribution in the female population. */
/* is it normal with the specified parameters?     */

PROC CAPABILITY DATA=RNDPOP NORMALTEST LINEPRINTER;
    VAR HEIGHT;
    WHERE GENDER='F';
    QQPLOT HEIGHT / NORMAL (MU=63.68 SIGMA=2.68);
    RUN;
```

Output 3.9
Distribution of
Randomly
Generated
Height

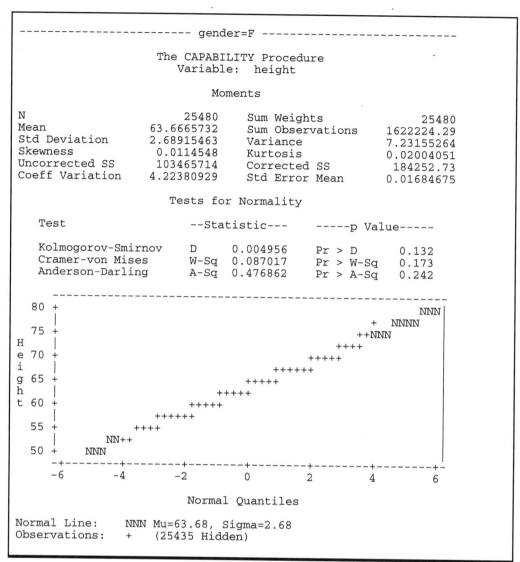

```
-------------------- gender=F --------------------------

                     The CAPABILITY Procedure
                       Variable:  height

                             Moments

N                           25480   Sum Weights              25480
Mean                   63.6665732   Sum Observations    1622224.29
Std Deviation          2.68915463   Variance            7.23155264
Skewness               0.0114548    Kurtosis            0.02004051
Uncorrected SS          103465714   Corrected SS          184252.73
Coeff Variation        4.22380929   Std Error Mean      0.01684675

                       Tests for Normality

     Test                  --Statistic---      -----p Value-----

     Kolmogorov-Smirnov    D    0.004956    Pr > D       0.132
     Cramer-von Mises      W-Sq 0.087017    Pr > W-Sq    0.173
     Anderson-Darling      A-Sq 0.476862    Pr > A-Sq    0.242

        ------------------------------------------------------------
     80 +                                                    NNN|
        |                                           +  NNNN
     75 +                                           ++NNN
   H    |                                         ++++
   e 70 +                                      +++++
   i    |                                   ++++++
   g 65 +                               +++++
   h    |                             +++++
   t 60 +                         +++++
        |                      ++++++
     55 +                  ++++
        |           NN++
     50 +      NNN
        -+--------+--------+--------+--------+--------+--------+-
        -6       -4       -2        0        2        4        6

                         Normal Quantiles

   Normal Line:     NNN Mu=63.68, Sigma=2.68
   Observations:     +   (25435 Hidden)
```

3.8.2 Random Sample of Stock Prices (Lognormal Distribution)

In this example, we generate random samples of stock prices that follow the distribution of the S&P 500 stock prices as of February 29, 2000. Program 3.10 reads all 500 prices and probes whether they form a normal distribution. Knowing the negative answer in advance, it also calculates the logarithm of the price and finds that to be normal. Output 3.10 shows the non-normal distribution of PRICE with a mean of 42.14 and a standard deviation of 30.22. The distribution of the variable LPRICE = LOG(PRICE) with a mean of 3.53 and a variance of 0.66 can be considered normal, based on the 0.1108 p-value of the Shapiro-Wilk normality test. (The stock prices in many other months follow different distributions.)

Program 3.10 *Distribution of Stock Prices*

```
DATA SPPRICE;
     INPUT PRICE @@;
     LPRICE=LOG(PRICE);
     DATALINES;
  3.6875    4.8750    5.6250    5.6875    6.1875    6.5000    6.8125    6.8750    7.0000
  7.0000    8.0000    8.3125    8.5000    8.6250    8.7500    8.8125    8.9375    9.3750
  9.6250    9.8125   10.0625   10.0625   10.8125   11.2500   11.7500   11.8125   12.1875
 12.3750   13.1875   13.2500   13.3750   13.5625   13.6250   13.7500   13.8125   13.8125
 13.8750   14.0000   14.3125   14.3125   14.5000   14.6250   14.8750   14.9375   15.0000
 15.6250   15.7500   15.7500   15.7500   15.7500   15.9375   16.0625   16.1250   16.3125
 16.3750   16.3750   16.5000   16.6875   16.7500   16.8125   16.8125   16.8125   16.9375
 16.9375   17.1875   17.1875   17.2500   17.3750   17.4375   17.5000   17.5000   17.5625
 17.6875   17.8125   17.8125   17.8750   18.0000   18.2500   18.3125   18.4375   18.5000
 18.5000   18.5000   18.5625   18.6875   18.8125   19.0000   19.0000   19.1250   19.1250
 19.1250   19.2500   19.3125   19.3125   19.3750   19.6875   19.6875   19.6875   19.7500
 19.7500   19.8125   19.8125   19.8750   19.8750   20.1250   20.1250   20.1875   20.2500
 20.2500   20.5625   20.6250   20.6250   20.6875   20.8750   20.9375   21.0000   21.0625
 21.1875   21.3125   21.3750   21.3750   21.3750   21.6250   21.7500   21.8125   21.8750
 21.8750   22.1250   22.1250   22.1250   22.1875   22.1875   22.3750   22.4375   22.5625
 22.6875   22.8750   22.8750   22.9375   23.0000   23.2500   23.3750   23.4375   23.4375
 23.5000   23.7500   23.9375   23.9375   24.0000   24.0625   24.2500   24.5000   24.6250
 24.6875   24.6875   24.7500   24.8750   24.8750   24.9375   25.0625   25.1250   25.3125
 25.7500   25.8125   25.8750   25.8750   26.0000   26.0000   26.0625   26.1875   26.1875   26.2500
 26.4375   26.6250   26.7500   26.7500   26.8125   27.0000   27.0625   27.0625   27.1875
 27.2500   27.2500   27.3750   27.5000   27.5625   27.5625   27.5625   27.6250   27.6250
 28.1250   28.2500   28.3125   28.3750   28.3750   28.4375   28.4375   28.5000   28.6250
 28.8125   28.9375   29.0000   29.0625   29.5000   29.6875   29.7500   29.7500   29.7500
 29.8125   29.8750   29.8750   29.9375   30.0000   30.0000   30.1250   30.1875   30.2500
 30.3125   30.3750   30.7500   31.0000   31.1250   31.2500   31.3125   31.7500   31.9375
 31.9375   32.1250   32.1250   32.6250   32.7500   32.8125   32.9375   32.9375   32.9375
 33.0000   33.0000   33.0000   33.0625   33.0625   33.2500   33.3125   33.4375   33.6250
 33.7500   33.8750   34.0000   34.0000   34.4375   34.6875   34.9375   35.0000   35.0000
 35.0625   35.2500   35.4375   35.7500   35.9375   36.2500   36.5000   36.5625   36.6875
 36.6875   36.6875   36.8125   36.8125   36.8125   36.9375   37.0000   37.0625   37.3125
 37.3750   37.4375   37.7500   37.8125   37.9375   38.0000   38.0000   38.0000   38.1250
 38.1875   38.2500   38.3125   38.3750   38.5625   38.5625   38.6250   38.6875   38.8125
 38.9375   38.9375   39.2500   39.4375   39.5000   39.5000   40.0000   40.0000   40.1875
 40.2500   40.4375   40.4375   40.5625   40.8125   40.8125   41.0000   41.1250   41.6250
 41.7500   41.8125   41.8125   41.9375   42.0000   42.0625   42.2500   42.5000   42.6250
 42.8125   43.0625   43.2500   43.4375   43.5000   43.5625   43.8750   43.8750   43.9375
 44.5000   44.6250   44.6875   44.7500   44.8750   45.0000   45.2500   45.3125   45.5000
 45.5625   45.6250   46.0000   46.0000   46.6250   46.8750   47.1250   47.4375   47.6250
 47.6250   47.8125   47.8125   48.0000   48.0000   48.1250   48.3125   48.3125   48.4375
 48.5000   48.6250   48.7500   48.9375   49.0000   49.1875   49.3750   49.3750   49.5000
 49.6250   49.6875   49.6875   50.0625   50.3125   50.5000   50.5000   50.5625   50.8125
 50.8750   50.9375   51.0000   51.1250   51.1250   51.3125   51.5000   51.6875   51.7500
 51.7500   51.7500   52.0625   52.0625   52.1875   52.1875   52.7500   52.7500   52.8750
 53.0000   53.3750   53.4375   53.6875   53.9375   54.3125   54.5000   54.6250   55.7500
 55.8750   56.5000   57.1875   57.2500   57.3125   57.5000   57.8750   58.0000   58.0000
 58.7500   58.9375   59.0000   59.0000   59.0000   59.4375   59.5000   59.5000   59.5625
 60.6875   61.0000   61.0000   61.5625   62.3750   63.5000   64.0000   64.0000   64.2500
 64.5000   64.6250   64.6875   65.1875   65.5000   66.6250   67.3750   67.5000   67.6250
 68.1250   68.1875   68.5000   68.7500   68.7500   70.1875   70.4375   72.0000   72.5000
 72.6250   72.8750   73.8125   73.8750   74.2500   74.6875   74.9375   75.1250   75.3125
 75.8125   76.0625   77.3750   77.9375   78.5000   78.7500   78.8125   79.6250   79.7500
 83.8125   85.2500   85.5625   87.0000   87.8750   88.1875   88.4375   89.3750   94.1875
 95.2500   96.0000   98.0000   98.2500  102.0000  102.5000  102.6875  102.7500  105.0000
105.4375  107.9375  108.5000  111.1875  113.0000  114.6250  115.7500  119.0000  119.2500
132.1875  132.3750  134.1875  134.5000  136.7500  142.4375  157.2500  159.6875  166.1250
172.0000  182.9375  188.0000  188.7500  196.8750
;
 'OC UNIVARIATE DATA=SPPRICE NORMAL PLOT;
       VAR PRICE LPRICE;
       RUN;
```

Output 3.10
Lognormal
Distribution of
Stock Prices

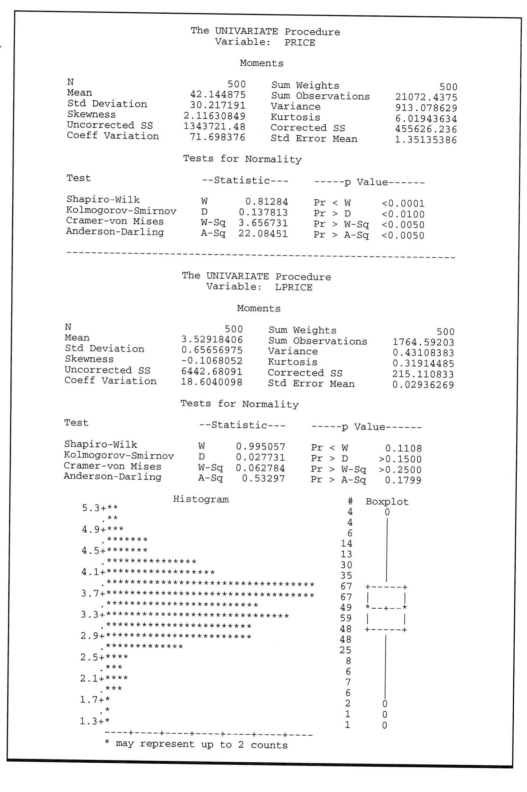

```
                    The UNIVARIATE Procedure
                      Variable:  PRICE

                           Moments

N                        500      Sum Weights              500
Mean                42.144875     Sum Observations    21072.4375
Std Deviation       30.217191     Variance            913.078629
Skewness           2.11630849     Kurtosis            6.01943634
Uncorrected SS     1343721.48     Corrected SS        455626.236
Coeff Variation     71.698376     Std Error Mean      1.35135386

                     Tests for Normality

Test                    --Statistic---      -----p Value------

Shapiro-Wilk          W     0.81284      Pr < W      <0.0001
Kolmogorov-Smirnov    D    0.137813      Pr > D      <0.0100
Cramer-von Mises      W-Sq 3.656731      Pr > W-Sq   <0.0050
Anderson-Darling      A-Sq 22.08451      Pr > A-Sq   <0.0050


-------------------------------------------------------------

                    The UNIVARIATE Procedure
                      Variable:  LPRICE

                           Moments

N                        500      Sum Weights              500
Mean                3.52918406    Sum Observations    1764.59203
Std Deviation       0.65656975    Variance            0.43108383
Skewness           -0.1068052     Kurtosis            0.31914485
Uncorrected SS     6442.68091     Corrected SS        215.110833
Coeff Variation     18.6040098    Std Error Mean      0.02936269

                     Tests for Normality

Test                    --Statistic---      -----p Value------

Shapiro-Wilk          W    0.995057      Pr < W       0.1108
Kolmogorov-Smirnov    D    0.027731      Pr > D      >0.1500
Cramer-von Mises      W-Sq 0.062784      Pr > W-Sq   >0.2500
Anderson-Darling      A-Sq  0.53297      Pr > A-Sq    0.1799

                        Histogram                    #  Boxplot
        5.3+**                                       4    0
           .**                                       4
        4.9+***                                      6
           .******                                  14
        4.5+*******                                 13
           .**************                          30
        4.1+******************                      35
           .*********************************       67
        3.7+*********************************       67   +-----+
           .************************              49   |     |
        3.3+*****************************         59 *--+--*
           .***********************               48   +-----+
        2.9+***********************               48
           .*************                         25
        2.5+****                                   8
           .***                                    6
        2.1+****                                   7
           .***                                    6
        1.7+*                                      2    0
           .*                                      1    0
        1.3+*                                      1    0
           ----+----+----+----+----+----+----
            * may represent up to 2 counts
```

A variable is lognormally distributed if its logarithm is normally distributed. If the lognormal distribution has a mean of m and a standard deviation of s, then the variable PRICE in the statement below will follow lognormal distribution.

```
PRICE=EXP(M+S*RANNOR(123));
```

Program 3.11 generates a sample of 10,000 random stock prices that follow the desired lognormal distribution. Output 3.11 shows a mean of 41.79 and a standard deviation of 31.33. Figure 3.2 presents the frequency histogram of the random sample superimposed on the theoretical lognormal distribution. The histogram of the random sample closely follows the theoretical curve. The histogram gets much smoother and closer to the theoretical one when we increase the sample size to 100,000. The program rounds the generated prices in two ways.

```
PRICE=ROUND(PRICE,1/16);
PRICERND=ROUND(PRICE,1);
```

The first one rounds prices to 1/16 of a dollar, which is the precision with which the stock prices were quoted (before the change to decimalization), and the second one rounds them to whole values in order to facilitate the production of the frequencies with PROC FREQ later in the program.

Program 3.11 *Generation of 10,000 Random Stock Prices*

```
DATA RNDPRICE;
    DO I=1 TO 10000;
        PRICE=EXP(3.52918406+0.65656975*RANNOR(123));
        PRICE=ROUND(PRICE,1/16);    *** round the price to 1/16.;
        PRICERND=ROUND(PRICE,1);
        OUTPUT;
    END;
PROC UNIVARIATE DATA=RNDPRICE;
    VAR PRICE;
    RUN;
PROC FREQ DATA=RNDPRICE;
    TABLE PRICERND / OUT=FREQHIST(RENAME=(PRICERND=PRICE)
                                  KEEP=PRICERND PERCENT);
    RUN;

/* create the theoretical probability density  */
/* function of stock prices as of 31/1/1999.   */

DATA PDFLOGN;
    DO PRICE=0 TO 200 BY 0.1;
        PROB=100*PDF('LOGNORMAL',PRICE,3.52918406,0.65656975);
        OUTPUT;
    END;
DATA BOTH;
    SET PDFLOGN FREQHIST;
    RUN;
PROC GPLOT DATA=BOTH;
    PLOT (PROB PERCENT)*PRICE / OVERLAY VAXIS=AXIS1
                               HAXIS=AXIS2;
    AXIS1 LABEL=(A=90 R=0 F=SWISS H=1.5 'Probability (%)')
          ORDER=0 TO 2.5 BY 0.5 VALUE=(H=1.2 F=SWISS)
          MINOR=(N=1);
```

```
AXIS2 LABEL=(F=SWISS H=1.5 'Stock Price ($)')
      ORDER=0 TO 200 BY 25 VALUE=(H=1.2 F=SWISS)
      MINOR=(N=3);
SYMBOL1 I=JOIN C=BLACK W=1 R=1;
SYMBOL2 I=STEPCJ C=BLACK W=2 R=1;
TITLE F=SWISS H=1.5 'Theoretical and Randomly Generated
      Distributions of Stock Prices';
TITLE2 F=SWISS H=1.5 'Size of Random Sample is 10,000';
RUN;
QUIT;
```

Output 3.11
Distribution of
Randomly
Generated
Stock Prices

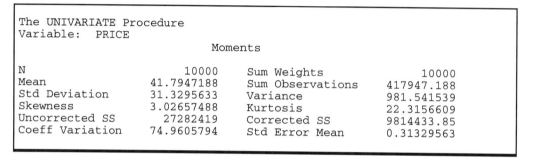

```
The UNIVARIATE Procedure
Variable:   PRICE
                              Moments

N                       10000    Sum Weights              10000
Mean               41.7947188    Sum Observations     417947.188
Std Deviation      31.3295633    Variance             981.541539
Skewness           3.02657488    Kurtosis             22.3156609
Uncorrected SS       27282419    Corrected SS         9814433.85
Coeff Variation    74.9605794    Std Error Mean       0.31329563
```

Figure 3.2 *Distribution of Randomly Generated 10,000 and 100,000 Stock Prices*

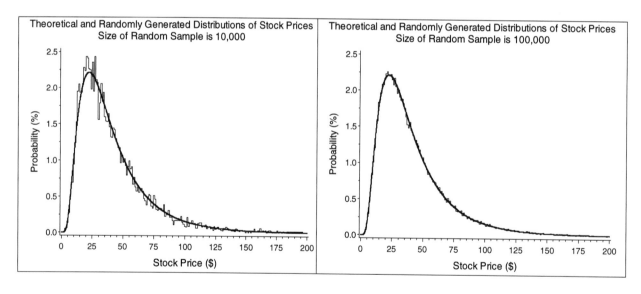

3.9 The RANTBL Function

The RANTBL function is one of the most widely used random number generators. When we need random numbers from a discrete distribution, RANTBL is the choice. Or when the theoretical distribution is unknown and we only possess a stepwise approximation of it, RANTBL is the generator of choice again. The RANTBL function has the form

$$R = \text{RANTBL}(seed, p_1, p_2, \ldots p_n);$$

and the RANTBL CALL routine has the form

$$\text{CALL RANTBL}(seed, p_1, p_2, \ldots p_n, r);$$

where p_i are probabilities and $\sum_{i=1}^{n} p_i = 1$. Variable r receives a value of

1	with probability of p_1,
2	with probability of p_2,
...	
n	with probability of p_n.

If we need different values to be generated, we have to map $1, 2, \ldots n$ into the desired set of values. Sometimes $\sum_{i=1}^{n} p_i < 1$ due to rounding error, and the RANTBL function may return an unexpected extra value of $n+1$. In order to avoid this problem, we can increase the value of p_n or leave it out entirely. In this latter case, SAS will automatically assign the remaining probabilities ($1 - \sum_{i=1}^{n-1} p_i$) to p_n and the execution time will also decrease. The p_i probabilities can be spelled out individually in RANTBL, or they can be placed into an array, which is then referenced instead of the p_i 's. The following two methods result in the same random numbers:

```
R=RANTBL(123,0.1,0.2,0.3,0.4);

ARRAY PROB(4) P1-P4 (0.1,0.2,0.3,0.4);
R=RANTBL(123,OF PROB(*));
```

As mentioned earlier, the following solutions provide the same results, but take a little less time to execute because we leave out the last probability:

```
R=RANTBL(123,0.1,0.2,0.3);

ARRAY PROB(3) P1-P3 (0.1,0.2,0.3);
R=RANTBL(123,OF PROB(*));
```

The execution time of the RANTBL function, in general, increases linearly with the number of probabilities specified, and it does not depend on the above two methods.

In the following example, we will demonstrate the RANTBL function's use for generating random samples of bonds with a given distribution of bond ratings. Then we pretend that the lognormal distribution in Section 3.8.2 is unknown, and we generate the random stock prices with the help of RANTBL in Section 3.10.2.

3.10 Examples Using the RANTBL Function

3.10.1 Random Sample of Bonds with Bond Ratings

The riskiness of bonds is measured by so-called bond ratings, determined by rating agencies such as Moody's or Standard and Poor's. This example generates a sample portfolio of 10,000 bonds following the rating composition of U.S. bonds rated by Moody's at the end of 1998. In Moody's bond rating scale, 'Aaa' indicates the lowest level of risk, 'Aa' the second lowest level of risk and 'Caa' (including 'Ca' and 'C') the highest. Program 3.12 reads the theoretical composition and loads the frequencies (probabilities) into array PROB, which makes up the probability mass function for RANTBL. The heart of the program is the statement

```
BRATING=BRATINGS(RANTBL(123,OF PROB(*)));
```

which generates a random integer between 1 and 7 and maps it to the character string of the corresponding rating category. This program determines what the ideal composition of the portfolio would be in a sample of 10,000 bonds, and compares the random sample to this one using the chi-square test. The non-significant result of the chi-square test (p-value of 0.216 in Output 3.12) means that the random and theoretical portfolios are statistically identical.

Program 3.12 Generation of 10,000 Random Bond Ratings

```
/* Read the theoretical distribution of Moody's */
/* bond ratings as of 12/1998.                  */

DATA BRATINGS;
    INPUT BRATING $3. MDPROB;
    MDPROB=MDPROB/100;
    CARDS;
Aaa     0.707    *** The sum of these frequencies is 100.
Aa      4.302
A      11.903
Baa    17.030
Ba     21.332
B      33.942
Caa    10.785
;
DATA RNDBONDS(KEEP=BRATING);
    SET BRATINGS END=ENDOFRT;

    /* set up arrays for the bond ratings ('BRTNGS') */
    /* and the percent of companies in those rating  */
```

```
      /* categories ('PROB').                                    */

      ARRAY BRATINGS(7) $5 BRTNGS1-BRTNGS7;
      ARRAY PROB(7) PROB1-PROB7;
      RETAIN BRTNGS1-BRTNGS7 PROB1-PROB7;
      BRATINGS(_N_)=BRATING;
      PROB(_N_)=MDPROB;

      /* generate the 10,000 random bond ratings. */

      IF ENDOFRT THEN DO;
         DO I=1 TO 10000;

            /* function RANTBL is called with the probabilities */
            /* stored in array 'PROB'. The integer returned by  */
            /* RANTBL is mapped into the rating category.       */

            BRATING=BRATINGS(RANTBL(123,OF PROB(*)));
            OUTPUT;
         END;
         END;

/* check the random distribution to the theoretical one using */
/* the chi-square test of PROC FREQ. Obtain the frequencies   */
/* by rating category in the random sample.                   */

PROC FREQ DATA=RNDBONDS;
     TABLE BRATING / NOPRINT OUT=FREQHIST(RENAME=(PERCENT=RNDPNT)
                                   KEEP=BRATING PERCENT COUNT);
     RUN;

/* set up a special file where there is a record for each       */
/* rating category and for each sample (theoretical and random).*/
/* both theoretical and random samples have 10,000 bonds each.  */
/* variable 'FRQ' holds the frequency in each record.           */

PROC SORT DATA=BRATINGS;
     BY BRATING;
DATA BOTH;
     MERGE BRATINGS FREQHIST;
     BY BRATING;
     SAMPLE='Theoretical';
     FRQ=ROUND(10000*MDPROB);
     OUTPUT;
     SAMPLE='Random';
     FRQ=COUNT;
     OUTPUT;
     RUN;

/* execute PROC FREQ to determine whether or not the   */
/* random sample is from the theoretical distribution. */

PROC FREQ DATA=BOTH;
     TABLE SAMPLE*BRATING / CHISQ;
     WEIGHT FRQ;
     RUN;
```

Output 3.12 *The Random Bond Ratings Follow the Theoretical Distribution*

```
SAMPLE          BRATING

Frequency
Percent
Row Pct
Col Pct     |A      |Aa     |Aaa    |B      |Ba     |Baa    |Caa    |  Total
------------+-------+-------+-------+-------+-------+-------+-------+
Random      |  1125 |   462 |    68 |  3461 |  2215 |  1664 |  1005 |  10000
            |  5.63 |  2.31 |  0.34 | 17.31 | 11.08 |  8.32 |  5.03 |  50.00
            | 11.25 |  4.62 |  0.68 | 34.61 | 22.15 | 16.64 | 10.05 |
            | 48.60 | 51.79 | 48.92 | 50.49 | 50.94 | 49.42 | 48.22 |
------------+-------+-------+-------+-------+-------+-------+-------+
Theoretical |  1190 |   430 |    71 |  3394 |  2133 |  1703 |  1079 |  10000
            |  5.95 |  2.15 |  0.36 | 16.97 | 10.67 |  8.52 |  5.40 |  50.00
            | 11.90 |  4.30 |  0.71 | 33.94 | 21.33 | 17.03 | 10.79 |
            | 51.40 | 48.21 | 51.08 | 49.51 | 49.06 | 50.58 | 51.78 |
------------+-------+-------+-------+-------+-------+-------+-------+
Total          2315     892     139    6855    4348    3367    2084   20000
              11.58    4.46    0.70   34.28   21.74   16.84   10.42  100.00

Statistic                   DF     Value        Prob
-----------------------------------------------------
Chi-Square                   6     8.318       0.216
```

3.10.2 Generating Random Stock Prices Using the RANTBL Function

If the theoretical distribution of a variable is not known, but a stepwise approximation of it is available, we can utilize the RANTBL function to generate the random samples that follow the distribution given by that stepwise function. Let us assume that the stock prices in the example in Section 3.8.2 follow an unknown theoretical distribution. We will show how to generate the random stock prices with the RANTBL function.

Program 3.13 first establishes the theoretical cumulative density function of the S&P 500 stock prices (using the file SPPRICE from Program 3.10 in Section 3.8.2). Then these prices and their probabilities are loaded into two arrays used in conjunction with the RANTBL function. Note the compact reference to array PROB, which has 414 elements during the execution (414 is the number of unique stock prices among the S&P 500 stocks). Since the RANTBL function returns an integer, it is mapped to an actual stock price. The program finally determines the cumulative distribution function of the random stock prices and plots it along with the theoretical one. The closeness of the two curves is clear in Figure 3.3 even with 1,000 random prices. The first ten randomly generated values are shown in Output 3.13.

Program 3.13   *Generating Random Stock Prices with RANTBL*

```
/* determine the probability mass function of the stock prices. */
/* file 'SPPRICE' was created in Program 3.10.                   */

PROC FREQ DATA=SPPRICE;
    TABLE PRICE / NOPRINT OUT=SPFREQ(KEEP=PRICE PERCENT);

/* macro variable 'N' holds the number of unique stock prices.  */

DATA _NULL_;
    IF 0 THEN SET SPFREQ NOBS=N;
    IF _N_=1 THEN CALL SYMPUT('N',COMPRESS(PUT(N,8.0)));
    STOP; RUN;

/* generate 1,000 random stock prices according to the          */
/* probabilities determined before (file 'RNDPRICE'). File       */
/* 'SPCDF' holds the theoretical cumulative density function     */
/* of the S&P 500 stock prices.                                  */

DATA RNDPRICE(KEEP=PRICE) SPCDF(KEEP=PRICE SPPROB);
    SET SPFREQ END=ENDOFPRC;

    /* arrays 'PRICES' and 'PROB' hold the unique stock prices */
    /* and their probabilities of the S&P 500 stocks. Load     */
    /* them into the arrays from the output of 'PROC FREQ'.    */

    ARRAY PRICES(&N) PRC1-PRC&N;
    ARRAY PROB (&N) PRB1-PRB&N;
    RETAIN PRC1-PRC&N PRB1-PRB&N;
    PRICES(_N_)=PRICE;
    PROB(_N_)=PERCENT/100;

    /* the arrays are loaded. Create the theoretical cdf (file */
    /* 'SPCDF') and generate the 1,000 random stock prices.    */

    IF ENDOFPRC THEN DO;

        /* calculate and save the theoretical cdf. */

        SPPROB=0;
        DO I=1 TO DIM(PRICES);
            PRICE=PRICES(I);
            SPPROB=SPPROB+PROB(I);
            OUTPUT SPCDF;
        END;

        /* generate random stock prices using function RANTBL. */

        DO I=1 TO 1000;

            /* function RANTBL is called with the probabilities */
            /* in array 'PROB'. The returned integer is mapped  */
            /* to the actual stock price.                       */

            PRICE=PRICES(RANTBL(123,OF PROB(*)));
            OUTPUT RNDPRICE;
        END;
    END;
    RUN;

/* determine the cumulative distribution */
```

```
/* function of the random stock prices.  */

PROC FREQ DATA=RNDPRICE;
    TABLE PRICE / NOPRINT OUT=RNDCDF(KEEP=PRICE PERCENT);
    RUN;
DATA RNDCDF(KEEP=PRICE RNDPROB);
    SET RNDCDF;
    RETAIN RNDPROB 0;
    RNDPROB=RNDPROB+PERCENT/100;
    RUN;

/* concatenate the theoretical (file 'SPCDF') and the randomly  */
/* generated (file 'RNDCDF') cdf's. Set up a sample identifier. */

DATA BOTH;
    SET SPCDF(RENAME=(SPPROB=PROB))
        RNDCDF(RENAME=(RNDPROB=PROB) IN=RND);
    RETAIN SAMPLE 'Theoretical';
    IF RND THEN SAMPLE='Random';
    OUTPUT;
    RUN;

/* create an annotate file for the legend. */

DATA ANNO;
    XSYS='2'; YSYS='2';
    FUNCTION='LABEL'; POSITION='6'; STYLE='DUPLEX'; SIZE=1.2;
    X=170; Y=0.20; TEXT='THEORETICAL'; OUTPUT;
          Y=0.10; TEXT='RANDOM';       OUTPUT;
    LINE=1;  FUNCTION='MOVE'; X=150; Y=0.1; OUTPUT;
             FUNCTION='DRAW'; X=168; Y=0.1; OUTPUT;
    LINE=20; FUNCTION='MOVE'; X=150; Y=0.2; OUTPUT;
             FUNCTION='DRAW'; X=168; Y=0.2; OUTPUT;

/* plot the two cdf's. */

PROC GPLOT DATA=BOTH ANNOTATE=ANNO;
    PLOT PROB*PRICE=SAMPLE / VAXIS=AXIS1 HAXIS=AXIS2 NOLEGEND;
    AXIS1 LABEL=(A=90 R=0 F=DUPLEX H=1.2 'Probability')
          ORDER=0 TO 1 BY 0.2 VALUE=(H=1.2 F=DUPLEX) MINOR=(N=1);
    AXIS2 LABEL=(F=DUPLEX H=1.2 'Stock Price ($)')
          ORDER=0 TO 200 BY 25 VALUE=(H=1.2 F=DUPLEX) MINOR=(N=3);
    TITLE  F=SWISS H=1.3 'Theoretical and Randomly Generated
Cumulative Distribution Functions';
    TITLE2 F=SWISS H=1.3 'Size of Random Sample is 1,000. Function
Used: RANTBL';
    SYMBOL1 I=JOIN C=BLACK R=1 L=1;
    SYMBOL2 I=JOIN C=BLACK R=1 L=20;
    RUN;
    QUIT;
```

Output 3.13
Random Stock
Prices
Generated
with the
RANTBL
Function

```
            The first 10 Random Stock Prices

                   OBS      PRICE

                    1     62.0000
                    2     33.6875
                    3     26.6875
                    4     85.0000
                    5     35.0625
                    6     28.3125
                    7     64.5625
                    8     37.0000
                    9     21.7500
                   10     26.9375
```

Figure 3.3 *Distribution of Random Stock Prices Generated by RANTBL*

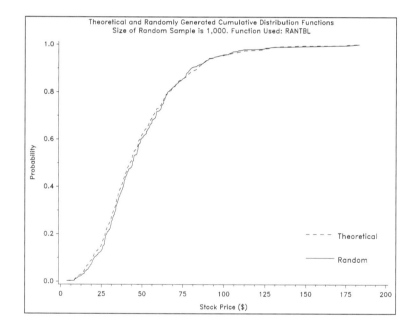

3.11 Summary

The random number generator functions available in SAS satisfy the requirements of producing random numbers of any distribution for Monte Carlo simulations. They are invoked in a DATA step or in PROC IML, either as functions or CALL routines. When we create more than one random variable, the CALL form should be used with carefully picked seed values in order to avoid overlapping or correlated streams of random numbers. Various SAS procedures help verify the distribution of the generated random numbers.

3.12 References

Brainard, J., and D. E. Burmaster. 1992. "Bivariate Distributions for Height and Weight of Men and Women in the United States." *Risk Analysis* 12:267-275

Clark, M. R., and D. E. Woodward. 1992. "Generating Random Numbers with Base SAS Software." *Observations* 1(4):12-19.

Felsővályi, Á. 1994. "Solving the Monty Hall Problem with SAS Simulation." *Observations* 3(3):43-53.

Fishman, G. S., and L. R. Moore. 1982. "A Statistical Evaluation of Multiplicative Congruential Random Number Generators with Modulus 2^{31}-1." *Journal of the American Statistical Association* 77 (377):129-136.

Hamer, R. M., and T. J. Breen. 1985. "The SAS System as a Statistical Simulation Language." *Proceedings of the Tenth Annual SAS Users Group International Conference*, Reno, Nevada, 982-989.

Killam, B. 1987. "An Overview of the SAS System Random Number Generators."*Proceedings of the Twelfth Annual SAS Users Group International Conference*, Dallas, Texas, 1059-1065.

Knuth, D. E. 1982. *The Art of Computer Programming: Seminumerical Algorithms*. Vol. 2. 2d ed. Reading, MA: Addison-Wesley.

Lehmer, F. H. 1951. Second *Symposium on Large-Scale Digital Calculating Machinery*. Cambridge: Harvard University Press.

Moody's Investor Services. 1999. *Bond Rating Distribution*. New York: Moody's Investor Services.

Ralston, A., ed. 1976. *Encyclopedia of Computer Science*. New York: Van Nostrand Reinhold.

Rubinstein, R. Y. 1981. *Simulation and the Monte Carlo Method*. New York: John Wiley & Sons.

U.S. Bureau of the Census. "Resident Population of the United States: Estimates, by Age and Sex." http://www.census.gov/population/estimates/nation/intfile2-1.txt (12/28/1998).

Chapter 4 Generating Data in Monte Carlo Studies

4.1 Introduction

In Chapter 3, we discussed how to generate random numbers from different distributions in SAS (e.g., uniform or normal distributions). This chapter is a continuation of that discussion. A Monte Carlo study is ". . . the use of random sampling techniques ... to obtain approximate solutions ..." (Merriam-Webster, Inc. 1994, pp. 754-755). To conduct a Monte Carlo study, it is obviously necessary to generate sample data in such a fashion that the generated sample data adequately represent random samples from a population with known population characteristics, such as population central tendency (e.g., population mean) and population variability (e.g., population standard deviation). Furthermore, population characteristics also include whether or not the population is normally distributed, and in the case of non-normal distributions, the nature and degree of non-normality (e.g., degree of skewness and/or kurtosis).

When the analysis involves more than one variable, as is usually the case in most analysis situations, not only individual variable distribution characteristics (i.e., mean, standard deviation, skewness, and kurtosis of each individual variable) need to be simulated, but the inter-variable relationship patterns among the variables must also be adequately simulated. Fundamentally, the validity of any Monte Carlo study results hinges on the adequacy of data generation, both for individual variables and for inter-variable relationship patterns. Data generation is so crucial in Monte Carlo studies that it is no exaggeration to say that unless we are able to generate sample data according to our specified population characteristics, no Monte Carlo studies can be attempted.

The purpose of this chapter is to present procedures for data generation, and to present SAS program examples to implement the data generation procedures. The theoretical aspects of data generation are briefly covered when necessary to provide readers with the necessary theoretical underpinnings of the data generation procedures. SAS programming examples of data generation are provided for all important aspects of data generation so that readers will be able to apply these data generation procedures in SAS in their own work.

4.2 Generating Sample Data for One Variable

Most Monte Carlo studies involve more than one variable. But we must be able to generate samples of a single variable before we can attempt to tackle the situation involving multiple variables. This section discusses how such a task can be accomplished in SAS. Simulating data as if they were sampled from a standard normal distribution—i.e., N(0,1), normally distributed with a population mean of zero, and a population standard deviation of one—is easily accomplished in SAS by using the RANNOR function, as discussed in Chapter 3. So the major focus of this chapter is on generating sample data for a population with a known degree of *non-normality*. Because many statistical analyses assume data normality, the impact of violating data normality assumption on the validity of statistical results often becomes an area of focus for empirical investigations. Consequently, data non-normality is often one important area of research interest in Monte Carlo simulation studies.

4.2.1 Generating Sample Data from a Normal Distribution with the Desired Mean and Standard Deviation

As discussed in Chapter 3, the SAS normal variate generator RANNOR makes it relatively easy to generate samples from a normally distributed population with a mean of zero and a standard deviation of one [N(0, 1)]. The numerical values obtained through repeated generation of the SAS normal variate generator RANNOR can be considered as *z* scores from a normally distributed Z score distribution, which is used widely in many statistical analyses. In many Monte Carlo studies, however, we need variables with population means and standard deviations other than those provided by the SAS normal variate generator RANNOR. To linearly transform normally distributed data to a new distribution with the desired population mean and variance requires only a simple linear transformation. Linear transformation only changes the mean and variance of a distribution, but not the shape of the distribution as defined by the distribution's third and fourth statistical moments (i.e., skewness and kurtosis). The formula used for such linear transformation is as follows:

$$X' = \mu_{X'} + z(\sigma_{X'})$$

(4.1)

where

X' is the transformed variable.

$\mu_{x'}$ is the desired population mean of the transformed variable.

z the z score values generated by the SAS random normal variate generator RANNOR.

$\sigma_{x'}$ is the desired population standard deviation of the transformed variable.

Such simple linear transformation is readily implemented in the data generation process in SAS. For example, we are interested in generating a sample of 10,000 observations (cases) on three uncorrelated variables (X_1, X_2, X_3) from the following three normal distributions with their respective population means and standard deviations:

X_1: $\mu = 100$, $\sigma = 15$ (e.g., IQ Score Distribution)

X_2: $\mu = 50$, $\sigma = 10$ (e.g., T-Score Distribution)

X_3: $\mu = 0$, $\sigma = 1$ (e.g., Z-Score Distribution)

A SAS program example (Program 4.1) is provided below to accomplish this task. Please notice that the linear transformations based on Formula 4.1, implemented for X_1 and X_2 in the SAS program, easily accomplish the goal of imposing the specified population means and standard deviations on X_1 and X_2.

Program 4.1 *Generating Three Independent Normal Variables*

```
DATA A;
  DO I = 1 TO 10000;
     X1 = 100 + 15*RANNOR (0);
     X2 =  50 + 10*RANNOR (0);
     X3 = RANNOR (0);
   OUTPUT;
  END;
PROC MEANS DATA=A N MEAN VAR SKEWNESS KURTOSIS;
  VAR X1 X2 X3;
PROC CORR NOSIMPLE;
  VAR X1 X2 X3;
RUN;
```

Sample statistics (for N=10,000) based on one execution of Program 4.1 are presented in Output 4.1. These results indicate that the variables in the sample closely resemble normal distributions with specified means and standard deviations. In addition, as expected, the three variables are not correlated with each other except by chance.

Output 4.1
Sample
Statistics of
Three
Independent
Variables
(Program
4.1)

```
                         The MEANS Procedure

    Variable      N        Mean        Variance      Skewness      Kurtosis
    ----------------------------------------------------------------------
    X1         10000   100.1210242   225.5664422    0.0089585    -0.0961917
    X2         10000    50.2067529   101.1253957   -0.0118714     0.0306617
    X3         10000     0.0139093     1.0228762    0.0087563     0.0473664
    ----------------------------------------------------------------------
                          The CORR Procedure

               Pearson Correlation Coefficients, N = 10000
                      Prob > |r|  under H0: Rho=0

                              X1             X2             X3

                  X1       1.00000        0.01188        0.00158
                                          0.2349         0.8749

                  X2       0.01188        1.00000        0.00809
                           0.2349                        0.4183

                  X3       0.00158        0.00809        1.00000
                           0.8749         0.4183
```

4.2.2 Generating Data from Non-Normal Distributions

Although it is relatively easy to generate sample data from a normal distribution with any desired population mean and standard deviation, as seen in the previous section, generating data from a *non-normal* distribution is considerably more complicated. But since non-normality tends to be an important condition for empirical investigation in a variety of statistical Monte Carlo simulation studies, it is crucial that a Monte Carlo researcher be able to accomplish this task.

A variety of mathematical algorithms have been developed over the years to simulate non-normality distribution conditions (Burr 1973; Fleishman 1978; Johnson 1949, 1965; Johnson & Kitchen 1971; Pearson & Hartley 1972; Ramberg & Schmeiser 1974; Ramberg et al. 1979; Schmeiser & Deutch 1977). In this section, we introduce two algorithms for simulating population distributional non-normality conditions. These two algorithms have been popular among Monte Carlo researchers in different disciplines. Also, these two systems are relatively easy to implement in SAS programming.

4.2.2.1 Using the Generalized Lambda Distribution (GLD) System

Based on Tukey's earlier work (Tukey 1960), Ramberg and Schmeiser (1974) developed algorithms for obtaining a generalized lambda distribution (GLD) for simulating non-normal distributions with desired degrees of skewness and kurtosis:

$$X' = \lambda_1 + \frac{u^{\lambda_3} - (1 - u)^{\lambda_4}}{\lambda_2} \tag{4.2}$$

where

X' is the simulated non-normal distribution.

u is a *uniform* distribution ranging from 0 to 1 (see Chapter 3 for details about the SAS uniform distribution generator RANUNI).

λ_i (i=1 to 4)   represents values needed to simulate sample data from a non-normal distribution with specified degrees of skewness and kurtosis; these four λ values are determined once the degrees of skewness and kurtosis of the simulated non-normality are specified.

Ramberg et al. (1979) elaborated on the GLD algorithms and tabulated the parameters λ_1, λ_2, λ_3, and λ_4 needed in (4.2) for selected values of skewness and kurtosis. Part of the tabulated parameters of λ_1, λ_2, λ_3, and λ_4 are adapted from Ramberg et al. (1979) and presented in Table 4.1. Table 4.1 is intended as an illustrative example, and it only covers those λ values for non-normality conditions with skewness of +.75 or -.75, and kurtosis ranging from -.2 to +3.2. Readers should consult the tabulated values in Ramberg et al. (1979) for other non-normality conditions as defined by the population skewness and kurtosis of a distribution.

Table 4.1 *GLD Method Coefficients for Non-Normality Transformation*

SKEWNESS[1]	KURTOSIS	λ_1	λ_2	λ_3	λ_4
.75	-.20	-1.3340	.2104	.0000	.3903
.75	.00	-1.0970	.2003	.0183	.3119
.75	.40	- .7850	.1658	.0360	.1974
.75	.80	- .5900	.1206	.0355	.1179
.75	1.20	- .4660	.0726	.0246	.0614
.75	1.60	- .3840	.0266	.9663(+)	.0202
.75	2.00	- .3240	-.0157	-.5915(+)	-.0109
.75	2.40	- .2840	-.0539	-.0207	-.0352
.75	2.80	- .2540	-.0884	-.0342	-.0547
.75	3.20	- .2290	-.1195	-.0464	-.0706

1:    For negative skewness, see the explanation later in this section.
(+): Multiply by 10^{-2}.

One potential confusion related to the tabulated λ_i values in the tables of Ramberg et al. (1979) is the kurtosis values listed in their tables. Ramberg et al. defined skewness (α_3) and kurtosis (α_4) respectively as:

$$\alpha_3 = \frac{E(X - \mu)^3}{\sigma^3}$$

$$\alpha_4 = \frac{E(X - \mu)^4}{\sigma^4}$$

(4.3)

where

E is a symbol meaning "expected value".

μ is the population mean.

σ is the population standard deviation.

α_3 is the skewness.

α_4 is the kurtosis.

While the definition for skewness (α_3) is consistent with what is commonly used elsewhere, the definition for kurtosis (α_4) is not. Although their definition for kurtosis is technically correct and not uncommon, the more commonly known definition for kurtosis is:

$$\alpha_4 = \frac{E(X - \mu)^4}{\sigma^4} - 3$$

(4.4)

The difference between the two definitions of kurtosis is simple: Based on the more common definition of kurtosis (4.4), a normal distribution will have a skewness of zero and a kurtosis of zero. But based on the kurtosis definition in Ramberg et al. (1979), as expressed in (4.3), a normal distribution would have a skewness of zero and a kurtosis of 3. For this reason, readers should be careful in reading the tables in Ramberg et al. (1979) for different kurtosis values: simply subtract 3 from their tabulated kurtosis values to make those values conform to the more common definition. For example, the kurtosis values in Table 4.1 above originally ranged from +2.8 to +6.2 in Ramberg et al. (1979). We simply subtracted 3 from their listed kurtosis values in order to make them conform to the convention that normal distributions have a kurtosis of zero instead of +3.

The tabulated λ_i values in Ramberg et al. (1979) for the GLD algorithm, as represented in Table 4.1, do not list any condition of negative skewness. But the probability density with a negative skewness is the mirror image of the probability density with a positive skewness of the same absolute value. So to obtain the λ_i values for a negative skewness condition, do the following:

1. Find the λ_i values for the positive skewness with the same absolute value.

2. Interchange the λ_3 and λ_4 values—i.e., use the λ_3 as the new λ_4, and λ_4 as the new λ_3.

3. Change the sign of λ_1.

These three steps will allow us to generate sample data from distributions with negative skewness.

It also warrants readers' attention that, in using the GLD algorithm as presented above in simulating non-normal conditions, the *uniform distribution* generator (RANUNI in SAS) is needed instead of the *normal variate* generator (RANNOR). A SAS program example is presented below (Program 4.2) in which the GLD method is used to simulate a sample (N=10,000) with three uncorrelated non-normal variables with the following population non-normality conditions:

$$X_1: \mu = 100, \ \sigma = 15, \ \text{skewness} = .75, \ \text{kurtosis} = .80$$

$$X_2: \mu = 50, \ \ \sigma = 10, \ \text{skewness} = -.75, \ \text{kurtosis} = .80$$

$$X_3: \mu = 0, \ \ \ \sigma = 1, \ \text{skewness} = .75, \ \text{kurtosis} = 2.40$$

Program 4.2 *GLD Method for Generating Three Non-Normal Variables*

```
DATA A;
  DO I = 1 TO 10000;
     X1 = RANUNI(0);
     X2 = RANUNI(0);
     X3 = RANUNI(0);
     X1 = -.59 + (X1**.0355 - (1-X1)**.1179)/.1206;
     X2 =  .59 + (X2**.1179 - (1-X2)**.0355)/.1206;
     X3 = -.284 + (X3**(-.0207) - (1-X3)**(-.0352))/(-.0539);
     X1 = 100 + 15*X1;
     X2 =  50 + 10*X2;
     X3 =  X3;
   OUTPUT;
  END;
PROC MEANS N MEAN STD SKEWNESS KURTOSIS;
  VAR X1 X2 X3;
PROC CORR NOSIMPLE;
  VAR X1 X2 X3;
RUN;
```

The descriptive statistics for the simulated sample of three uncorrelated variables based on one execution of this SAS program are presented in Output 4.2 below. These results indicate that the sample generated using the GLD method closely approximates the desired population non-normality conditions specified for the three variables. Furthermore, the sample correlations among the three variables do not exceed chance level, as expected theoretically.

Output 4.2
Three Non-
Normal
Variables
Based on
GLD Method
(Program 4.2)

```
                            The MEANS Procedure

   Variable      N          Mean      Std Dev     Skewness      Kurtosis
   ---------------------------------------------------------------------
   X1         10000   100.0306527   14.7541618    0.7329213     0.8436068
   X2         10000    50.0614385    9.9028254   -0.7390503     0.7232249
   X3         10000     0.0015703    0.9900119    0.6779757     2.4359533
   ---------------------------------------------------------------------
                            The CORR Procedure
                 Pearson Correlation Coefficients, N = 10000
                      Prob > |r| under H0: Rho=0

                              X1            X2            X3
              X1         1.00000       0.00274       0.00319
                                       0.7838        0.7497

              X2         0.00274       1.00000      -0.00231
                         0.7838                      0.8175

              X3         0.00319      -0.00231       1.00000
                         0.7497        0.8175
```

4.2.2.2 Using Fleishman's Power Transformation Method

Fleishman (1978) also introduced a method for generating sample data from a population with desired degrees of skewness and kurtosis. This method uses polynomial transformation to transform a normally distributed variable to a variable with specified degrees of skewness and kurtosis. The polynomial transformation developed by Fleishman takes the form:

$$Y = a + bZ + cZ^2 + dZ^3 \tag{4.5}$$

where

Y	is the transformed non-normal variable with specified population skewness and kurtosis.
Z	is a normally distributed variable with a population mean of zero and a variance of one—i.e., a unit normal variate.
a, b, c, d	are coefficients needed for transforming the unit normal variate to a non-normal variable with specified degrees of population skewness and kurtosis. Of the four coefficients, $a = -c$.

The coefficients (a, b, c, d) needed for the transformation are tabulated in Fleishman (1978) for selected combinations of degrees of skewness and kurtosis. Table 4.2 presents a small example set of Fleishman power transformation coefficients for skewness of .75, and for kurtosis ranging from -.20 to +3.20. Because $a = -c$, the table does not list the values for a.

Once the coefficients for the desired transformation are available, generating non-normal data becomes a relatively simple matter. While the GLD method discussed above requires a *uniform* distribution random number generator (the RANUNI function in SAS), Fleishman's method requires a *normal variate* generator (the RANNOR function in SAS) for generating random numbers from a normal distribution with a mean of zero and a variance of one.

Table 4.2 *Selected Coefficients for Non-Normality Transformation*

SKEWNESS[1]	KURTOSIS	b	c	d
.75	-.20	1.173302916	.207562460	-.079058576
.75	.00	1.112514484	.173629896	-.050334372
.75	.40	1.033355486	.141435163	-.018192493
.75	.80	.978350485	.124833577	.001976943
.75	1.20	.935785930	.114293870	.016737509
.75	1.60	.900640275	.106782526	.028475848
.75	2.00	.870410983	.101038303	.038291124
.75	2.40	.843688891	.096435287	.046773413
.75	2.80	.819604207	.092622898	.054275030
.75	3.20	.797581770	.089386978	.061023176

Note: a = -c

1: For negative skewness, see the discussion in the text.

Since positive and negative skewness can be considered symmetrical, the tabulated transformation coefficients in Fleishman (1978) did not list negative skewness conditions. But the coefficients for negative skewness conditions can be obtained simply by reversing the signs of *c* and *a*. In other words, to generate a sample from a negatively skewed distribution, do the following:

1. Obtain the coefficients (*b, c, d*) for the desired kurtosis and *positive* skewness of the same absolute value.

2. Obtain *a* (*a = -c*).

3. Reverse the signs of *a* and *c*.

4. Apply the coefficients in the formula.

An example SAS program (Program 4.3) is presented below in which the Fleishman power transformation method is used for generating a sample (N=10,000) of three uncorrelated variables with the same univariate non-normality conditions as those specified in the example for the GLD method. That is,

X_1: $\mu = 100$, $\sigma = 15$, skewness = .75, kurtosis = .80

X_2: $\mu = 50$, $\sigma = 10$, skewness = -.75, kurtosis = .80

X_3: $\mu = 0$, $\sigma = 1$, skewness = .75, kurtosis = 2.40

Program 4.3 *Fleishman Method for Generating Three Non-Normal Variables*

```
DATA A;
  DO I = 1 TO 10000;
      X1 = RANNOR (0);
      X2 = RANNOR (0);
      X3 = RANNOR (0);
                                  *** Fleishman non-normality transformation;

      X1 = -.124833577 + .978350485*X1 + .124833577*X1**2 + .001976943*X1**3;
      X2 =  .124833577 + .978350485*X2 - .124833577*X2**2 + .001976943*X2**3;
      X3 = -.096435287 + .843688891*X3 + .096435287*X3**2 + .046773413*X3**3;

      X1 = 100 + 15*X1;          ***linear transformation;
      X2 =  50 + 10*X2;
      X3 =  X3;
    OUTPUT;
  END;
PROC MEANS N MEAN STD SKEWNESS KURTOSIS;
  VAR X1 X2 X3;
PROC CORR NOSIMPLE;
  VAR X1 X2 X3;
RUN;
```

The resultant sample descriptive statistics based on one execution of Program 4.3 are presented in Output 4.3 below. These results indicate that the sample represents the theoretical population well in terms of the specified non-normality conditions (i.e., specified degrees of skewness and kurtosis). Note that the negative skewness of X_2 was easily achieved by reversing the signs of *a* and *c*. In addition, the three variables are not correlated beyond what can be expected by sampling error.

Output 4.3
Three Non-Normal Variables Based on the Fleishman Method (Program 4.3)

```
                          The MEANS Procedure

Variable     N        Mean      Std Dev     Skewness     Kurtosis
-----------------------------------------------------------------------
X1        10000   99.9971162   15.1025922   0.7038539    0.7563708
X2        10000   50.0069170   10.0722888  -0.7547759    0.9121069
X3        10000    0.0014170    1.0133944   0.7898695    2.6114542
-----------------------------------------------------------------------

                          The CORR Procedure
                Pearson Correlation Coefficients, N = 10000
                    Prob > |r| under H0: Rho=0

                           X1           X2           X3

             X1        1.00000     -0.00943      0.01024
                                    0.3456       0.3060

             X2       -0.00943      1.00000      0.00668
                        0.3456                   0.5040

             X3        0.01024      0.00668      1.00000
                        0.3060       0.5040
```

Both the GLD and Fleishman methods for generating sample data from non-normal distributions are easy to use, because the coefficients needed for the non-normal transformation are tabulated in the authors' original articles for many selected combinations of skewness and kurtosis.

In case non-normality conditions other than those tabulated in Ramberg et al. (1979) or in Fleishman (1978) are desired, and consequently no coefficients are available for generating sample data with the desired non-normality conditions, we provide a SAS/IML program (Program 4.4) below for deriving your own Fleishman coefficients for any possible univariate non-normality conditions permitted by the Fleishman method. To derive the Fleishman coefficients for any desired non-normality conditions, one simply specifies the desired degree of skewness and kurtosis for each variable, and then runs the SAS/IML program. The program will then output the Fleishman coefficients (*a*, *b*, *c*, and *d*). These coefficients can then be used for generating sample data, as in Program 4.3 above. As an example, in Program 4.4, Fleishman coefficients are derived for the following four skewness/kurtosis conditions:

1. skewness = -1, kurtosis = 2.5

2. skewness = 2, kurtosis = 7

3. skewness = 0, kurtosis = 0

4. skewness = -2, kurtosis = 7

Program 4.4 Deriving Fleishman Coefficients for Desired Skewness and Kurtosis

```
/*  This program calculates the coefficients for Fleishman's power transformation in
    order to obtain univariate non-normal variables.  For references, see  Allen I.
    Fleishman, (1978).  A method for simulating non-normal distributions,
    Psychometrika, 43, 521-532.  Also see Vale, C. David and Maurelli, Vincent A.
    (1983).  Simulating multivariate non-normal distributions, Psychometrika, 48,
    465-471.                                                                      */

    PROC IML;

/*  In the following matrix 'SKEWKURT', specify the skewness and kurtosis for each
    variable.  Each row represents one variable. In each row, the 1st number is the
    skewness, the 2nd is the kurtosis of the variable;                           */
    SKEWKURT={-1 2.5,
               2 7,
               0 0,
              -2 7};

    START NEWTON;
      RUN FUN;
      DO ITER = 1 TO MAXITER
      WHILE(MAX(ABS(F))>CONVERGE);
            RUN DERIV;
            DELTA=-SOLVE(J,F);
            COEF=COEF+DELTA;
            RUN FUN;
      END;
    FINISH NEWTON;
    MAXITER=25;
    CONVERGE=.000001;
    START FUN;
      X1=COEF[1];
      X2=COEF[2];
```

```
   X3=COEF[3];
   F=(X1**2+6*X1*X3+2*X2**2+15*X3**2-1)//
     (2*X2*(X1**2+24*X1*X3+105*X3**2+2)-SKEWNESS)//
     (24*(X1*X3+X2**2*(1+X1**2+28*X1*X3)+X3**2*
       (12+48*X1*X3+141*X2**2+225*X3**2))-KURTOSIS);
FINISH FUN;
START DERIV;
   J=((2*X1+6*X3)||(4*X2)||(6*X1+30*X3))//
     ((4*X2*(X1+12*X3))||(2*(X1**2+24*X1*X3+105*X3**2+2))
     ||(4*X2*(12*X1+105*X3)))//
     ((24*(X3+X2**2*(2*X1+28*X3)+48*X3**3))||
      (48*X2*(1+X1**2+28*X1*X3+141*X3**2))||
      (24*(X1+28*X1*X2**2+2*X3*(12+48*X1*X3+141*X2**2+225*X3**2)
      +X3**2*(48*X1+450*X3))));
FINISH DERIV;
DO;
NUM = NROW(SKEWKURT);
DO VAR=1 TO NUM;
   SKEWNESS=SKEWKURT[VAR,1];
   KURTOSIS=SKEWKURT[VAR,2];
   COEF={1.0, 0.0, 0.0};
   RUN NEWTON;
   COEF=COEF`;
   SK_KUR=SKEWKURT[VAR,];
   COMBINE=SK_KUR || COEF;
   IF VAR=1 THEN RESULT=COMBINE;
   ELSE IF VAR>1 THEN RESULT=RESULT // COMBINE;
END;
   PRINT "COEFFICIENTS OF B, C, D FOR FLEISHMAN'S POWER TRANSFORMATION";
   PRINT "Y = A + BX + CX^2 + DX^3";
   PRINT " A = -C";
   MATTRIB RESULT COLNAME=({SKEWNESS KURTOSIS B C D})
                  FORMAT=12.9;
   PRINT RESULT;
END;
QUIT;
```

In Program 4.4, the Fleishman coefficients for four variables with varying degrees of skewness/kurtosis combinations (-1/2.5, 2/7, 0/0, and -1/7 respectively) are derived at the same time. A versatile iterative estimation method called the Newton-Raphson method is used to obtain a solution for the Fleishman coefficients for the variables with the desired degrees of skewness and kurtosis. It is not necessary for readers to understand the Newton-Ralphson method implemented in the program, nor is it necessary to understand the details of the SAS PROC IML program in Program 4.4. The user only needs to provide the matrix called "SKEWKURT" in the program. The number of rows in this matrix represents the number of variables for which Fleishman coefficients are needed. Each row of the matrix has two numbers. The first is the desired skewness of the variable, and the second is the desired kurtosis of the variable. The execution of Program 4.4 produces the results shown in Output 4.4. These coefficients (*a*, *b*, *c*, and *d*) can then be used to generate sample data drawn from non-normal populations with the desired degrees of skewness and kurtosis.

Output 4.4
Fleishman
Coefficients
for Four
Variables
(Program
4.4)

```
       COEFFICIENTS OF B, C, D FOR FLEISHMAN'S POWER TRANSFORMATION

                      Y = A + BX + CX^2 + DX^3

                               A = -C

                              RESULT
       SKEWNESS      KURTOSIS          B             C             D


      -1.000000000  2.500000000  0.865574890  -0.136404884  0.037138751

       2.000000000  7.000000000  0.761585275   0.260022598  0.053072274

       0.000000000  0.000000000  1.000000000   0.000000000  0.000000000

      -2.000000000  7.000000000  0.761585275  -0.260022598  0.053072274
```

One disadvantage of both the GLD and Fleishman methods is that neither of the two covers all possible combinations of skewness and kurtosis. In other words, the two methods cannot generate data for some combinations of skewness and kurtosis conditions (Fleishman 1978; Tadikamalla 1980). The comparative study by Tadikamalla (1980) indicated that the two methods cover approximately the same parameter space of non-normality as defined by skewness and kurtosis, but the Fleishman method is more efficient. Readers interested in this limitation may consult these references about the approximate parameter space (non-normality conditions as defined by skewness and kurtosis) for which the two methods can generate non-normal data.

Besides the two methods discussed here, other methods exist for the same purpose, such as those by Johnson (1949, 1965), Ramberg and Schmeiser (1974), Schmeiser and Deutch (1977), and Burr (1973). Interested readers may consult the original papers for these alternative methods. Despite the fact that the Fleishman method cannot cover some non-normality conditions, the Fleishman method may be easier to use compared with other methods when *multivariate* non-normal data are desired in Monte Carlo simulations, as will be discussed later in this chapter.

4.3 Generating Sample Data from a Multivariate Normal Distribution

Methods for generating *univariate* normal and non-normal sample data have been discussed in the previous sections. In most Monte Carlo studies, however, multiple variables are involved. For example, in any regression analysis, there must be two correlated variables at a minimum: the dependent variable (Y) and one predictor (X). The same is true for many other *univariate* statistical techniques (i.e., where there is only one dependent variable). Any *multivariate* statistical technique (i.e., where there are multiple dependent variables), by definition, must have multiple variables in the system.

When multiple variables are involved in a Monte Carlo study, not only does the researcher have to control *univariate* distributional characteristics as discussed above, he/she must also be able to control the multiple-variable sample data in such a way that the sample data generated can be considered as samples drawn from a multiple-variable population with known *inter-variable correlations*. This is the topic to be discussed in this section.

The degree of complexity in generating multiple variables with desired degrees of inter-variable correlations depends partially on whether the individual variables involved are normally distributed or not. Because of this, we divide our discussion into two sections, with this section covering normal univariate variables, and with section 4.4 covering non-normal univariate variables.

When all individual variables are normally distributed, imposing a specified population inter-correlation pattern on the sample data of multiple variables is a relatively straightforward procedure. Kaiser and Dickman (1962) presented a matrix decomposition procedure that imposes a specified correlation matrix on a set of otherwise uncorrelated random normal variables, as if the data were sampled from a population with specified population correlations as represented by the imposed correlation matrix. Given a desired population correlation matrix **R**, the basic matrix decomposition procedure takes the following form (Kaiser & Dickman 1962):

$$\hat{Z}_{(k \times N)} = F_{(k \times k)} \, \hat{X}_{(k \times N)} \tag{4.6}$$

where

k is the number of variables involved.

N is the number of observations (sample N).

$\hat{X}$ is a k×N data matrix, with N observations, each with k uncorrelated random normal variables (mean of zero and standard deviation of one).

F: is a k×k matrix containing principal component factor pattern coefficients obtained by applying principal component factorization to the given population correlation matrix **R**.

$\hat{Z}$ is the resultant k×N sample data matrix (N observations on k variables), as if sampled from a population with the given population correlation matrix **R**.

k×N represents the matrix dimensions (k rows and N columns).

To generate sample data of k variables with the desired population inter-correlation pattern as represented by **R**, take the following steps:

1. For a specified population correlation matrix **R**, conduct a factor analysis (SAS/STAT PROC FACTOR) using principal component as the factor extraction method (the default option in PROC FACTOR). Request the option of keeping the same number of factors (PROC FACTOR N=K) as the number of variables in the specified population correlation matrix **R**, and obtain the matrix of factor pattern **F**, which is called "factor pattern" in SAS output.

2. Generate k uncorrelated random normal variables (mean of zero and standard deviation of one), each with N observations. The dimension of this matrix is originally N×k. It is then transposed to a k×N dimension matrix $\hat{X}$, i.e., the matrix has k rows to represent k variables, and N columns to represent N observations.

3. Premultiply the uncorrelated data matrix $\hat{X}$ with the factor pattern matrix **F**. The resultant $\hat{Z}$ matrix (k×N) contains N observations on k correlated variables, as if the N observations were sampled from a population with the population correlation pattern represented by **R**. This correlated data matrix is then transposed back to an N×k dimension sample data matrix for later use in analysis.

The matrix manipulations involved in the above discussion can easily be implemented in SAS. When individual variables are univariate normal, the multivariate data generated through this matrix decomposition procedure are multivariate normal (Vale & Maurelli 1983). To illustrate the steps for generating correlated multivariate normal data, we plan to generate sample data for three variables (X1, X2, and X3) with the following population parameters:

Table 4.3 *Specification of Three Correlated Normal Variables*

	Mean	STD	Skew	Kurtosis	Correlation Matrix		
X1	100	15	.00	.00	1.00		
X2	50	10	.00	.00	.70	1.00	
X3	0	1	.00	.00	.20	.40	1.00

For obtaining the factor pattern of the desired population correlation matrix, we use the following SAS FACTOR procedure:

```
DATA A (TYPE=CORR);   _TYPE_='CORR';
  INPUT X1-X3;
CARDS;
1.00   .    .
 .70 1.00   .
 .20   .40 1.00
;
PROC FACTOR N=3;
RUN;
```

The execution of the SAS program above produces the following factor pattern matrix:

	FACTOR1	FACTOR2	FACTOR3
X1	0.84267	-0.42498	0.33062
X2	0.91671	-0.12476	-0.37958
X3	0.59317	0.79654	0.11694

Using the previous pattern matrix, we can then generate three correlated normal variables with specified population correlation coefficients and variable means and standard deviations as in Program 4.5. More specifically, Program 4.5 accomplishes the following:

❏ generates sample data of three uncorrelated univariate normal variables of 10,000 observations

❏ transforms the three uncorrelated variables to correlated variables as if sampled from a population with the desired correlation pattern, as specified in the population correlation matrix

❏ linearly transforms the variables to have the specified population means and standard deviations.

Program 4.5   *Generating Three Correlated Normal Variables*

```
PROC IML;
F={0.84267  -0.42498   0.33062,
   0.91671  -0.12476  -0.37958,
   0.59317   0.79654   0.11694};
DATA=RANNOR(J(10000,3,0));      *** generate data matrix (10000x3);
DATA=DATA`;                     *** transpose data matrix (3x10000);
Z = F*DATA;                     *** impose inter-correlations;
Z = Z`;                         *** transpose data matrix back (10000x3);

X1=Z[,1]*15 + 100;              *** linear transformation for specified mean and std;
X2=Z[,2]*10 + 50;
X3=Z[,3];
                                *** output data to a temporary SAS data set'A';
Z=X1||X2||X3;
CREATE A FROM Z [COLNAME={X1 X2 X3}];
APPEND FROM Z;
                                *** obtain sample descriptive statistics;
PROC MEANS DATA=A N MEAN STD SKEWNESS KURTOSIS;
  VAR X1 X2 X3;
PROC CORR DATA=A NOSIMPLE;
  VAR X1 X2 X3;
RUN;
```

One execution of the program produces the results shown in Output 4.5. As can be seen from these results, the sample data that we obtained closely resemble the desired population characteristics both in terms of univariate descriptive statistics (sample mean and standard deviation) and in terms of the sample inter-variable correlation pattern. In Program 4.5, linear transformation is carried out for the three correlated variables to impose the specified univariate population means and standard deviations. As discussed previously, such linear transformation will not affect the inter-variable correlation pattern.

Output 4.5
Three
Correlated
Normal
Variables
(Program 4.5)

```
                         The MEANS Procedure

     Variable    N         Mean       Std Dev       Skewness       Kurtosis
     ------------------------------------------------------------------------
     X1        10000   100.2838455   14.9544748    -0.0548380    -0.0099831
     X2        10000    50.1804325    9.9780623     0.0058695    -0.0204076
     X3        10000     0.0168731    0.9968740     0.0165395     0.1349200
     ------------------------------------------------------------------------

                         The CORR Procedure

             Pearson Correlation Coefficients, N = 10000
                     Prob > |r| under H0: Rho=0

                           X1            X2            X3

            X1          1.00000       0.70128       0.19828
                                      <.0001        <.0001

            X2          0.70128       1.00000       0.40052
                        <.0001                      <.0001

            X3          0.19828       0.40052       1.00000
                        <.0001        <.0001
```

Program 4.5a is almost identical to Program 4.5, except that the factor pattern matrix is obtained within this program. Previously, the factor pattern matrix was obtained first, and it was then used in Program 4.5. In Program 4.5a, the two steps are combined, and the program becomes more automated.

Program 4.5a *Generating Three Correlated Normal Variables*

```
DATA A (TYPE=CORR);   _TYPE_='CORR';
  INPUT X1-X3;
CARDS;
1.00   .    .
 .70 1.00   .
 .20  .40 1.00
;

    * obtain factor pattern matrix for later data generation;

PROC FACTOR N=3 OUTSTAT=FACOUT;
DATA PATTERN; SET FACOUT;
  IF _TYPE_='PATTERN';
  DROP _TYPE_ _NAME_;
RUN;

PROC IML;
   USE PATTERN;                       * read in the factor pattern as a matrix 'F';
   READ ALL VAR _NUM_ INTO F;
  F=F`;

DATA=RANNOR(J(10000,3,0));    *** generate data matrix (10000x3);
DATA=DATA`;                   *** transpose data matrix (3x10000);
Z = F*DATA;                   *** impose inter-correlations;
Z = Z`;                       *** transpose data matrix back (10000x3);
```

```
X1=Z[,1]*15 + 100;                 *** linear transformation for specified mean and std;
X2=Z[,2]*10 + 50;
X3=Z[,3];
                                   *** output data to a temporary SAS data set 'A';
Z=X1||X2||X3;
CREATE A FROM Z [COLNAME={X1 X2 X3}];
APPEND FROM Z;
                                   *** obtain sample descriptive statistics;
PROC MEANS DATA=A N MEAN STD SKEWNESS KURTOSIS;
  VAR X1 X2 X3;
PROC CORR DATA=A NOSIMPLE;
  VAR X1 X2 X3;
RUN;
```

Program 4.6 presents a fully automated base SAS macro program (%RMNC) comparable to Program 4.5a. However, Program 4.6 is fully automated, and as a SAS macro program, it can be called in whenever it is needed. As the explanation in Program 4.6 indicates, once the correlation matrix plus means and standard deviations are used as data input, and the three parameters are specified (DATA=, OUT=, SEED=,) in the macro, sample data generation is fully automated. In addition, to use macro RMNC, there is no need to specify information about the number of variables, sample size, etc.; all information is contained in the input data in the form of the correlation matrix plus means, standard deviations, and sample size N.

Program 4.6 *SAS Macro for Generating Correlated Normal Variables (Any Number)*

```
/*-----------------------------------------------------------------------*/
/* Macro RMNC generates Random variables of Multivariate Normal distribution */
/* with given means, standard deviations and Correlation matrix.         */
/*                                                                       */
/*                                                                       */
/* Parameters                                                            */
/* DATA       the name of the input file that determines the characteristics */
/*            of the random numbers to be generated. The file specifies  */
/*            the mean, standard deviation, number of observations of each */
/*            random number and the correlation coefficients between the */
/*            variables. It must be a TYPE=CORR file and its structure must */
/*            comply with that of such file (see 'Chapter 15: The CORR   */
/*            Procedure' in SAS Procedures Guide). The file has           */
/*            to have the following and only the following observations:  */
/*            _TYPE_=MEAN, STD, N, CORR. Its variables are _TYPE_, _NAME_ and */
/*            the variables to be generated. If the number of observations */
/*            is not the same for all variables, the macro takes the minimum */
/*            number of observations for all random variables.            */
/* OUT        the name of the output file that has the random variables  */
/*            generated according to the file given in parameter DATA.   */
/* SEED       seed of the random number generator.                       */
/*                                                                       */
/* Example                                                               */
/* The code below sets up an input file, calls the macro to request three */
/* random variables, and it checks their distributions and correlation  */
/* matrix.                                                               */
/*                                                                       */
/*     data a(type=corr);                                                */
/*          input _name_ $ _type_ $ x1-x3;                               */
/*          cards;                                                       */
/*      .   MEAN    100     50      0                                    */
/*      .   STD      15     10      1                                    */
/*      .   N     10000  10000  10000                                    */
/*      x1  CORR   1.00      .      .                                    */
/*      x2  CORR    .70   1.00      .                                    */
/*      x3  CORR    .20    .40   1.00                                    */
```

```
/*        ;                                                                */
/*           run;                                                         */
/*       %rmnc(data=a,out=b,seed=123)                                     */
/*       proc means data=b n mean std skewness kurtosis maxdec=2;         */
/*       proc corr data=b;                                                */
/*            var x1-x3;                                                   */
/*            run;                                                        */
/*                                                                        */
/* Output of Example                                                      */
/* Variable Label                       N   Mean Std Dev  Skewn.  Kurt.   */
/* ---------------------------------------------------------------------- */
/* X1         St.Normal Var., m=100, std=15 10000  99.99  14.93   0.02  -0.01 */
/* X2         St.Normal Var., m=50, std=10  10000  50.04   9.95   0.02  -0.04 */
/* X3         St.Normal Var., m=0, std=1    10000  -0.01   1.00  -0.01  -0.06 */
/* ---------------------------------------------------------------------- */
/*                                                                        */
/* Pearson Correlation Coefficients / Prob > |R| under Ho: Rho=0 / N = 10000 */
/*                                                                        */
/*                                 X1          X2          X3             */
/*                                                                        */
/* X1                          1.00000     0.70462     0.20305            */
/* St.Normal Var., m=100, std=15  0.0       0.0001      0.0001            */
/*                                                                        */
/* X2                          0.70462     1.00000     0.39276            */
/* St.Normal Var., m=50, std=10   0.0001    0.0         0.0001            */
/*                                                                        */
/* X3                          0.20305     0.39276     1.00000            */
/* St.Normal Var., m=0, std=1     0.0001    0.0001      0.0               */
/*                                                                        */
/*----------------------------------------------------------------------*/

%MACRO RMNC (DATA=,OUT=,SEED=0);

  /* obtain the names of the random variables to be generated. */
  /* the names are stored in macro variables V1, V2,...        */
  /* macro variable VNAMES has all these variable names        */
  /* concatenated into one long string.                        */

PROC CONTENTS DATA=&DATA(DROP=_TYPE_ _NAME_) OUT=_DATA_(KEEP=NAME) NOPRINT;
     RUN;
DATA _DATA_;
     SET _LAST_ END=END;
     RETAIN N 0;
     N=N+1;
     V=COMPRESS('V'||COMPRESS(PUT(N,6.0)));
     CALL SYMPUT(V,NAME);
     IF END THEN CALL SYMPUT('NV',LEFT(PUT(N,6.)));
     RUN;
%LET VNAMES=&V1;
%DO I=2 %TO &NV;
    %LET VNAMES=&VNAMES &&V&I;
%END;


  /* obtain the matrix of factor patterns and other statistics. */

PROC FACTOR DATA=&DATA NFACT=&NV NOPRINT
          OUTSTAT=_PTTRN_(WHERE=(_TYPE_ IN ('MEAN','STD','N','PATTERN')));
     RUN;

  /* generate the random numbers.*/

%LET NV2=%EVAL(&NV*&NV);
DATA &OUT(KEEP=&VNAMES);

     /* rename the variables to be generated to V1, V2,... in order */
     /* to avoid any interference with the DATA step variables.     */
```

```
      SET _PTTRN_(KEEP=&VNAMES _TYPE_ RENAME=(          %DO I=1 %TO &NV;
                                         &&V&I=V&I
                                                  %END;
                                            )) END=LASTFACT;
RETAIN;

/* set up arrays to store the necessary statistics. */
ARRAY FPATTERN(&NV,&NV) F1-F&NV2;   /* factor pattern                  */
ARRAY VMEAN(&NV)        M1-M&NV;    /* mean                            */
ARRAY VSTD(&NV)         S1-S&NV;    /* standard deviation              */
ARRAY V(&NV)            V1-V&NV;    /* random variables to be generated */
ARRAY VTEMP(&NV)        VT1-VT&NV;  /* temporary variables             */
LENGTH LBL $40;

/* read and store the matrix of factor patterns. */

IF _TYPE_='PATTERN' THEN DO; DO I=1 TO &NV;

                              /* here we utilize the fact that the  */
                              /* observations of the factor pattern */
                              /* start at observation #4.           */

                              FPATTERN(_N_-3,I)=V(I);
                          END;
                       END;

/* read and store the means. */

IF _TYPE_='MEAN' THEN DO; DO I=1 TO &NV;
                           VMEAN(I)=V(I);
                          END;
                       END;

/* read and store the standard deviations. */

IF _TYPE_='STD' THEN DO; DO I=1 TO &NV;
                          VSTD(I)=V(I);
                         END;
                      END;

/* read and store the number of observations. */

IF _TYPE_='N' THEN NNUMBERS=V(1);

/* all necessary statistics have been read and stored. */
/* start generating the random numbers.                */

IF LASTFACT THEN DO;

    /* set up labels for the random variables. The labels */
    /* are stored in macro variables LBL1, LBL2,... and   */
    /* used in the subsequent PROC DATASETS.              */

    %DO I=1 %TO &NV;
        LBL="ST.NORMAL VAR., M="||COMPRESS(PUT(VMEAN(&I),BEST8.))||
           ", STD="||COMPRESS(PUT(VSTD(&I), BEST8.));
        CALL SYMPUT("LBL&I",LBL);
    %END;

    DO K=1 TO NNUMBERS;

        /* generate the initial random numbers of standard  */
        /* normal distribution. Store them in array 'VTEMP.' */

        DO I=1 TO &NV;
           VTEMP(I)=RANNOR(&SEED);
        END;
```

```
         /* impose the intercorrelation on each variable. The */
         /* transformed variables are stored in array 'V'.    */

         DO I=1 TO &NV;
            V(I)=0;
            DO J=1 TO &NV;
               V(I)=V(I)+VTEMP(J)*FPATTERN(J,I);
            END;
         END;

         /* transform the random variables so they will have */
         /* means and standard deviations as requested.      */

         DO I=1 TO &NV;
            V(I)=VSTD(I)*V(I)+VMEAN(I);
         END;
         OUTPUT;
      END;
   END;

   /* rename V1,V2,... to the requested variable names. */

   RENAME          %DO I=1 %TO &NV;
         V&I=&&V&I
                   %END;
      ;
   RUN;

/* set the label of each random variable. The label contains */
/* the mean and standard deviation of the variable.          */

PROC DATASETS NOLIST;
   MODIFY &OUT;
   LABEL %DO I=1 %TO &NV;
            &&V&I="&&LBL&I"
         %END;
         ;
   RUN;
%MEND;
```

4.4 Generating Sample Data from a Multivariate Non-Normal Distribution

Although it is relatively straightforward to generate sample data from a multivariate normal distribution with desired univariate means and standard deviations and the desired population inter-variable correlation pattern, as demonstrated in the previous section, it is considerably more difficult to generate sample data from a multivariate *non-normal* distribution. The nature of the increased difficulty in data generation for multivariate *non-normal* distributions will be discussed momentarily.

4.4.1 Examining the Effect of Data Non-normality on Inter-variable Correlations

As is discussed in previous sections, generating sample data from a *univariate* non-normal distribution can be accomplished through several procedures, and Fleishman's method was one of them. Although it was pointed out that, for univariate non-normal variables, Fleishman's method has some weakness because it does not cover certain combinations of degrees of skewness and kurtosis, Fleishman's method does offer "an advantage over the other procedures in that it can easily be extended to generate multivariate random numbers with specified intercorrelations and univariate means, variances, skews, and kurtoses" (Vale & Maurelli 1983, p. 465). In other words, when we need to generate sample data from a *multivariate* non-normal distribution with specified population univariate skewness and kurtosis, and with a specified population inter-variable correlation pattern among the variables, Fleishman's method is appropriate.

In the generation of multivariate *non-normal* data, Vale and Maurelli (1983) showed that the application of matrix decomposition procedure for controlling the sample inter-variable correlations among the variables is no longer as straightforward as demonstrated previously. On the surface, the goal of generating multivariate *non-normal* data can be accomplished by

1. generating multivariate *normal* data with specified inter-variable correlations through the matrix decomposition procedure.

2. transforming each variable to the desired distributional shapes with specified population univariate skewness and kurtosis.

Unfortunately, the two processes interact, and the resultant multivariate non-normal data will have an inter-variable correlation pattern that may differ from that specified in the matrix decomposition procedure.

This point is illustrated in Program 4.7 for data population parameters specified in Table 4.4. The output from one execution of Program 4.7 is presented in Output 4.7. Table 4.3 presented an example of multivariate normal data (three correlated variables from normal distributions), and Program 4.5 demonstrates that, through the application of the matrix decomposition procedure, the sample inter-variable correlation pattern closely approximates that specified for the population of normally distributed variables.

In the example in Table 4.4, the same inter-variable correlation pattern as that in Table 4.3 is imposed on the same three variables using the same matrix decomposition procedure. But this time, the three variables are not normal, as indicated by their respective population parameters of the third and the fourth moments (skewness and kurtosis). By applying the Fleishman power transformation method, the specified univariate skewness and kurtosis conditions are achieved. The resultant sample descriptive statistics indicate that the univariate non-normality conditions are modeled adequately. But compared with the sample data generated from normal distributions by Program 4.5 (see Output 4.5), the sample inter-variable correlations generated by Program 4.7 have deviated considerably more from the population inter-variable correlation pattern implemented in the matrix decomposition procedure (see Output 4.7). This example illustrates that the two processes (the matrix decomposition procedure, and the Fleishman procedure) interact with each other, and this interaction will typically cause some non-trivial deviation in the generated sample data from the specified population inter-variable correlation pattern when non-normality exists. In other words, when non-normal distributions are simulated, the simple combination of the two procedures is not adequate.

Table 4.4 *Non-Normal Data Conditions and Inter-Variable Correlations*

		POPULATION PARAMETERS					
	Mean	STD	Skew	Kurtosis	Correlation Matrix		
X1	100	15	.75	.80	1.00		
X2	50	10	-.75	.80	.70	1.00	
X3	0	1	.75	2.40	.20	.40	1.00

Program 4.7 *Generating Three Correlated Non-Normal Variables – Inadequate Approach*

```
PROC IML;
                                        *read in factor pattern matrix;
F={0.84267   -0.42498    0.33062,
   0.91671   -0.12476   -0.37958,
   0.59317    0.79654    0.11694};

DATA=RANNOR(J(10000,3,0));              *GENERATE DATA MATRIX (10000x3);
DATA=DATA`;                            *TRANSPOSE DATA MATRIX (3x10000);
Z = F*DATA;                            *TRANSFORM TO 3 CORRELATED VAR;
Z = Z`;                               *TRANSPOSE DATA MATRIX BACK (10000X3);

                                        *FLEISHMAN NON-NORMALITY TRANSFORMATION;

X1 = -.124833577 + .978350485*Z[,1] + .124833577*Z[,1]##2 + .001976943*Z[,1]##3;
X2 =  .124833577 + .978350485*Z[,2] - .124833577*Z[,2]##2 + .001976943*Z[,2]##3;
X3 = -.096435287 + .843688891*Z[,3] + .096435287*Z[,3]##2 + .046773413*Z[,3]##3;

X1=X1*15 + 100;                        *LINEAR TRANSFORMATION FOR MEAN & STD;
X2=X2*10 + 50;
X3=X3;
Z=X1||X2||X3;

CREATE A FROM Z [COLNAME={X1 X2 X3}];   *OUTPUT DATA FOR DESCRIPTIVE STATS;
APPEND FROM Z;

PROC MEANS DATA=A N MEAN VAR SKEWNESS KURTOSIS;
  VAR X1 X2 X3;
PROC CORR DATA=A NOSIMPLE NOPROB;
  VAR X1 X2 X3;
RUN;
```

Output 4.7
Results of
Program 4.7

```
                               The MEANS Procedure

Variable      N          Mean         Std Dev      Skewness      Kurtosis

X1         10000     99.9754373     15.1008345     0.7601219     0.7667669

X2         10000     49.9041591     10.0024051    -0.7203833     0.7196319

X3         10000     -0.0173893      0.9966803     0.7651695     2.4459113

                               The CORR Procedure

                  Pearson Correlation Coefficients, N = 10000
                        Prob > |r|  under H0: Rho=0

                            X1            X2            X3

              X1         1.00000       0.66905       0.18441
                                       <.0001        <.0001

              X2         0.64905       1.00000       0.37367
                         <.0001                      <.0001

              X3         0.18041       0.36367       1.00000
                         <.0001        <.0001
```

4.4.2 Deriving Intermediate Correlations

Because inter-variable correlations and variable non-normality conditions interact with each other to cause sample data to deviate from the specified population inter-variable correlation pattern, the interaction must be taken into account in the process of generating sample data from multivariate non-normal distributions. Vale and Maurelli (1983) presented a procedure for decomposing an "intermediate" inter-variable correlation matrix to counteract the effect of non-normality on the inter-variable correlations. This *intermediate correlation procedure* is described in detail in the following sections to illustrate the implementation of this procedure.

The intermediate correlation procedure presented by Vale and Maurelli (1983) demonstrates that, for multiple correlated variables, a simple implementation of the matrix decomposition procedure does not work as expected when the variables are not normally distributed. To counteract the effect of non-normal conditions on the inter-variable correlations in the process of data generation, inter-variable correlations that are different from those specified as population inter-variable correlations must be derived and used in the matrix decomposition procedure. These derived correlations are called *intermediate correlations*, and the derivation of these intermediate correlations is based both on the specified population inter-variable correlation pattern to be modeled, and on the specified univariate non-normality conditions.

Once all the intermediate inter-variable correlations are derived, they can be assembled in proper order into an intermediate inter-variable correlations matrix. It is this intermediate inter-variable correlation matrix that will be factor analyzed (decomposed). The resultant factor pattern matrix derived from this intermediate inter-variable correlation matrix will be used in the matrix decomposition procedure to impose the specified population inter-variable correlation pattern on a set of non-normal variables. The end result will be correlated multivariate non-normal sample data that has the population inter-variable correlation pattern as originally specified.

Obviously, derivation of all pairwise intermediate correlations is essential when population non-normal conditions exist. The derivation process takes into account both the originally specified population correlation between two variables, and the population non-normality conditions of the two variables as defined by univariate skewness and kurtosis. It is here that the Fleishman power transformation method is appropriate, since the coefficients in Fleishman's power transformation can readily be used to derive the needed intermediate correlation coefficients. It is not obvious that other non-normality transformation procedures can have the same direct extension to multivariate non-normality data situations (Vale & Maurelli 1983).

Any two normal variates Z_1 and Z_2 can be transformed into two non-normal variables X_1 and X_2, each with its known skewness and kurtosis, as follows (see previous equation 4.5):

$$X_1 = a_1 + b_1 Z_1 + c_1 Z_1^2 + d_1 Z_1^3$$
$$X_2 = a_2 + b_2 Z_2 + c_2 Z_2^2 + d_2 Z_2^3$$

Once the degrees of skewness and kurtosis are known, the coefficients (a_i, b_i, c_i, and d_i, for i=1, 2) become available (either by consulting Fleishman's table in the original article, or by executing Program 4.4, presented previously). These coefficients (a_i, b_i, c_i, and d_i) in the Fleishman power transformation above are what is needed for deriving intermediate correlations. In addition to these coefficients, the modeled population correlation between the two non-normal variables X_1 and X_2 can be specified as R_{x1x2}. Once R_{x1x2} is set and the Fleishman coefficients are obtained based on the specified skewness and kurtosis conditions of the two variables (X_1 and X_2), Vale and Maurelli (1983) demonstrate that the following relationship exists:

$$R_{X_1 X_2} = \rho(b_1 b_2 + 3 b_1 d_2 + 3 d_1 b_2 + 9 d_1 d_2) + \rho^2 (2 c_1 c_2) + \rho^3 (6 d_1 d_2) \tag{4.7}$$

where ρ is the correlation between the two normal variates Z_1 and Z_2. This correlation is termed an "intermediate" correlation. In (4.7), all elements are known except the intermediate correlation ρ. The bivariate intermediate correlation coefficient must be solved for all possible pairs of the variables involved. These intermediate correlation coefficients are then assembled in proper order into an intermediate correlation matrix. This intermediate correlation matrix is then factor analyzed to obtain the factor pattern matrix needed to transform uncorrelated variables into correlated ones.

There is no direct algebraic solution for solving this polynomial function for ρ, and an iterative approach has to be taken to arrive at an estimated solution. Again, we use the versatile iterative Newton-Raphson method to solve for ρ, as we did in Program 4.4 for solving for Fleishman coefficients for generating sample data from univariate non-normal distributions. Table 4.5 presents population parameters for three correlated non-normal variables, as well as the Fleishman's power transformation coefficients for generating the three variables for the specified non-normality conditions.

Table 4.5 *Parameters of Three Non-Normal Variables and Fleishman Coefficients*

POPULATION PARAMETERS

	Mean	STD	Skew	Kurtosis	Target Correlation Matrix		
X1	100	15	.75	.80	1.00		
X2	50	10	-.75	.80	70	1.00	
X3	0	1	.75	2.40	20	.40	1.00

FLEISHMAN COEFFICIENTS FOR THE THREE VARIABLES

	a	b	c	d
X1	-.124833577	.978350485	.124833577	.001976943
X2	.124833577	.978350485	-.124833577	.001976943
X3	-.096435287	.843688891	.096435287	.046773413

Program 4.8 presents an example for deriving an intermediate correlation coefficient. In Table 4.5, the three variables to be modeled are correlated with each other as specified in the population correlation matrix, and each of them is non-normal as specified by the univariate skewness and kurtosis. Program 4.8 derives the intermediate correlation coefficient between the first two variables (X_1 and X_2). Here, it is not necessary for readers to fully understand the Newton-Raphson method, nor is it necessary to fully understand the base SAS program itself.

Program 4.8 *Deriving a Pairwise Intermediate Correlation (X_1 & X_2)*

```
DATA D1;
  B1=.978350485; C1=-.124833577; D1=.001976943;  * use Fleishman coefficients;
  B2=.978350485; C2= .124833577; D2=.001976943;
  TARGET=.70;                                      * target population correlation;
  R=.5;                                            * starting value for iteration;

DO I=1 TO 5;
  FUNCTION=(R**3*6*D1*D2+R**2*2*C1*C2+R*(B1*B2+3*B1*D2+3*D1*B2+9*D1*D2)-TARGET);
  DERIV=(3*R**2*6*D1*D2+2*R*2*C1*C2+(B1*B2+3*B1*D2+3*D1*B2+9*D1*D2));
  RATIO=FUNCTION/DERIV;
  R_TEMP = R - RATIO;
  IF ABS(R_TEMP - R)>.00001 THEN R = R_TEMP; OUTPUT;
END;
PROC PRINT; WHERE I=5;     * print intermediate correlation r for the last iteration;
  VAR I RATIO R;
RUN;
```

One execution of Program 4.8 produces the following result:

```
        OBS    I     RATIO       R

         5     5    -0.00000    0.74015
```

Although the specified population correlation coefficient between X_1 and X_2 is 0.70, the result above indicates that for the given univariate non-normality conditions, the intermediate correlation between the two variables is 0.74. It is this intermediate correlation coefficient that will be used in the matrix decomposition procedure for sample data generation of these three correlated non-normal variables.

By substituting the appropriate Fleishman coefficients and the specified population pair-wise correlation coefficient (TARGET=?), all pair-wise intermediate correlations can be solved with Program 4.8. Once this is done, all the intermediate correlation coefficients can then be assembled in proper order into a correlation matrix. The following is the resultant intermediate correlation matrix for the three non-normal variables as specified in Table 4.5.

```
              Intermediate Correlation Matrix

           X1    1.0000
           X2     .7402  1.0000
           X3     .2054   .4173  1.0000
```

After all the pair-wise intermediate correlation coefficients are assembled into an intermediate correlation matrix, this intermediate correlation matrix is then factor analyzed in the usual fashion, and the factor pattern matrix is obtained. This factor pattern matrix based on the intermediate correlation matrix is then used in transforming uncorrelated non-normal variables into correlated ones. Program 4.9 presents an example of generating sample data for the three correlated non-normal variables described earlier in Table 4.5. In Program 4.9, the step for obtaining the factor pattern matrix is incorporated, as in Program 4.5a.

Program 4.9 *Generating Non-Normal Multivariate Sample Data*

```
DATA A (TYPE=CORR);  _TYPE_='CORR';
  INPUT X1-X3;
CARDS;
1.0000   .     .
 .7402 1.0000   .
 .2054  .4173 1.0000
;

     * obtain factor pattern matrix for later data generation;

PROC FACTOR N=3 OUTSTAT=FACOUT;
DATA PATTERN; SET FACOUT;
  IF _TYPE_='PATTERN';
  DROP _TYPE_ _NAME_;
RUN;

PROC IML;
   USE PATTERN;                      * read in the factor pattern as a matrix 'F';
   READ ALL VAR _NUM_ INTO F;
  F=F`;

DATA=RANNOR(J(10000,3,0));    *** generate data matrix (10000x3);
DATA=DATA`;                   *** transpose data matrix (3x10000);
Z = F*DATA;                   *** impose inter-correlations;
Z = Z`;                       *** transpose data matrix back (10000x3);

                                 * Fleishman non-normality transformation;
X1 = -.124833577 + .978350485*Z[,1] + .124833577*Z[,1]##2 + .001976943*Z[,1]##3;
X2 =  .124833577 + .978350485*Z[,2] - .124833577*Z[,2]##2 + .001976943*Z[,2]##3;
X3 = -.096435287 + .843688891*Z[,3] + .096435287*Z[,3]##2 + .046773413*Z[,3]##3;

X1=X1*15 + 100;                         * linear transformation for mean & std;
X2=X2*10 + 50;
X3=X3;
Z=X1||X2||X3;
CREATE A FROM Z [COLNAME={X1 X2 X3}];   * output a temporary SAS data set 'A';
APPEND FROM Z;


                                  * obtain descriptive stats for sample data;
PROC MEANS DATA=A N MEAN STD SKEWNESS KURTOSIS;
  VAR X1 X2 X3;
PROC CORR DATA=A NOSIMPLE NOPROB;
  VAR X1 X2 X3;
RUN; QUIT;
```

The descriptive statistics of the sample data (N=10,000) from one execution of Program 4.9 are presented in Output 4.9. These results indicate that the sample statistics closely approximate the specified population parameters, both in terms of the correlations among the variables, and in terms of the univariate skewness and kurtosis of the three variables. This is especially true when we compare the sample correlation matrix in Output 4.9 with that in Output 4.7, where the intermediate correlation procedure was *not* implemented for non-normal distributions in the process (Program 4.7). The sample correlations in Output 4.9 are much closer to the specified population correlations than those in Output 4.7.

Output 4.9
Results of
Program 4.9

Variable	N	Mean	Std Dev	Skewness	Kurtosis
X1	10000	99.9721150	15.0763019	0.7540160	0.8112059
X2	10000	50.0248158	10.1009159	-0.8062380	0.7873609
X3	10000	-0.0103037	1.0042507	0.7850528	2.5621595

The CORR Procedure

Pearson Correlation Coefficients, N = 10000
Prob > |r| under H0: Rho=0

	X1	X2	X3
X1	1.00000	0.70038 <.0001	0.20824 <.0001
X2	0.70038 <.0001	1.00000	0.39828 <.0001
X3	0.20824 <.0001	0.39828 <.0001	1.00000

4.5 Converting between Correlation and Covariance Matrices

During the data generation process of a Monte Carlo study, sometimes there is a need to convert a covariance matrix to a correlation matrix, or vice versa. The relationship between a covariance and a correlation between two variables (*X* and *Y*) is simple, as shown below:

$$r_{xy} = \frac{\text{Cov}_{xy}}{s_x * s_y} \tag{4.8}$$

$$\text{Cov}_{xy} = r_{xy} * s_x * s_y \tag{4.9}$$

where r_{xy} is the correlation between X and Y, Cov_{xy} is the covariance between X and Y, and s_x and s_y are standard deviations for X and Y, respectively.

But when you have a covariance matrix and need to convert it to a correlation matrix, you may not want to do the computation for each covariance (correlation) in the matrix one by one. Instead, you may rely on matrix algebra and use SAS PROC IML for the conversion. In matrix algebra, the equivalents of (4.8) and (4.9) are as follows:

$$\mathbf{R} = (\mathbf{S})^{-1} * \Sigma * (\mathbf{S})^{-1} \tag{4.10}$$

$$\Sigma = (\mathbf{S}) * \mathbf{R} * (\mathbf{S}) \tag{4.11}$$

where $\mathbf{R}$ is the correlation matrix, Σ is the covariance matrix, and $\mathbf{S}$ is a diagonal matrix containing standard deviations for each variable as its diagonal elements, as in the following example matrix for three variables (X_1, X_2, and X_3):

$$S = \begin{bmatrix} s_{x1} & 0 & 0 \\ 0 & s_{x2} & 0 \\ 0 & 0 & s_{x3} \end{bmatrix}$$

Once we have the covariance matrix Σ, the $\mathbf{S}$ matrix can easily be obtained through SAS PROC IML, and the correlation matrix $\mathbf{R}$ can be derived for use in the data generation process, as used in Program 4.5, for example. Conversely, if we have the correlation matrix and the standard deviations for the variables, we can also obtain the covariance matrix easily. As an example, we use the correlation matrix and standard deviations for the three variables (X_1, X_2, and X_3) in Table 4.4 to illustrate the use of SAS PROC IML for such a conversion. Program 4.10 presents the SAS PROC IML code for such conversions.

Program 4.10 *Converting between Correlation and Covariance Matrices*

```
***** Program 4.10  PROC IML **********;
***** Converting a correlation matrix to covariance matrix, and vice versa;
***** Example data from Table 4.4   ;

     ****** Part I: Converting correlation matrix to covariance matrix;
PROC IML;
        *** define the correlation matrix;
R={1.00 0.70 0.20,
   0.70 1.00 0.40,
   0.20 0.40 1.00};

        *** define the diagonal matrix with standard deviations on the diagonal;
S={15  0  0,
    0 10  0,
    0  0  1};

COV=S*R*S;      *** obtain the covariance matrix;

PRINT COV;      *** print the covariance matrix;

RUN;
```

```
     ***** Part II: Converting covariance matrix to correlation matrix;
PROC IML;

          *** define the covariance matrix;
COV={225 105 3,
     105 100 4,
       3   4 1};

S=SQRT(DIAG(COV));    *** obtain the matrix with standard deviations on the diagonal;

S_INV=INV(S);         *** the inverse of S matrix;

R=S_INV*COV*S_INV;    *** obtain correlation matrix;

PRINT COV;            *** print out the three matrices;
PRINT S;
PRINT R;
RUN;
```

Program 4.10 has two parts. Part I (the top portion) converts a correlation matrix to a covariance matrix, and Part II (the bottom portion) converts a covariance matrix to a correlation matrix. If you run the two parts separately, you obtain the matrices shown in Output 4.10. As can be seen, from the correlation matrix and standard deviations given in Table 4.4, the covariance matrix (**COV**) is:

$$COV = \begin{bmatrix} 225 & 105 & 3 \\ 105 & 100 & 4 \\ 3 & 4 & 1 \end{bmatrix}$$

Part II of Program 4.10 converts the covariance matrix above (**COV**) to the original correlation matrix (**R**) and a diagonal matrix (**S**) containing the standard deviations of the three variables.

Output 4.10
Results from
Program 4.10

```
                              COV

           225          105           3
           105          100           4
             3            4           1

                              COV

           225          105           3
           105          100           4
             3            4           1

                               S

            15            0           0
             0           10           0
             0            0           1

                               R

             1          0.7         0.2
           0.7            1         0.4
           0.2          0.4           1
```

4.6 Generating Data That Mirror Your Sample Characteristics

In quantitative research, there is often a need to define statistical populations based on the sample data the researcher has. For example, suppose a researcher is interested in comparing two groups via a *t*-test. But the sample data from the two groups are highly non-normal, and transformation is not of interest nor meaningful for the researcher. In this situation, the researcher may be interested in determining the *empirical* distribution of the *t*-statistic for these highly non-normal data, because the empirical *t*-statistic distribution for these kinds of data may deviate considerably from the theoretical *t* distribution that assumes data normality.

To accomplish the researcher's goal described above, i.e., to obtain the empirical distribution of the *t*-statistic for the researcher's non-normal data, the researcher can (a) define statistical populations by using sample characteristics, (b) conduct a Monte Carlo study based on these defined populations, and (c) derive empirical distributions for the statistic of interest from the Monte Carlo study results. These and similar tasks can be readily accomplished by using the data generation procedures discussed in this chapter. More specifically, the following steps need to be taken:

1. Obtain the first four moments (i.e., mean, standard deviation, skewness, kurtosis; these four moments should be sufficient for most applications) of a variable from the sample data (e.g., using PROC UNIVARIATE).

2. If multiple correlated variables are involved, obtain the inter-variable correlations from the sample data (e.g., using PROC CORR).

3. Use sample data moments and inter-variable correlations as *population* parameters, and generate data accordingly, as we did in Section 4.2.2.2 (e.g., Program 4.3), Section 4.3 (e.g., Program 4.5, Program 4.5a), and/or Section 4.4.2 (Program 4.9).

In other words, generating data from statistical populations that mirror your sample characteristics is not any different from what we have been presenting so far. We simply need to obtain sample characteristics (e.g., four statistical moments, and inter-variable correlations), and use these sample characteristics as population parameters for later data generation. Once we have the population parameters as defined by the sample characteristics, we use exactly the same procedures as we have shown in this chapter.

For example, in Table 4.4, we could assume that these statistical moments and inter-variable correlations for the three variables (X_1, X_2, and X_3) are actually obtained from a sample. Of course obtaining these sample moments and correlations is a simple matter, because only simple analysis based on PROC UNIVARIATE and PROC CORR is needed. Once we have obtained these sample statistics, we will treat them as population parameters and will generate data for our Monte Carlo experiments as described in detail in the sections following Table 4.4.

4.7 Summary

In this and the previous chapters, we spent a considerable amount of time discussing different aspects of sample data generation as part of any Monte Carlo study. As is obvious in our discussions in these four chapters up to now, a Monte Carlo study is based on drawing random samples from a theoretical population with known population parameters. Our ability to simulate the process of drawing random samples from a population with specified population characteristics determines the validity of the results of our Monte Carlo study. In this sense, the importance of correct data generation procedures in a Monte Carlo study can never be overemphasized.

In this chapter, we discussed in some detail the following relevant topics: (1) generating sample data from a univariate normal distribution; (2) generating sample data from a univariate non-normal distribution as defined by univariate skewness and kurtosis; (3) generating sample data from a multivariate normal distribution with correlated variables; and (4) generating sample data from a multivariate non-normal distribution with correlated variables. As is seen in the presentation of this chapter, the process of generating sample data becomes increasingly complicated as we proceed from a univariate to multivariate situation, and as we proceed from a multivariate normal distribution to a multivariate non-normal distribution.

We hope that Chapter 3 and Chapter 4 have provided an adequate working knowledge base for generating sample data for conducting a Monte Carlo study in general, and for implementing the procedures for generating sample data in SAS in particular. In the following chapters, we will focus more on procedural and/or programmatic issues for implementing Monte Carlo studies in SAS. For that purpose, we will discuss program automation in SAS (Chapter 5), and we will present a series of SAS examples for conducting Monte Carlo studies in Chapters 6-9.

4.8 References

Burr, I. W. 1973. "Parameters for a General System for Distributions to Match a Grid of α_3 and α_4." *Communications in Statistics* 2:1-21.

Fleishman, A. I. 1978. "A Method for Simulating Non-Normal Distributions." *Psychometrika* 43: 521-531.

Johnson, N. L. 1949. "Systems for Frequency Curves Generated by Methods of Translation." *Biometrika* 36:149-176.

Johnson, N. L. 1965. "Tables to Facilitate Fitting S_U Frequency Curves." *Biometrika* 52:547-558.

Johnson, N. L., and J. O. Kitchen. 1971. "Tables to Facilitate Fitting S_B Curves." *Biometrika* 58: 223-226.

Kaiser, H. F., and K. Dickman. 1962. "Sample and Population Score Matrices and Sample Correlation Matrices from an Arbitrary Population Correlation Matrix." *Psychometrika* 27:179-182.

Merriam-Webster, Inc. 1994. *Merriam-Webster's Collegiate Dictionary*. 10th ed. Springfield, MA: Merriam-Webster, Inc.

Pearson, E. S., and H. O. Hartley, eds. 1972. *Biometrika Tables for Statisticians*. Vol. 2. London: Cambridge University Press.

Ramberg, J. S., E. J. Dudewicz, P. R. Tadikamalla, and E. F. Mykytka. 1979. "A Probability Distribution and Its Use in Fitting Data." *Technometrics* 21:201-214.

Ramberg, J. S., and B. W. Schmeiser. 1974. "An Approximate Method for Generating Asymmetric Random Variables." *Communications of the Association for Computing Machinery* 17:78-82.

Schmeiser, B. W., and S. J. Deutch. 1977. "A Versatile Four Parameter Family of Probability Distributions Suitable for Simulation." *AIIE Transactions* 9:176-182.

Tadikamalla, P. R. 1980. "On Simulating Non-Normal Distributions." *Psychometrika* 45:273-279.

Tukey, J. W. 1960. "A Survey of Sampling from Contaminated Distributions." In *Contributions to Probability and Statistics*, ed. I. Olkin, 448-485. Palo Alto, CA: Stanford University Press.

Vale, C. D., and V. A. Maurelli. 1983. "Simulating Multivariate Nonnormal Distributions." *Psychometrika* 48:465-471.

Chapter 5 Automating Monte Carlo Simulations

5.1 Introduction

The SAS System is an excellent choice for conducting Monte Carlo simulations (Hamer & Breen 1985) because it is a whole environment providing the following features: ease of programming, portability (the same code runs on different hardware platforms and operating systems), good quality and a broad variety of random number generators, readily available statistical procedures, convenient database storage, and report writing capabilities.

In this chapter, we will discuss the steps involved in conducting Monte Carlo simulations, the various ways of controlling the random number generators, placing the simulation into a macro shell for flexible and automatic execution, monitoring the execution of the simulation, and saving and presenting the results. The chapter will utilize the simple problem of "Matching Birthdays" for illustration purposes. At the end of the chapter, we will present a full-fledged solution to the so-called Parking Problem.

5.2 Steps in a Monte Carlo Simulation

The full implementation of a Monte Carlo simulation problem in SAS usually includes the following steps:

1. Designing the system (What are the parameters of the system? What are the relationships among these parameters? What is the unknown we are after? What are the parameters changing by chance? What precision do we wish to achieve?).

2. Identifying the *a priori* distributions of the probability variables in the system.

3. Programming the whole system in SAS.

4. Executing the simulation.

5. Saving all relevant results and necessary intermediate values.

6. Checking the required randomness in the system.

7. Calculating the results.

8. Presenting the results.

5.3 The Problem of Matching Birthdays

We will use the problem of Matching Birthdays to illustrate the complete solution to a simulation problem in the SAS System. There are at least 366 people in a room. Their birthdays (birthday in this problem means month and day only) are random in the sense that each person's birthday has the same probability of being any of the 365 days of the year. We select people randomly until the newly selected person's birthday matches *any* of the birthdays of the people already selected. The problem that we want to solve is: What is the average number of people needed to obtain the first pair of matching birthdays?

Before we start solving the problem, let us emphasize an important aspect of the problem/solution: When a new person is selected, his birthday is compared to the birthdays of all people previously selected. For simplicity's sake, we ignore leap years.

The problem has a simple analytical solution,[1] but we intend to solve it with simulation. The problem's parameters are the birthdays, up to 366 of them (the first 365 birthdays could be all different). They are random and independent of each other. During the simulation, we have to compare each newly selected birthday to each of the birthdays already chosen. The distribution of the birthdays is uniform from 1 to 365, because we will represent a birthday as day-of-the-year. We will utilize the RANUNI function and convert its random number to an integer between 1 and 365. We will save all birthdays selected randomly (in order to check the necessary uniform distribution of the

---

[1] Let *P(n)* denote the probability of having the *first* pair of matching birthdays after selecting *n* people. Then $P(n) = \frac{n-1}{365} \prod_{i=1}^{n-1} \left(\frac{366-i}{365} \right)$. The average number of people is given by $E(n) = \sum_{n=1}^{365} nP(n)$, which results in approximately 24.62.

birthdays) and the number of people required to have two matching birthdays (in order to answer the question). PROC UNIVARIATE will calculate and present the results: the average number of people needed for the first matching pair of birthdays.

A crucial step in the simulation is the design and programming of the system in the SAS environment. It is usually done in a DATA step because it provides the user with almost all the capabilities of a programming language. A clever approach and good programming help to simplify the task and speed up the simulation. In the case of the matching birthdays, we have to generate random birthdays and compare them pair-wise. It is clear that a birthday in this problem should not contain a year, since we are only interested in the month and day. The generation of the day of the year, i.e., an integer between 1 (January 1st) and 365 (December 31st) would be sufficient.

The other important simplification regards the comparison. We could program the comparison of the newly generated birthday to each of the birthdays obtained earlier, but it would take a lot of time. Instead, we keep track of a birthday by setting a flag associated with that particular date. Then, when we generate a new birthday, we only have to see whether or not that date has a flag and we do not have to compare it to all dates already obtained. These design- and programming tricks will speed up the simulation tremendously.

The solution is given in Program 5.1. The simulation is executed 10,000 times in a DO LOOP of a DATA step. The data set RESULTS from that DATA step captures not only the number of people needed for the first matching pair of birthdays, but all intermediate birthdays selected randomly, so we can examine whether our program generates uniformly distributed random birthdays. Each record corresponds to one simulation. In a subsequent DATA step, the program creates the data set DAYS, which has every birthday of every simulation in a separate record, in order to check their uniform distribution. PROC CAPABILITY is utilized to see if these birthdays follow the uniform distribution between 1 and 365. (The uniform distribution is a special beta distribution with ALPHA=BETA=1.) PROC UNIVARIATE answers the problem by calculating the average number of people.

The results are presented in Output 5.1: the randomly selected birthdays distribute uniformly (their Q-Q plot is a straight line), and the average number of people is 24.69 (the precise rounded value is 24.62—see the analytic solution in the footnote on page 94). The presentation of the results in Output 5.1 also reveals the distribution of the number of people needed for the first matching birthdays (see the histogram of PROC UNIVARIATE).

Program 5.1 *Matching Birthdays*

```
DATA RESULTS;

     /* array of day indicators. A value of one in an element of this array   */
     /* indicates the selection of that birthday. Zero means that birthday    */
     /* has not been selected.                                                */

     ARRAY DAYS(365) $1 D1-D365;
     LENGTH NPEOPLE 3;
     DO SIM=1 TO 10000;   *** execute 10,000 simulations of the problem.;
        DO I=1 TO 365;
           DAYS(I)='0';   *** the day indicators are set to zero initially.;
        END;
        DO NPEOPLE=1 TO 366;
           D=1+INT(365*RANUNI(123));   *** generate a random birthday between 1
                                   and 365.;
           IF  DAYS(D)='1'  THEN  LEAVE;   *** was that birthday previously
                                   selected?;
                               *** if yes, leave the loop.;
                            ELSE  DAYS(D)='1';   *** If not, mark the day as
                                   'selected'.;
        END;
        OUTPUT;
     END;
     RUN;

/* check the distribution of all birthdays selected during the simulation. */
/* they should form a uniform distribution between 1 and 365. Place each   */
/* birthday into an individual observation.                                */

DATA DAY(KEEP=DAY);
     SET RESULTS;
     ARRAY DAYS(365) D1-D365;
     DO I=1 TO 365;
        IF DAYS(I)='1' THEN DO; DAY=I;
                                OUTPUT; END;
     END;
     RUN;

/* test whether or not the days generated randomly follow the uniform   */
/* distribution between 1 and 365. Use PROC CAPABILITY with the 'beta'   */
/* distribution, because the uniform distribution is a special beta      */
/* distribution (alpha=beta=1). Set the threshold and scale parameters   */
/* to 1 and 365 respectively.                                           */

PROC CAPABILITY DATA=DAY;
     VAR DAY;
     QQPLOT DAY / BETA (ALPHA=1 BETA=1 THETA=1 SIGMA=365)
                HAXIS=AXIS1 VAXIS=AXIS2 NOLEGEND;
     AXIS1 LABEL=(F=SWISS H=1.5 'Uniform Distribution (1-365)')
           ORDER=0 TO 1 BY 0.2 VALUE=(H=1.2 F=SWISS) MINOR=(N=1);
     AXIS2 LABEL=(A=90 R=0 F=SWISS H=1.5 'Random Birthday')
           ORDER=0 TO 400 BY 100 VALUE=(H=1.2 F=SWISS) MINOR=(N=1);
     TITLE  F=SWISS H=1.5 'Q-Q Plot of Randomly Selected Birthdays';
     SYMBOL1 R=8;
     SYMBOL9 I=JOIN C=BLACK W=40;
     RUN;
PROC UNIVARIATE DATA=RESULTS PLOT;   *** calculate and present the answer.;
     VAR NPEOPLE;
     RUN;
```

Output 5.1 *Results of the Matching Birthday Problem*

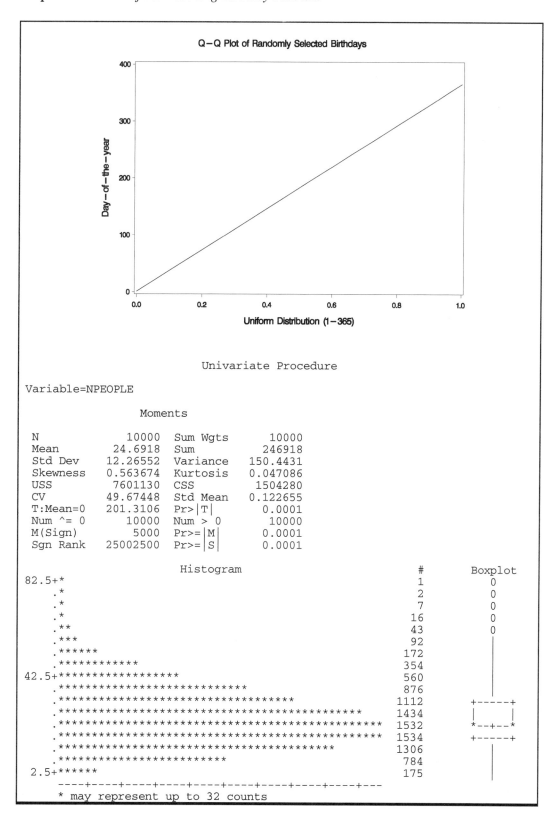

```
                    Q-Q Plot of Randomly Selected Birthdays

   400


   300

Day-of-the-year
   200


   100


     0
       0.0       0.2       0.4       0.6       0.8       1.0
                    Uniform Distribution (1-365)
```

```
                        Univariate Procedure

Variable=NPEOPLE

                        Moments

   N              10000    Sum Wgts          10000
   Mean          24.6918   Sum              246918
   Std Dev      12.26552   Variance        150.4431
   Skewness     0.563674   Kurtosis        0.047086
   USS           7601130   CSS             1504280
   CV           49.67448   Std Mean        0.122655
   T:Mean=0     201.3106   Pr>|T|           0.0001
   Num ^= 0        10000   Num > 0           10000
   M(Sign)          5000   Pr>=|M|          0.0001
   Sgn Rank     25002500   Pr>=|S|          0.0001

                      Histogram                        #      Boxplot
 82.5+*                                                 1        0
     .*                                                 2        0
     .*                                                 7        0
     .*                                                16        0
     .**                                               43        0
     .***                                              92        |
     .******                                          172        |
     .************                                    354        |
 42.5+*****************                                560        |
     .*************************                       876        |
     .**********************************            1112     +-----+
     .*******************************************   1434     |     |
     .********************************************  1532     *--+--*
     .********************************************  1534     +-----+
     .*****************************************     1306        |
     .***********************                       784         |
  2.5+******                                        175         |
     ---+----+----+----+----+----+----+----+----+---
       * may represent up to 32 counts
```

5.4 The Seed Value

The role of a seed value in a random number generator function is discussed fully in Chapter 3. Here we give some practical advice for setting its value. During testing of the simulation program, we should use a known seed value, so we could replicate the results and make the debugging process possible. (Otherwise, when we alter our program, we do not know whether the different outcome is due to the changes we just administered to the code or to different random numbers.) We use SEED=123 in many sample programs in this book, so you could run the examples and generate the same results. When the program is completely debugged and we start the simulation, we should use random seeds. The SAS System applies randomly selected starting values to the random generator functions if SEED=0 is specified. We can also generate special seed values satisfying certain criteria (see the SEEDGEN macro in section 3.6 of Chapter 3). If we wish to use random seed values and know their values as well, we can invoke the TIME function to obtain the current time from the operating system and enter that value into the random number generators. For example, Program 5.1 could be expanded:

```
SEED = 1+ROUND(1000*TIME());
PUT SEED=;
DO SIM=1 TO 10000;
...
   DO I=1 TO 365;
      D=1+INT(365*RANUNI(SEED));
      ...
```

Since the TIME function returns a fraction and the seed must be an integer, the program forces the value of SEED to be a positive integer. The statement PUT SEED=; displays the current seed value in the LOG window for possible re-use.

5.5 Monitoring the Execution of a Simulation

Simulations usually take a long time to perform. There is a need to monitor the execution and know its speed, so we can estimate the total time required to finish the entire simulation or so we can know how many simulations we can perform in a given time unit. A simple statement placed at the head of the *simulation loop* in Program 5.1 can provide a message at a given number of iterations.

```
DO SIM=1 TO 10000;
   IF NOT MOD(SIM,1000) THEN PUT 'Simulation Number: ' SIM;
   ...
```

The above IF statement displays the messages

```
Simulation Number: 1000
Simulation Number: 2000
...
```

in the LOG window, so we can estimate the required time and monitor the execution of the simulation. Of course, we can modify the frequency of this message by altering the second argument of the MOD function.

A more sophisticated way is to display starting and ending times, and time elapsed. Program 5.2 substitutes the DATA step of Program 5.1 and provides full-time monitoring. It displays the starting time at the beginning of the simulation loop, then shows the current time and the time elapsed between the previous and current messages at every 2,000 simulations. The message is constructed as a character variable (MSG) in order to line up its parts nicely. The solution utilizes the DATETIME function (instead of TIME) in order to correctly determine the elapsed time when midnight strikes between two messages.

Program 5.2 *Simulation with Full-Time Monitoring*

```
DATA RESULTS;
     ARRAY DAYS(365) $1 D1-D365;
     LENGTH NPEOPLE 3;
     SDT=DATETIME();
     STIME=TIMEPART(SDT);    *** take and display the time only.;
     PUT 'Starting Time: ' STIME TIME12.3;
     LENGTH MSG $72;    *** define a character variable for the message.;
     SUBSTR(MSG,1,13)='Simulation #:';      *** set the fixed parts of the message.;
     SUBSTR(MSG,21,16)=', Current Time: ';
     SUBSTR(MSG,49,16)=', Duration: ';
     DO SIM=1 TO 10000;

         /* Construct and display a message if this is a 2,000th simulation. */

         IF NOT MOD(SIM,2000)
             THEN DO; EDT=DATETIME();
                     ETIME=TIMEPART(EDT);
                     DURATION=EDT-SDT;    *** determine the elapsed time.;
                     SUBSTR(MSG,15,6)=PUT(SIM,6.);    *** build the message.;
                     SUBSTR(MSG,37,12)=PUT(ETIME,TIME12.3);
                     SUBSTR(MSG,61,12)=PUT(DURATION,TIME12.3);
                     PUT MSG;    *** display the message.;
                     SDT=EDT;    *** move the current time into the starting time;
                                 *** for the next message.;
                 END;
         DO I=1 TO 365;
             DAYS(I)='0';
         END;
         DO NPEOPLE=1 TO 366;
             D=1+INT(365*RANUNI(123));
             IF DAYS(D)='1' THEN LEAVE;
                         ELSE DAYS(D)='1';
         END;
         OUTPUT;
     END;
     RUN;
```

Log 5.2 *Messages in the LOG Window with Full-Time Monitoring*

```
Starting Time: 10:17:20.718
Simulation #:   2000, Current Time: 10:17:22.296, Duration:  0:00:01.578
Simulation #:   4000, Current Time: 10:17:23.937, Duration:  0:00:01.641
Simulation #:   6000, Current Time: 10:17:25.765, Duration:  0:00:01.828
Simulation #:   8000, Current Time: 10:17:27.390, Duration:  0:00:01.625
Simulation #:  10000, Current Time: 10:17:29.421, Duration:  0:00:02.031
```

Program 5.4 later in this chapter will simplify the code back to its original clarity by placing the extraneous statements of the time monitoring into macros.

5.6 Portability

One of the many advantages of conducting simulation with SAS is the portable nature of the SAS code. The same code runs on all hardware platforms and operating systems supported by the SAS System. There are slight variations in the input/output options due to differences in the operating systems, but that may affect only statements outside of the real simulation. Most importantly, the core statements of the SAS language and all random number generators (assuming the same seed values) produce the same results on all hardware. This means that we can code and test the simulation program on a micro computer and send it up to a more powerful machine for executing the time-consuming simulation.

5.7 Automating the Simulation

By definition, simulation is the repeated execution of a piece of code. As such, it is best implemented in the SAS macro framework. This book's aim is not teaching the SAS macro language, but we will show you in a simplified way how to implement a simulation as a macro. Many of the examples in the book are presented as macros.

The SAS macro language can be thought of as a super SAS language, which is not executed by the SAS System directly, but evaluated by the macro processor in order to produce *real* SAS code, which is then executed. The macro processor carries out all macro statements and replaces all macro variables with actual values, creating actual SAS code. Macro programs, in a simplified manner, have four components:

- ❑ opening and closing statements (%MACRO and %MEND).

- ❑ macro statements that are like regular SAS statements, but preceded by a % sign, and which only affect the creation of regular SAS statements.

- ❑ macro variables that are, in many ways, similar to SAS data set variables. (The most important differences include: the macro variables are preceded by a & sign when referenced, and they contain text, which replaces the reference during the macro processing phase.)

- ❑ regular SAS code that stays intact during the macro processing phase.

When we write a macro, we always have to think like the macro processor: *the macro code must result in correct SAS code when evaluated.* Macros provide essential flexibility for the simulation. Without discussing the macro language extensively, we will show its construction and usefulness through some examples in the rest of this chapter. For more information about the SAS macro facility, consult the *SAS Guide to Macro Processing.*

5.8 A Macro Solution to the Problem of Matching Birthdays

It is recommended that you start writing a macro by coding your program in the regular SAS language and testing it fully. Then you can alter the code to place it in the framework of a macro. To "convert" a piece of SAS code to a macro, first you have to identify the parts of the code that should be changeable (e.g., the number of simulations, the seed value, certain parameters of the problem. Then you replace them with macro variables written in the form &*macro-variable-name*. Finally, you wrap the code with a %MACRO and %MEND statement.

You list the macro variables (also called parameters) in the %MACRO statement, where you can assign default values to them. The macro, i.e., the code from %MACRO to %MEND, is only the definition of the macro. In order to execute it, you have to start the macro processor by referencing the name of the macro with the necessary parameters.

Let us use Program 5.1 to illustrate the process of writing a macro. The Original Solution in Program 5.3 is identical to Program 5.1 without saving the randomly selected birthdays and checking their distribution with PROC CAPABILITY. The first part of the code that we wish to change is the name of the data set that captures the results of the simulation. On the right hand side of Program 5.3, we replace it with the corresponding macro variable: &OUT. In the %MACRO statement, we list this macro variable and assign a default value to it after an equal sign (OUT=RESULTS). Then we make the number of days (365), the number of simulations (10000), the frequency of the monitoring messages (at every 2000 simulations), and the seed value (123) parameters by replacing them with the macro variables &NDAYS, &NSIMS, &MSG, and &SEED, respectively. The left hand side of Program 5.3 highlights all parts of the code that we will replace with macro variables, and the right hand side has all those replaced with the corresponding macro variables.

The second argument, the divisor, of function MOD becomes a macro variable (&MSG) in the macro solution. Since its value could be set to zero (i.e., we wish to suppress the monitoring messages), the execution of the MOD function should be restricted to non-zero values. In other words, the actual SAS code generated by the macro processor should not contain the IF statement with the MOD function, if macro variable &MSG is zero. Therefore, we enclose it in a %IF macro statement. This is like a regular IF statement, but it only controls the presence or disappearance of the statement containing the function call in the generated SAS program. During execution, the macro processor checks the value of &MSG, and it skips the following statement if the value is zero.

The last statement of the macro solution, %BDAY(SEED=123) invokes the macro and executes the simulation. (The missing semicolon here is not an error, because this command causes SAS to load and process the macro, and each statement of the macro and the generated code already contains the obligatory semicolon.) Since the simulation is executed with SEED=123 specified, the results are identical to those given in Output 5.1. The highlighted parts in the right hand side of Program 5.3 are the changes required to create the macro solution.

Program 5.3 Macro Solution to the Matching Birthdays Problem

Original Solution	Macro Solution
| | ```
/*****************************************/
/* Macro BDAY simulates the problem of   */
/* of Matching Birthdays.                */
/*                                       */
/* Parameters:                           */
/* NDAYS   # of days in a year.          */
/* NSIMS   # of simulations.             */
/* MSG     # of simulations at which to  */
/*         display a message in the LOG  */
/*         window to monitor the run.    */
/* SEED    Seed of function RANUNI.      */
/* OUT     the name of the file that     */
/*         captures the results.         */
/*****************************************/
%MACRO BDAY(NDAYS=365,NSIMS=10000,MSG=2000,
            SEED=0,OUT=RESULTS);
DATA &OUT(KEEP=NPEOPLE);
    ARRAY DAYS(&NDAYS) $1 D1-D&NDAYS;
    LENGTH NPEOPLE 3;
    DO SIM=1 TO &NSIMS;
        %IF &MSG^=0 %THEN %DO;
        IF NOT MOD(SIM,&MSG) THEN PUT
                'SIMULATION NUMBER: ' SIM;
                %END;
        DO I=1 TO &NDAYS;
            DAYS(I)='0';
        END;
        DO NPEOPLE=1 TO &NDAYS+1;
            D=1+INT(&NDAYS*RANUNI(&SEED));
            IF DAYS(D)='1' THEN LEAVE;
                            ELSE DAYS(D)='1';
        END;
        OUTPUT;
    END;
    RUN;
PROC UNIVARIATE DATA=&OUT PLOT;
    VAR NPEOPLE;
    RUN;
%MEND;
%BDAY(SEED=123)
``` |

Original Solution (full text):
```
DATA RESULTS(KEEP=NPEOPLE);
    ARRAY DAYS(365) $1 D1-D365;
    LENGTH NPEOPLE 3;
    DO SIM=1 TO 10000;

        IF NOT MOD(SIM,2000) THEN PUT
                    'SIMULATION NUMBER: '
SIM;

        DO I=1 TO 365;
            DAYS(I)='0';
        END;
        DO NPEOPLE=1 TO 366;
            D=1+INT(365*RANUNI(123));
            IF DAYS(D)='1' THEN LEAVE;
                            ELSE
DAYS(D)='1';
        END;
        OUTPUT;
    END;
    RUN;
PROC UNIVARIATE DATA=RESULTS PLOT;
    VAR NPEOPLE;
    RUN;
```

If we specify OPTION MPRINT; before a macro execution, the Log window displays the real SAS code generated by the macro processor. In our case, the contents of the Log window are as follows (except that the indentation has been added for clarity):
```

Log 5.3
SAS Code
Generated by
the Macro
Processor When
Executing
Program 5.3

```
DATA RESULTS(KEEP=NPEOPLE);
     ARRAY DAYS(365) $1 D1-D365;
     LENGTH NPEOPLE 3;
     DO SIM=1 TO 10000;
         IF NOT MOD(SIM,2000) THEN PUT 'Simulation Number: ' SIM;
         DO I=1 TO 365;
             DAYS(I)='0';
         END;
         DO NPEOPLE=1 TO 365+1;
             D=1+INT(365*RANUNI(123));
             IF DAYS(D)='1' THEN LEAVE;
                             ELSE DAYS(D)='1';
         END;
         OUTPUT;
     END;
     RUN;
PROC UNIVARIATE DATA=RESULTS PLOT;
     VAR NPEOPLE;
     RUN;
```

It is recommended to set the default value of parameter SEED to zero in the %MACRO statement. Otherwise, when we forget to control it, we obtain the same result every time we run the macro.

Also, to achieve the highest degree of flexibility, we should "parameterize" as much code as possible. One could ask, for example, why did we make the number of days a parameter? If we execute %BDAY(NDAYS=12,SEED=123), then we can solve the problem of Matching Birth Months, a variation of the original problem: What is the average number of people needed to obtain the first pair of matching birth months? The macro returns a value of 5.06, whereas the theoretical value is 5.04.

5.9 Full-Time Monitoring with Macros

Much of Program 5.2 is related to monitoring the execution of the simulation. These parts of the program can be removed and placed into macros for clarity's sake. One macro could contain the code for starting the monitoring process, and another one could contain the statements displaying the recurring message. These macros provide two benefits: they make the code clearer, and they can serve as building blocks for general use. Program 5.4 is a modified version of Program 5.3 with full-time monitoring implemented. In the macros %TMONST and %TMON, we use variable names starting with underscores, because the macros must not interfere with the simulation code, and they must reference variables different from the ones used in the simulation. The macro %TMONST sets up many variables that are utilized by the second macro, %TMON. The macros are designed to handle the case where the user does not wish to monitor (i.e., MSG=0).

Program 5.4 *Macro Solution to the Matching Birthdays Problem with Full-Time Monitoring*

```
LIBNAME MYMACLIB 'subdirectory';    *** define a location for the macro library.;
OPTION SASMSTORE=MYMACLIB MSTORED;

/* Macro TMONST starts the time monitoring.                      */
/* Parameter                                                     */
/* MSG        # of simulations at which the program displays a   */
/*            a message in the LOG window. Specify zero if you   */
/*            wish to suppress the monitoring.                    */

%MACRO TMONST(MSG=2000) / STORE;
  _MSGCNT=0;
  %IF &MSG^=0 %THEN %DO;
      _MSGCNT=&MSG;
      _SDT=DATETIME();
      _STIME=TIMEPART(_SDT);
      PUT 'Starting Time: ' _STIME TIME12.3;
      LENGTH _MSG $72;
      SUBSTR(_MSG,1,13)='Simulation #:';
      SUBSTR(_MSG,21,16)=', Current Time: ';
      SUBSTR(_MSG,49,16)=', Duration: ';
  %END;
%MEND;

/* macro TMON displays the simulation number, current time and */
/* elapsed time after a certain number of simulations.         */

%MACRO TMON / STORE;
  IF _MSGCNT^=0 THEN DO;
      _SIM+1;
      IF NOT MOD(_SIM,_MSGCNT) THEN DO; _EDT=DATETIME();
                                        _ETIME=TIMEPART(_EDT);
                                        _DUR=_EDT-_SDT;
                                        SUBSTR(_MSG,15,6)=PUT(_SIM,6.);

SUBSTR(_MSG,37,12)=PUT(_ETIME,TIME12.3);SUBSTR(_MSG,61,12)=PUT(_DUR,TIME12.3);
                                        PUT _MSG;
                                        _SDT=_EDT;
                                    END;
                        END;
%MEND;

/* a new SAS session starts here. */
```

```
LIBNAME MYMACLIB 'subdirectory';   *** this is the location of the macro library.;
OPTION SASMSTORE=MYMACLIB;
%MACRO BDAY(NDAYS=365,NSIMS=10000,MSG=2000, SEED=0,OUT=RESULTS);
   DATA &OUT(KEEP=NPEOPLE);
        ARRAY DAYS(&NDAYS) $1 D1-D&NDAYS;
        LENGTH NPEOPLE 3;
        %TMONST(MSG=2000)
        DO SIM=1 TO &NSIMS;
           %TMON
           DO I=1 TO &NDAYS;
              DAYS(I)='0';
           END;
           DO NPEOPLE=1 TO &NDAYS+1;
              D=1+INT(&NDAYS*RANUNI(&SEED));
              IF DAYS(D)='1' THEN LEAVE;
                             ELSE DAYS(D)='1';
           END;
           OUTPUT;
        END;
        RUN;
   PROC UNIVARIATE DATA=&OUT PLOT;
        VAR NPEOPLE;
        RUN;
%MEND;
%BDAY(SEED=123)
```

Program 5.4 also illustrates how we can seamlessly incorporate macros in our programs. We can set up a macro library, store our macros there, and later reference them without repeating the macro codes in our program. The statements

```
LIBNAME MYMACLIB 'subdirectory';
OPTION SASMSTORE=MYMACLIB MSTORED;
```

define the location of a macro library and let SAS know that we wish to permanently store macros there. Storing a macro in that library requires the STORE option in the %MACRO statement (see, e.g., %MACRO TMONST/STORE;). In a future SAS session, we only need to point to this macro library and the macros become available with a simple reference.

5.10 Simulation of the Parking Problem (Rényi's Constant)

In the rest of the chapter, we will solve the Parking Problem with a macro. We will see the advantages of using a macro solution, the many and convenient ways SAS enables us to analyze and present the results, and we will answer additional interesting questions concerning the original problem.

The Parking Problem is as follows. What is the average number of cars of unit length that can randomly park along a street of length x? If M(x) denotes that average, then the problem can also ask:

$$\lim_{x \to \infty} \frac{M(x)}{x} = C = ?$$

The problem was first solved by Alfréd Rényi,[2] and C is called Rényi's constant. We assume an ideal situation, i.e., that cars can park with their bumpers touching (but not overlapping) each other.

First, let us design an algorithm that can be programmed in SAS. At the beginning, there is one parking space, the whole street. After parking the first car, there may be two parking spaces—one in front of that car, the other one behind it. When we park a car, we have to choose an available parking space first, and then we have to randomly place the car somewhere in that parking space. During the simulation, we need to store the parking locations of the cars, keep track of the available parking spaces, and stop the parking process when the available parking space decreases to zero. The parking locations and the number of parking spaces are constantly updated during the simulation. We choose the centrum of a car for its parking location.

The macro %PARKING in Program 5.5 is the complete solution to the simulation. The simulation itself is performed in a DATA step. In that DATA step, we have to dimension an array (PARKGLOC) for the parking locations. The number of elements in that array depends on the maximum number of cars that can park along the street of a given length. That value is determined in a preceding DATA _NULL_ step and is carried over in a macro variable (&MAXNCARS). If the parameters are specified such that no car can park (the street is shorter than the length of a car), the macro jumps to the end of the macro without starting the simulation.

Note the use of the macro parameters: their values are assigned to regular DATA step variables in a RETAIN statement to avoid the excessive presence of macro variables. The macro provides added flexibility by controlling the level of output: whether to output the intermediate information after parking each car, or only the end result (see the parameter LEVEL), and whether to keep only the number of cars parked or all parking locations as well (see the parameter KEEP).

---

[2] Rényi showed (Rényi, 1958) that $M(0) = 0$ and $M(x) = 1 + \dfrac{2}{x-1} \displaystyle\int_0^x M(u)\,du$ if x>0. By a Laplace transform, he obtained

$C = \displaystyle\int_0^\infty \exp\left(-2 \int_0^t \frac{1-e^{-u}}{u}\,du\right) dt = 0.74759...$ For a survey of the problem, see Solomon 1986. For calculating the value of C with high precision, see Marsaglia 1989.

Program 5.5 *Macro PARKING*

```
LIBNAME MYMACLIB 'subdirectory';   *** this is the location of;
OPTION SASMSTORE=MYMACLIB;         *** the macro library.;
/*************************************************************/
/* Macro PARKING simulates the parking problem and returns  */
/* the number of cars that park along a given street.       */
/*                                                          */
/* Parameters                                               */
/* OUT       name of the data set that captures the results */
/*           of the simulations.                            */
/* STRLNGTH  the length of the street.                      */
/* CARLNGTH  the uniform length of a car.                   */
/* NSIMS     # of simulations.                              */
/* SEED      Seed of function RANUNI.                       */
/* MSG       # of simulations at which to display a         */
/*           a monitoring message in the LOG window.        */
/* LEVEL     MAIN or PARKING. It controls the level of      */
/*           detail in the output data set. MAIN creates    */
/*           one record per simulation. PARKING creates     */
/*           one record for every car parked.               */
/* KEEP      NCARS or ALL. It controls the variables in the */
/*           output data set. NCARS saves only variable     */
/*           NCARS (# of cars parked), ALL saves all        */
/*           auxiliary variables along with NCARS.          */
/*************************************************************/

%MACRO PARKING(OUT=TEMP,STRLNGTH=10,CARLNGTH=1,
               NSIMS=1,SEED=123,MSG=0,LEVEL=MAIN,KEEP=NCARS);

 /* calculate the maximum number of cars that can park + 2. */
 /* do it in a data _null_ step and save the result in      */
 /* macro variable MAXNCARS using the SYMPUT CALL routine.   */
 /* macro variable &MAXNCARS will be used to dimension an    */
 /* array, which holds the locations of the parked cars.     */

DATA _NULL_;
     IF &STRLNGTH.<&CARLNGTH.
        THEN MAXNCARS=0;
        ELSE MAXNCARS=2+INT(&STRLNGTH/&CARLNGTH);
     CALL SYMPUT('MAXNCARS',COMPRESS(PUT(MAXNCARS,16.)));
     STOP; RUN;

 /* if parameters are invalid, jump to the end of the       */
 /* macro and do nothing.                                   */

%IF &MAXNCARS=0 %THEN %DO;
    %PUT Error: Invalid relative values for parameters 'STRLNGTH';
    %PUT Error: and 'CARLNGTH'.;
    %GOTO FINISH; %END;

 /* data step of the simulation. */

DATA &OUT;

     /* The parameters are placed in the corresponding SAS  */
     /* variables through a RETAIN statement.               */

     LENGTH STRLNGTH CARLNGTH 4;
     RETAIN STRLNGTH &STRLNGTH CARLNGTH &CARLNGTH;
     RETAIN NSIMS &NSIMS SEED &SEED;
```

```
/* array PRKGLOC stores the centrum of each car parked. */
/* its dimension is the maximum number of cars that      */
/* can park + 2 (see macro variable &MAXNCARS).          */
/* the minimum parking location can be half the length   */
/* of a car from the start of the street and the         */
/* maximum parking location can be half the length of a  */
/* car from the end of the street.                       */
/* to let our algorithm work, we park two imaginary      */
/* cars just before and after the street.                */

ARRAY PRKGLOC(&MAXNCARS) P1-P&MAXNCARS;
LENGTH NCARS 4;
%TMONST(MSG=&MSG)     *** start the time monitoring.;

DO SIM=1 TO NSIMS;   *** the main LOOP of the simulations.;
   %TMON             *** display the monitoring message.;
   NCARS=0;          *** NCARS holds the number of cars;
                     *** currently parked.;

   /* set the parking locations of the two imaginary  */
   /* cars. All cars that the simulation parks will be */
   /* parked between these two cars.                   */

   PRKGLOC(1)=-CARLNGTH/2;
   PRKGLOC(2)= STRLNGTH+CARLNGTH/2;

   /* NAVAILPS: # of available parking spaces. At the  */
   /* beginning, it is one, because the whole street   */
   /* is one continuous parking space.                 */

   NAVAILPS=1;

   /* LOOP that parks cars. It keeps parking until     */
   /* there is only one available parking space.       */

   DO WHILE (NAVAILPS>0);

      /* Choose from the available parking spaces. */

      CURRPARK=1+INT(RANUNI(SEED)*NAVAILPS);

      /* find the possible parking spaces between the   */
      /* cars already parked and stop when the randomly */
      /* chosen parking space is reached.               */

      NPS=0;
      DO I=1 TO NCARS+1 WHILE (CURRPARK^=NPS);
         IF PRKGLOC(I)+2*CARLNGTH <= PRKGLOC(I+1) THEN DO;

            /* the space between car i and car i+1 is  */
            /* long enough to be a parking space.      */

            NPS=NPS+1;   *** Keep counting the parking spaces.;

            /* the randomly chosen parking space       */
            /* (see above: CURRPARK) is found.         */

            IF CURRPARK=NPS THEN DO;

               /* choose the parking location within the */
               /* parking space randomly. The parking    */
               /* location is held in variable NEWPRKG.  */
```

```
             NEWPRKG=PRKGLOC(I)+CARLNGTH+RANUNI(SEED)*
                      (PRKGLOC(I+1)-PRKGLOC(I)-2*CARLNGTH);

             /* insert the car into the sequence of    */
             /* parked cars. Push up all cars behind    */
             /* it.                            -        */

             DO J=NCARS+2 TO I+1 BY -1;
                 PRKGLOC(J+1)=PRKGLOC(J);
             END;
             NCARS=NCARS+1;
             PRKGLOC(I+1)=NEWPRKG;

             /* update the number of available parking */
             /* spaces. Is there enough space for      */
             /* another car in front of and behind     */
             /* this newly parked car?                 */

             NAVAILPS=NAVAILPS-1;
             IF PRKGLOC(I)+2*CARLNGTH<=PRKGLOC(I+1)
                 THEN NAVAILPS=NAVAILPS+1;
             IF PRKGLOC(I+1)+2*CARLNGTH<=PRKGLOC(I+2)
                 THEN NAVAILPS=NAVAILPS+1;
            END;
          END;
        END;

        /* output record after each parking. */

        %IF %UPCASE(&LEVEL)=PARKING %THEN OUTPUT;
      END;

    /* output record after all cars are parked and no    */
    /* more cars can be parked.                          */

    %IF %UPCASE(&LEVEL)=MAIN %THEN OUTPUT;;
  END;
  %IF %UPCASE(&KEEP)=NCARS %THEN %STR(KEEP NCARS;);
                    %ELSE %STR(KEEP NCARS CARLNGTH STRLNGTH
                    P1-P&MAXNCARS;);
    RUN;
 %FINISH:;
%MEND;
```

Before we run a large number of simulations, let us call the macro to execute one simulation only and use a SAS/GRAPH procedure to present the process of parking visually. Program 5.6 calls the macro with one simulation requested, saving all intermediate data (note the utilization of the default values of the macro parameters). After adjusting the output file, we draw the parked cars along the street using PROG GPLOT (see Output 5.6). This sample simulation and its graphical presentation help us to understand the algorithm and the internal working of the macro.

Program 5.6 *One Simulation of Parking*

```
%PARKING(OUT=ONESIM,LEVEL=PARKING,KEEP=ALL)
PROC PRINT DATA=ONESIM;
     FORMAT P1-P12 5.3;
     TITLE F=SWISS H=1.5 'One Random Parking (Street=10, Car=1)';
     RUN;

/* data set ONESIM contains all parked cars of one simulation.*/
/* prepare the data set for drawing the sequence of parking   */
/* with PROC GPLOT using the SYMBOL INTERPOL=HILOBC;          */
/* statement that draws a rectangle representing a car.       */

DATA ONESIM(KEEP=CARS STREET);
     SET ONESIM;
     ARRAY PRKGLOC(12) P1-P12;
     DO I=2 TO _N_+1;

          /* make the 'x' coordinate of each car unique by    */
          /* adding a unique fudging factor to each.          */

          CARS=_N_+0.00000001*I;
          STREET=PRKGLOC(I)+0.5; OUTPUT;
          STREET=PRKGLOC(I)-0.5; OUTPUT;

          /* create two 'y' values in order to have the       */
          /* vertical sides of the rectangle.                 */

          STREET=PRKGLOC(I)-0.5; OUTPUT;
     END;
PROC FORMAT;
     VALUE FCARS 0=' ' 8=' ';
PROC GPLOT DATA=ONESIM;
     PLOT STREET*CARS / VAXIS=AXIS1 HAXIS=AXIS2;
     FORMAT CARS FCARS.;
     SYMBOL INTERPOL=HILOBC;
     AXIS1 LABEL=(A=90 R=0 F=SWISS H=1.5 'Street')
           ORDER=0 TO 10 BY 1 VALUE=(H=1.2 F=SWISS) MINOR=NONE;
     AXIS2 LABEL=(F=SWISS  H=1.5 'Cars')
           ORDER=0 TO 8 BY 1 VALUE=(H=1.2 F=SWISS) MINOR=NONE;
RUN;
```

Output 5.6 *Graphical Representation of One Simulation*

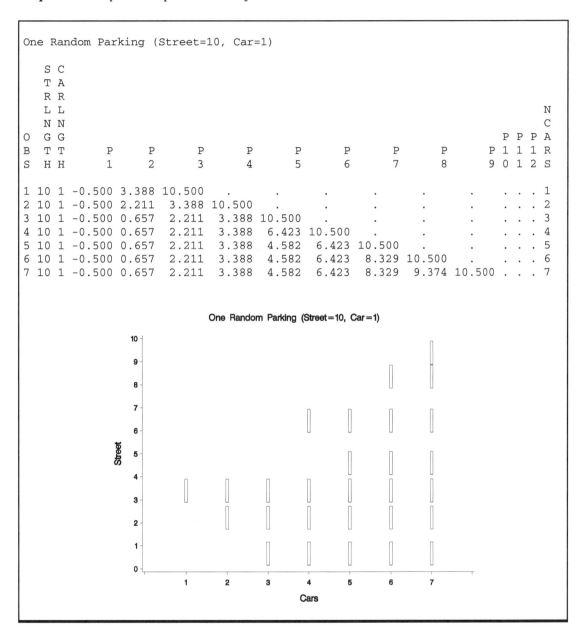

```
One Random Parking (Street=10, Car=1)

     S  C
     T  A
     R  R
     L  L                                                                         N
     N  N                                                                         C
 O   G  G                                                      P  P  P  A
 B   T  T      P      P      P      P      P      P      P      P   P  1  1  1  R
 S   H  H      1      2      3      4      5      6      7      8   9  0  1  2  S

 1  10  1  -0.500  3.388 10.500     .      .      .      .      .      .  . . .  1
 2  10  1  -0.500  2.211  3.388 10.500     .      .      .      .      .  . . .  2
 3  10  1  -0.500  0.657  2.211  3.388 10.500     .      .      .      .  . . .  3
 4  10  1  -0.500  0.657  2.211  3.388  6.423 10.500     .      .      .  . . .  4
 5  10  1  -0.500  0.657  2.211  3.388  4.582  6.423 10.500     .      .  . . .  5
 6  10  1  -0.500  0.657  2.211  3.388  4.582  6.423  8.329 10.500     .  . . .  6
 7  10  1  -0.500  0.657  2.211  3.388  4.582  6.423  8.329  9.374 10.500 . . .  7
```

Now we can run a real simulation and obtain the average number of cars. In Program 5.7, we specify the length of the street as 100 (the cars still have unit length), and we request 100,000 simulations. The output data set of the macro (RES100) is processed by PROC UNIVARIATE to return the answer: 74.5 cars. Rényi's constant would be 0.7451... .

Program 5.7 *100,000 Simulations with Street=100 and Car Length=1*

```
%PARKING(OUT=RES100,STRLNGTH=100,NSIMS=100000)
PROC UNIVARIATE DATA=RES100 PLOT;
    VAR NCARS;
    RUN;
```

Output 5.7 *Average Number of Parked Cars on Street=100*

```
Univariate Procedure

Variable=NCARS

              Moments                          Quantiles(Def=5)

N              100000  Sum Wgts    100000   100% Max     83    99%    79
Mean         74.51164  Sum        7451164    75% Q3       76    95%    78
Std Dev      1.969904  Variance   3.880523   50% Med      75    90%    77
Skewness     0.003419  Kurtosis   -0.00247   25% Q1       73    10%    72
USS          5.5559E8  CSS        388048.5    0% Min      66     5%    71
CV           2.643754  Std Mean   0.006229                      1%    70
T:Mean=0     11961.32  Pr>|T|       0.0001   Range        17
Num ^= 0       100000  Num > 0      100000   Q3-Q1         3
M(Sign)         50000  Pr>=|M|      0.0001   Mode         75
Sgn Rank        2.5E9  Pr>=|S|      0.0001
D:Normal     0.101038  Pr>D           <.01

              Extremes

     Lowest      Obs    Highest      Obs
         66(   79423)       82(   82446)
         66(   71606)       82(   87088)
         66(   53040)       82(   91180)
         67(   89263)       82(   95423)
         67(   87120)       83(   89658)

                      Histogram                      #    Boxplot
    83.5+*                                            1      0
        .*                                           13      0
        .*                                           95      0
        .**                                         416      |
        .****                                      1538      |
        .**********                                4245      |
        .********************                      8969      |
        .************************************     15296   +-----+
        .*************************************************  19741   *-----*
        .************************************************   19506   |  +  |
        .*************************************              14992   +-----+
        .**********************                             9110      |
        .*********                                          4119      |
        .****                                               1462      |
        .*                                                   400      |
        .*                                                    79      0
        .*                                                    15      0
    66.5+*                                                     3      0
         ----+----+----+----+----+----+----+----+---
         * may represent up to 412 counts
```

Using the macro solution, it is easy to approximate Rényi's constant by executing the macro with increasing street lengths. In Program 5.8, we simulate the problem with street lengths of 10, 100, 1000 and 10,000 units. Note that the last macro call requests only 10,000 simulations because of the increase in the execution time. The program concatenates the results of the four macro calls, sets up a variable for the length of the street (STREET), and calculates Rényi's constant with PROC MEANS and a subsequent DATA step. The results show an ever-increasing approximation of the true value. When the length of the street is 10,000 units, the error is less than 0.000003 (0.74760044... vs. the true value of 0.74759792...).

Program 5.8 *Approximation of Rényi's Constant*

```
%PARKING(OUT=RES10,STRLNGTH=10,NSIMS=100000)
%PARKING(OUT=RES100,STRLNGTH=100,NSIMS=100000)
%PARKING(OUT=RES1000,STRLNGTH=1000,NSIMS=100000)
%PARKING(OUT=RES10000,STRLNGTH=10000,NSIMS=10000)
DATA RESALL;    *** concatenate the results of all simulations;
    SET RES10(IN=S10)      RES100(IN=S100)
        RES1000(IN=S1000) RES10000(IN=S10000);
    IF S10    THEN STREET=10;  *** set up the length of the street.;
    IF S100   THEN STREET=100;
    IF S1000  THEN STREET=1000;
    IF S10000 THEN STREET=10000;
PROC MEANS DATA=RESALL NOPRINT;   *** calculate average number of cars.;
    VAR NCARS STREET;
    BY STREET;
    OUTPUT OUT=RENYI(KEEP=RENYI STREET NSIMS) MEAN=RENYI N=NSIMS;
    RUN;
DATA RENYI;    *** calculate Renyi's constant (average number of ;
               *** cars over the length of the street).;
    SET RENYI;
    RENYI=RENYI/STREET;
    RUN;
PROC PRINT DATA=RENYI LABEL SPLIT='*' NOOBS;
    VAR STREET RENYI NSIMS;
    LABEL STREET='Length of*Street' RENYI="Renyi's*Constant"
          NSIMS='Number of*Simulations';
    TITLE  "Approximation of Renyi's Constant";
    TITLE2 "(Average Number of Cars / Length of Street)";
    RUN;
```

Output 5.8
Approximation of Rényi's Constant

```
                Approximation of Renyi's Constant
             (Average Number of Cars / Length of Street)

          Length of      Renyi's       Number of
            Street       Constant      Simulations

                10       0.72264        100000
               100       0.74511        100000
              1000       0.74731        100000
             10000       0.74760         10000
```

As we discussed in the introduction to this chapter, the SAS System provides an unparalleled richness of statistical procedures and convenient data handling capabilities for the simulations. We can raise many secondary questions about the simulation problem and answer them with ease.

For example, we may ask: What is the distribution of the gaps between the parked cars? Normal or uniform? Even when we are not equipped with the necessary mathematical knowledge and skill, we can answer these questions. Program 5.9 presents the code to execute the simulation, grab the parking locations of the cars, calculate the gaps between them and, finally, draw the distribution with PROC UNIVARIATE. Output 5.9 shows the distribution, which is neither normal nor uniform.

Program 5.9 *Analysis of Gaps Between the Cars*

```
/* execute a simulation by grabbing the locations of */
/* all parked cars (see parameter KEEP=ALL and        */
/* variables p1,p2,...)                               */

%PARKING(OUT=GAP,STRLNGTH=100,NSIMS=100000,KEEP=ALL)

/* calculate the gaps between the cars. Include the   */
/* distance from the beginning of the street and the  */
/* first car and the distance between the last car    */
/* and the end of the street. Place each gap into a   */
/* separate observation.                              */

DATA GAP(KEEP=GAP);
    SET GAP;
    ARRAY PRKGLOC(102) P1-P102;    *** locations of the cars.;
    LENGTH GAP 4;
    DO I=1 TO NCARS+1;
        GAP=PRKGLOC(I+1)-PRKGLOC(I)-1;    *** the length of a car is 1.;
        OUTPUT;
    END;
PROC UNIVARIATE DATA=GAP NORMAL PLOT;
    VAR GAP;
    TITLE 'Distribution of Gaps between the Cars';
    RUN;
```

Output 5.9: *Distribution of Gaps Between the Cars*

```
                    Distribution of Gaps between the Cars

Univariate Procedure

Variable=GAP

              Moments                           Quantiles(Def=5)

N            7551164  Sum Wgts   7551164   100% Max        1       99%   0.97653
Mean        0.337542  Sum        2548835    75% Q3   0.541009      95%   0.887918
Std Dev     0.281835  Variance   0.079431    50% Med   0.26276     90%   0.787126
Skewness    0.676533  Kurtosis  -0.70364     25% Q1   0.091603     10%   0.026726
USS          1460135  CSS        599796.5     0% Min  1.146E-9      5%   0.011197
CV          83.49629  Std Mean   0.000103                          1%   0.001641
T:Mean=0     3291.09  Pr>|T|       0.0001   Range           1
Num ^= 0     7551164  Num > 0    7551164    Q3-Q1    0.449406
M(Sign)      3775582  Pr>=|M|      0.0001   Mode     0.255009
Sgn Rank    1.426E13  Pr>=|S|      0.0001
D:Normal    0.115525  Pr>D          <.01

              Extremes

   Lowest      Obs      Highest     Obs
 1.146E-9( 4756845)  0.999999( 4362339)
 7.907E-9( 2295455)  0.999999( 5790184)
 1.685E-8( 7007323)  0.999999( 6480881)
   1.7E-8( 5455812)         1( 2429628)
 2.736E-8( 4460589)         1( 4932128)

                       Histogram                          #    Boxplot
 0.975+*******                                          163291    |
      .******                                           171630    |
      .*******                                          180089    |
      .*******                                          189543    |
      .*******                                          200874    |
      .********                                         212389    |
      .********                                         224685    |
      .*********                                        240839    |
      .*********                                        256294    |
      .*********                                        275069  +-----+
      .**********                                       295764  |     |
      .***********                                      321136  |     |
      .************                                     349358  |     |
      .**************                                   382718  |  +  |
      .***************                                  423905  *-----*
      .*****************                                475048  |     |
      .******************                               542824  |     |
      .************************                         637857  |     |
      .****************************                     791203  +-----+
 0.025+**********************************************1.22E6      |
      ----+----+----+----+----+----+----+----+---
       *   may represent up to 25347 counts
```

5.11 Summary

The SAS System is an outstanding environment for Monte Carlo simulations. It provides all necessary tools for conducting a simulation, and it makes a full discussion of the problem possible with its broad range of procedures and features. In this chapter, we have seen that the programming of a simulation can be done in the familiar DATA step, that we have full control over the seed values of the random number generators, that it is easy to implement monitoring during the time-consuming execution, that the SAS code can be ported to any hardware and operating system without significant change, and that we can automate the simulation process by building it with the SAS Macro Facility.

5.12 References

Hamer, R. M., and T. J. Breen. 1985. "The SAS System as a Statistical Simulation Language." *Proceedings of the Tenth Annual SAS Users Group International Conference,* Reno, Nevada, 982-989.

Marsaglia, G., A. Zaman, and J. Marsaglia. 1989. "Numerical Solution of Some Classical Differential Equations." *Mathematics of Computation* 53(187):191-201.

Rényi, A. 1958. "On a One-Dimensional Problem Concerning Random Space Filling." *Publications of the Mathematical Institute of the Hungarian Academy of Sciences* 3:109-127 (in Hungarian).

SAS Institute Inc. 1990. *SAS Guide to Macro Processing, Version 6.* 2d ed. Cary, NC: SAS Institute Inc.

Solomon, H., and H. Weiner. 1986. "A Review of the Packing Problem." *Commun. Statist. Theory Methods* 15:2571-2607.

Chapter 6 Conducting Monte Carlo Studies That Involve Univariate Statistical Techniques

6.1 Introduction

Chapters 1 to 5 have covered the basic concepts and procedures for conducting a Monte Carlo simulation study. At the same time, the basic components of SAS programs necessary for implementing a Monte Carlo study have also been explained. We are now ready to present and discuss some complete examples of Monte Carlo studies in which the SAS System is used for statistical analysis. The examples in this chapter involve the following statistical techniques:

❑　a t-test, to assess the effect of violating the assumption of equal population variances

❑　analysis of variance (ANOVA), for assessing the effect of violating the assumptions of data normality and equal population variances

❑　linear regression, for comparing different R^2 shrinkage formulas for correcting positive bias of sample R^2.

For each example, we will present a) the theoretical rationale for conducting the study, and the major issues involved; b) the annotated SAS program for implementing the Monte Carlo study, with a detailed explanation of the SAS code; c) some selected and relevant results from the actual simulation based on the SAS programs provided. The examples provided in this chapter, as well as those in the following three chapters (Chapters 7, 8 and 9), are designed to help readers put together all the puzzle pieces discussed in previous chapters.

6.2 Example 1: Assessing the Effect of Unequal Population Variances in a T-TEST

The t-test is a widely used statistical inferential test for assessing the equality of two population means on a variable of interest. For example, suppose that a large corporation has a complicated end-of-year bonus policy that involves some subjective decisions from each employee's immediate supervisors. A personnel officer in the corporation may be interested in knowing if there is a difference in bonus (as represented by percentage of salary) between the male and female employees in the corporation. As another example, an educational psychologist may be interested in assessing whether there is a difference in the level of self-esteem between those students who are in the regular classroom and those who have been assigned to a special education program because of their lower performance on some academic aptitude/achievement measures. In both of these cases, a t-test may be used to test if the observed sample difference could have occurred by sampling variation, i.e., by chance. If it is statistically determined that the observed difference between the two samples on the variable of interest is very unlikely to be the result of sampling error, the difference would be declared to be statistically significant, namely, there is a real difference between the two populations (e.g., male versus female employees) on the variable of interest (e.g., end-of-year bonus).

All statistical inferential tests have some fundamental theoretical assumptions, and the t-test is no exception. If the fundamental assumptions of a statistical test are not tenable for the data used, the validity of the statistical conclusion based on the inferential test is often compromised to an unknown degree. For the t-test, there are two prominent assumptions: a) the two populations have equal variances; b) the variable of interest is normally distributed. If these assumptions are violated, the actual Type I error rate may deviate from the theoretical Type I error rate such that our statistical conclusion may be in error.

In this Monte Carlo simulation example, we examine the issue of violating the first assumption, i.e., the two populations do not have equal variances. The effect of violating these two assumptions of the t-test is well known, because these issues have been studied by many researchers. In this sense, our interest here is not in the statistical issues themselves, but only to present an example to illustrate how a Monte Carlo study can be implemented in the SAS System.

6.2.1 Computational Aspects of T-Tests

The t statistic for testing the equality of two independent samples, with sample sizes of n_1 and n_2 respectively, is:

$$t = \frac{\overline{X}_1 - \overline{X}_2}{\sqrt{s^2_{pooled}(\frac{1}{n_1} + \frac{1}{n_2})}}, \quad (df = n_1 + n_2 - 2) \tag{6.1}$$

s^2_{pooled} is the pooled variance of the two samples under the assumption of equal population variances ($\sigma_1^2 = \sigma_2^2$):

$$s^2_{pooled} = \frac{(n_1 - 1)s_1^2 + (n_2 - 1)s_2^2}{n_1 + n_2 - 2} \tag{6.2}$$

s_1^2 and s_2^2 are the sample variances of the two samples, and $(n_1 - 1)s_1^2$ and

$(n_2 - 1)s_2^2$ represent the corrected sum of squares for the two samples, respectively. The corrected sum of squares of a sample is defined as:

$$SS_{corrected} = \sum (X_i - \overline{X})^2$$

and it can be computed via:

$$SS_{corrected} = \sum X_i^2 - \frac{(\sum X_i)^2}{n} \tag{6.3}$$

These formulas are presented to help readers follow some SAS programming code that will be presented and discussed in later sections.

6.2.2 Design Considerations

In this example, we want to assess the effect of unequal population variances on the actual Type I error rate of t-tests for samples drawn from populations with the same means. The simulation design, however, should include conditions of both equal and unequal population variances so that an empirical comparison can be made about the empirical Type I error rates for the data condition that satisfies the theoretical assumption of equal population variances, and for the other data condition that violates this assumption.

Under the condition of unequal population variances, there can be different degrees of inequality of population variances. For example, the variance of one population may be 50% larger than that of the other, or twice as large as that of the other, or four times as large, etc. A real Monte Carlo study may include a range of degrees of inequality in order to gain a fuller understanding of the effects caused by such data conditions. In our example here, however, for the sake of simplicity, we only consider one condition of unequal population variances: the standard deviation of one population is 10 (variance=100), and that of the other is 15 (variance=225). In short, for the dimension of population variances, we will consider two conditions: equal and unequal population variances.

Previous research in this area suggests that sample size plays a role in influencing the effect of unequal population variances on the actual Type I error rate of t-tests. More specifically, unequal population variances have a substantially stronger effect on the actual Type I error rate of t-test statistics when the sample sizes of the two samples are unequal than when they are equal. To investigate the interaction effect between sample size and unequal population variances, sample size should be considered as another dimension of design.

Although a real research Monte Carlo study may include a range of sample size conditions with different degrees of inequality of sample sizes in the two samples, we only include one condition of equal sample sizes (20 and 20 for the two samples) and one condition of unequal sample sizes (20 for the sample from the population with equal/smaller population variance, and 40 for the sample from the population with equal/larger population variance). The two dimensions (population variance and sample size) are fully crossed with each other, resulting in a 2×2 experimental design with four cell conditions. To obtain a reasonably accurate estimate of the actual Type I error rate for the conditions, 10,000 replications of the t-test will be conducted in each cell condition. This design requires a total number of 40,000 replications [(2×2) ×10000]. The Monte Carlo study design is represented schematically in Table 6.1.

Table 6.1 *Schematic Representation of the T-Test Monte Carlo Study Design*

		Sample Size	
		Equal (20, 20)	Unequal (20, 40)
Variance	Equal (100, 100)	10,000 replications	10,000 replications
	Unequal (100, 225)	10,000 replications	10,000 replications

6.2.3 Different SAS Programming Approaches

Because the SAS System is so flexible, for any Monte Carlo simulation study, different approaches can be taken. Different approaches may involve different amounts of statistical programming. It is usually the individual researcher's preference that often dictates which approach is taken.

In this chapter, we present two approaches for implementing the Monte Carlo simulation design as represented in Table 6.1 for assessing the effect of unequal population variances on the validity of the t statistic's Type I error rate. The first approach is to rely on base SAS only, and we do the programming for all the computations involved in a t-test by using base SAS functions and mathematical capabilities. The second approach is to use SAS/IML for data generation and to use SAS/STAT software's PROC TTEST to obtain the t statistic and its probability value. This approach of relying on SAS/STAT procedures for statistical computations allows us to avoid programming for statistical computations, instead of doing the computation programming ourselves as in the first approach.

As we progress through our examples in this and later chapters, it will become more obvious that the latter approach allows us to take full advantage of the SAS System and is often much more efficient and simpler to implement. This is especially true when we deal with complicated statistical procedures, for which programming by ourselves is either impossible or simply too complicated for us to deal with.

6.2.4 T-Test Example: First Approach

Program 6.1 presents a SAS macro program for simulating a t-test under the design conditions depicted in Table 6.1. This program relies only on base SAS for all the programming, including the programming for data generation and all the statistical computations involved in a t-test. Although the program contains many comments to explain the functions of the SAS programming code, for researchers who are novices in this area, some more detailed explanations may be beneficial. Following the program, a detailed explanation will be provided for some selected components of the program.

Program 6.1 *SAS Program for T-Test – First Approach*

```
LIBNAME TTEST 'C:\T_TEST\TRIALS';

            * -- to avoid the problem of SAS Log Window becoming full;
PROC PRINTTO LOG='C:\T_TEST\TRIALS\LOGFILE.TMP';
RUN;

%MACRO TTEST;      * beginning of the macro program 'TTEST';

%DO A=1 %TO 2;     * A=1:equal variance, A=2:unequal;
%DO B=1 %TO 2;     * B=1:equal sample size, B=2:unequal;

%DO I=1 %TO 10000;   * number of replications in each cell. 10,000 in this case;

DATA TTEST;

        /*** set parameters ***/
ALPHA=0.05;      * nominal TYPE I error rate;
MEAN=50;         * common mean for two populations;
SD1=10;          * STD for GRP 1 & 2 - equal variance condition;
N1=20;           * sample size for GRP 1 & 2 - equal N condition;
        /*** end of parameters ***/
  IF &A=1 THEN SD2=SD1;       * A=1:equal variance, A=2:unequal - 1.5 times sd1;
    ELSE SD2=SD1*1.5;

  IF &B=1 THEN N2=N1;         * B=1:equal sample size, B=2:unequal - 2 times n1;
    ELSE N2=N1*2;
                           * initiate the accumulators;
SUM1=0;        * group 1:  sum of x - sigma(x);
SUM2=0;        * group 2:  sum of x - sigma(x);
SSU1=0;        * group 1:  uncorrected sum of squares (ss);
SSU2=0;        * group 2:  uncorrected sum of squares (ss);

  DO I=1 TO N1;           * generate Group 1 data, carry out some computations;
    X1=MEAN + SD1*RANNOR(0);
    SUM1=SUM1 + X1;
    SSU1=SSU1 + X1**2;
  END;

  DO J=1 TO N2;           * generate Group 2 data, carry out some computations;
    X2=MEAN + SD2*RANNOR(0);
    SUM2=SUM2 + X2;
    SSU2=SSU2 + X2**2;
  END;
```

```
  SSC1 = SSU1 - ((SUM1**2)/N1);        * compute corrected SS for two groups;
  SSC2 = SSU2 - ((SUM2**2)/N2);

  MEAN1=SUM1/N1;  MEAN2=SUM2/N2;       * means of the two samples;

  VARP=(SSC1+SSC2)/(N1+N2-2);          * pooled variance;

  T=(MEAN1-MEAN2)/SQRT(VARP*(1/N1 + 1/N2));    * t statistic;

  DF = N1 + N2 - 2;                    * degrees of freedom;

  IF T<0 THEN PT=2*PROBT(T,DF);           * p value of the t statistic - two-tailed;
  ELSE IF T>0 THEN PT=2*(1-PROBT(T,DF));

  IF PT<ALPHA THEN SIG=1;       * classify each t-test as either significant or not;
    ELSE SIG=0;

  IF &A=1 THEN EQ_VAR='  EQUAL';   * add design conditions to the output data set;
    ELSE EQ_VAR='UNEQUAL';

  IF &B=1 THEN EQ_N='  EQUAL';
    ELSE EQ_N='UNEQUAL';
DATA NEW; SET TTEST;                   * append the results to a SAS data set on disk;
  KEEP T DF PT SIG EQ_VAR EQ_N;
  PROC APPEND BASE=TTEST.TTEST;
RUN;

%END;                 * end iteration do loop;
%END;                 * end B do loop;
%END;                 * end A do loop;
%MEND TTEST;          * close the macro program;
%TTEST;               * run the macro program;
RUN;
                      * check empirical rejection rate for each cell condition;
DATA A; SET TTEST.TTEST;
PROC SORT; BY EQ_VAR EQ_N;
PROC FREQ; BY EQ_VAR EQ_N;
  TABLES SIG;
RUN;
```

The first PROC PRINTTO as repeated below directs the SAS log to a file on disk instead of displaying log messages in the SAS Log window. In a Monte Carlo simulation study where literally thousands of replications of some procedures may be run, the SAS log may become so long that the SAS Log window may not be able to display it, because the SAS Log window has a certain display limit (32,000 lines). Once the limit is reached, the SAS program will pause, and then ask you what to do. To avoid the problem so that we can be away while the program is running, we can simply redirect the SAS log to a file on the hard disk, and the file is given the name LOGFILE.TMP.

```
             * -- to avoid the problem of SAS Log Window becoming full;
    PROC PRINTTO LOG='C:\T_TEST\TRIALS\LOGFILE.TMP';
    RUN;
```

In this program, we used a SAS macro to write the program. As discussed in Chapter 5, a SAS macro program has the structure of starting with %MACRO and ending with %MEND, as shown below:

```
%MACRO name;
.
. (other SAS program statements)
.
%MEND name;
```

SAS macro programs are extremely flexible, and almost anything can be included in them. When we use SAS for a Monte Carlo study, in many cases it is necessary to use a SAS macro program in order to run some SAS procedures repeatedly. For example, the DO loop in SAS works within the DATA step, before any PROC statements begin. But if we want to run a PROC statement repeatedly, we cannot use a regular DO loop. In other words, if we want to run PROC TTEST one hundred times, as in the following program, it will not work:

```
DO I = 1 TO 100;       * program that will not work;

  PROC TTEST;
    CLASS GROUP;
    VAR X;
  RUN;

END;
```

This problem, however, can easily be solved by using a SAS macro program, as shown below. As will be seen in the examples in this and the following chapters, for simulating complicated statistical procedures, this becomes absolutely necessary so that we can take advantage of the powerful SAS/STAT procedures.

```
%MACRO TTEST;
%DO I = 1 %TO 100;
.
.(other program statements)
.
  PROC TTEST;
    CLASS GROUP;
    VAR X;
  RUN;
.
.(other program statements)
.
%END;
%MEND TTEST;
%TTEST;                * to run the macro program 'ttest';
RUN;
```

Once we obtain all the results of this simulation study, there are a variety of ways of handling the data. One approach is to output the results in the SAS Output window, in which case the results are not saved as a data set. For example, in this t-test example, we can program in such a way that the actual Type I error rates for the four cell conditions will be directly output into the SAS Output window. This approach, however, does not allow future analysis. Once the SAS program is terminated, the data no longer exist.

Our preference is to save the results first as a permanent SAS data set, so future analysis is possible. This approach has some obvious advantages. In many Monte Carlo studies, especially those with complicated designs involving multiple factors and a variety of statistics, secondary analysis of the results can be complicated, and it is not always possible to anticipate what kinds of secondary analyses will be performed on the simulation results. In these situations, it is imperative to save the simulation results for future analysis.

In our t-test example, we use the base SAS APPEND procedure (PROC APPEND) to append the relevant information from each replication of PROC TTEST to a permanent SAS data set 'TTEST' (Notice the two-level name for the permanent SAS data set), as repeated below. This permanent SAS data set contains six variables: the t statistic (T), degrees of freedom (DF), the probability value of the t statistic (PT), statistically significant or not at 0.05 level (SIG: 1=significant, 0=non-significant), equal population variance or not (EQ_VAR: EQUAL=equal variances for the two groups, UNEQUAL=unequal population variances), and equal sample size or not (EQ_N, EQUAL=equal sample size, UNEQUAL=unequal sample size). Once the results are saved in the permanent SAS data set, future analysis of the results can be done at any time.

```
                *  append the results to a permanent SAS data set on disk;
DATA NEW; SET TTEST;
  KEEP T DF PT SIG EQ_VAR EQ_N;
  PROC APPEND BASE=TTEST.TTEST;
RUN;
```

Once all the results are obtained, we can run some simple analyses to check the actual Type I error rates of the t-test under each of the four cell conditions. PROC SORT and PROC FREQ statements accomplish the tasks, and the results based on one execution of Program 6.1 are in Output 6.1 below.

```
DATA A; SET TTEST.TTEST;
PROC SORT; BY EQ_VAR EQ_N;
PROC FREQ; BY EQ_VAR EQ_N;
  TABLES SIG;
RUN;
```

Output 6.1
T-Test
Simulation
Results
(Program 6.1)

```
------------------------ EQ_VAR=' EQUAL' EQ_N=' EQUAL' ---------------------

                                       Cumulative  Cumulative
         SIG   Frequency    Percent    Frequency    Percent
          0       9509        95.1        9509        95.1
          1        491         4.9       10000       100.0

------------------------ EQ_VAR=' EQUAL' EQ_N=UNEQUAL ----------------------

                                       Cumulative  Cumulative
         SIG   Frequency    Percent    Frequency    Percent
          0       9500        95.0        9500        95.0
          1        500         5.0       10000       100.0

------------------------ EQ_VAR=UNEQUAL EQ_N=' EQUAL' ----------------------

                                       Cumulative  Cumulative
         SIG   Frequency    Percent    Frequency    Percent
          0       9503        95.0        9503        95.0
          1        497         5.0       10000       100.0

------------------------ EQ_VAR=UNEQUAL EQ_N=UNEQUAL -----------------------

                                       Cumulative  Cumulative
         SIG   Frequency    Percent    Frequency    Percent
          0       9717        97.2        9717        97.2
          1        283         2.8       10000       100.0
```

In Output 6.1 it is seen that in three of the four conditions, the actual Type I error rates (0.049, 0.05, and 0.05, respectively) are almost right on the target of the nominal Type I error rate of 0.05 as we specified in the program. Only for the last condition (both unequal variance and unequal sample size) does the actual Type I error rate (0.028) deviate noticeably from the nominal Type I error rate. This shows that the t-test is much more robust to the violation of the equal population variances assumption when the two groups have approximately equal sample sizes, a finding that is consistent with previous research studies in this area (see Glass & Hopkins 1996, Chapter 12, for some detailed discussion).

6.2.5 T-Test Example: Second Approach

The second program for the same t-test Monte Carlo study is presented Program 6.2. This program is very similar to the previous one, but it also contains enough variations to warrant some explanation. The two most prominent areas where this program differs from the previous one are 1) SAS/IML is used for data generation, instead of base SAS, as in the previous program; 2) SAS/STAT software's PROC TTEST is used to obtain t-test results instead of programming all the statistical computation ourselves. This second feature may not seem to be a big deal here, because the computation for the t-test is quite simple. But for the more complicated statistical procedures that we will encounter later, this feature becomes absolutely essential, either because we do not fully understand the computational aspects of a statistical procedure, or because programming for such complicated statistical procedures is beyond our programming repertoire, or both. By taking full advantage of SAS/STAT procedures, we can easily overcome these barriers and conduct Monte Carlo studies for quite complicated statistical techniques.

Program 6.2 SAS Program for T-Test – Second Approach

```
LIBNAME TTEST 'C:\T_TEST\TRIALS';

             * -- to avoid the problem of SAS Log Window becoming full;
PROC PRINTTO LOG='C:\T_TEST\TRIALS\LOGFILE.TMP';
RUN;

%MACRO TTEST;

%DO A=1 %TO 2;     * A=1:equal variance, A=2:unequal;
%DO B=1 %TO 2;     * B=1:equal sample size, B=2:unequal;

%DO REP=1 %TO 10000;  * number of replications in each cell;

PROC IML;

/*** define parameters  ***/

%LET ALPHA=0.05;     * nominal Type I error rate;
MEAN=50;             * common mean for two populations;
SD1=10;              * STD for GRP 1 & 2 - equal variance condition;
N1=20;               * sample size for GRP 1 & 2 - equal N condition;

/*** end of parameters ***/
```

```
                           * A=1:equal variance, A=2:unequal - 1.5 times SD1;
   IF &A=1 THEN SD2=SD1;
      ELSE IF &A=2 THEN SD2=SD1*1.5;

                           * B=1:equal sample size, B=2:unequal - 2 times N1;
   IF &B=1 THEN N2=N1;
      ELSE IF &B=2 THEN N2=N1*2;


                              * generate group 1 data;
DAT1=SD1*RANNOR(J(N1,1,0)) + MEAN;
GRP1=J(N1,1,1);                        * assigning group number: group=1;
DAT1=DAT1||GRP1;                       * horizontal concatenation;

                              * generate group 2 data;
DAT2=SD2*RANNOR(J(N2,1,0)) + MEAN;
GRP2=J(N2,1,2);                        * assigning group number: group=2;
DAT2=DAT2||GRP2;

DATA=DAT1//DAT2;          * vertical concatenation - put data of both
                            groups together;

CREATE DATAALL FROM DATA[COLNAME={X GROUP}];    * create a temporary
                                                  data set;
APPEND FROM DATA;
                                       * direct the output to a file on
                                         disk;

FILENAME NEWOUT 'C:\T_TEST\TRIALS\OUTFILE';
PROC PRINTTO PRINT=NEWOUT NEW;
RUN;
                         * run the TTEST procedure;
PROC TTEST DATA=DATAALL;
   CLASS GROUP;
   VAR X;
RUN;
                         * redirect output to print;
PROC PRINTTO PRINT=PRINT; RUN;

                         * read proc ttest output from the disk file and
                           obtain t statistic, df, and p value;
DATA READIN; INFILE NEWOUT;
   INPUT WORD $ @@;
IF WORD='Equal' THEN DO;
   INPUT T DF PT;
                         * add simulation design information to data;
   IF PT<&ALPHA THEN SIG=1;
      ELSE SIG=0;
   IF &A=1 THEN EQ_VAR='  EQUAL';
      ELSE EQ_VAR='UNEQUAL';
    IF &B=1 THEN EQ_N='  EQUAL';
      ELSE EQ_N='UNEQUAL';
   OUTPUT;
   KEEP T DF PT SIG EQ_VAR EQ_N;
END;
RUN;

                   * append the relevant information to a SAS System
                     file;
DATA NEW; SET READIN;
   KEEP T DF PT SIG EQ_VAR EQ_N;
   PROC APPEND BASE=TTEST.TTEST;
RUN;

%END;              * end replication do loop;
```

```
%END;                  * end B do loop;
%END;                  * end A do loop;
%MEND TTEST;           * close the macro program 'TTEST';
%TTEST;                * Run macro program 'TTEST';
RUN;

PROC SORT; BY EQ_VAR EQ_N;
PROC FREQ; BY EQ_VAR EQ_N;      * check Type I error rate in four cells;
  TABLES SIG;
RUN;
```

Data generation in SAS/IML has been discussed in previous chapters, so it will not be repeated here. The first new feature in this program is the group of statements that are repeated below. These two program statements direct the output from PROC TTEST to a file named OUTFILE on disk instead of displaying the results in the SAS Output window. This is necessary because the results of PROC TTEST cannot be directly output as a SAS data set. To use the PROC TTEST results, we will read the output from the file OUTFILE later, and obtain the information we need from it.

```
                         * direct the output to a file on disk;
FILENAME NEWOUT 'C:\T_TEST\TRIALS\OUTFILE';
PROC PRINTTO PRINT=NEWOUT NEW;
RUN;
```

In order to understand how to obtain relevant information from an output file containing the results of PROC TTEST, we need to take a look at how this output file is structured. The following table displays the variations in the format of PROC TTEST output.

Table 6.2 *Variations in the Format of PROC TTEST Output*

FORMAT 1 (SAS 6.12)

```
                              TTEST PROCEDURE
Variable: X

GROUP1      N          Mean        Std Dev      Std Error       Minimum         Maximum
--------------------------------------------------------------------------------------
   1        10      4.00000000    0.66666667    0.21081851    3.00000000      5.00000000
   2        10      6.00000000    1.15470054    0.36514837    4.00000000      7.00000000

Variances        T      DF    Prob>|T|
---------------------------------------
Unequal      -4.7434   14.4    0.0003
Equal        -4.7434   18.0    0.0002

For H0: Variances are equal, F' = 3.00    DF = (9,9)    Prob>F' = 0.1173
```

FORMAT 2 (SAS 6.12)

```
                              TTEST PROCEDURE
Variable: X

GROUP1    N     Mean        Std Dev      Std Error    Variances        T      DF    Prob>|T|
-------------------------------------------------      ---------------------------------------
   1     10  4.00000000   0.66666667    0.21081851    Unequal      -4.7434   14.4    0.0003
   2     10  6.00000000   1.15470054    0.36514837    Equal        -4.7434   18.0    0.0002

For H0: Variances are equal, F' = 3.00    DF = (9,9)    Prob>F' = 0.1173
```

FORMAT 3 (SAS 8)

The TTEST Procedure

Statistics

Variable	Class	N	Lower CL Mean	Mean	Upper CL Mean	Lower CL Std Dev	Std Dev	Upper CL Std Dev	Std Err
X	1	10	3.5231	4	4.4769	0.4586	0.6667	1.2171	0.2108
X	2	10	5.174	6	6.826	0.7942	1.1547	2.108	0.3651
X	Diff (1-2)		-2.886	-2	-1.114	0.7124	0.9428	1.3942	0.4216

T-Tests

Variable	Method	Variances	DF	t Value	Pr > |t|
X	Pooled	**Equal**	**18**	**-4.74**	**0.0002**
X	Satterthwaite	Unequal	14.4	-4.74	0.0003

Equality of Variances

Variable	Method	Num DF	Den DF	F Value	Pr > F
X	Folded F	9	9	3.00	0.1173

In all these format variations, the information we want to obtain follows the word "Equal", and it is highlighted in the table. Once we know the format of the output file OUTFILE, extracting the relevant information is relatively easy using the SAS code below.

```
                         * read proc ttest output from the disk file and
                           obtain t statistic, df, and p value;
DATA READIN; INFILE NEWOUT;
   INPUT WORD $ @@;
IF WORD='Equal' THEN DO;
  INPUT T DF PT;
                         * add simulation design information to data;
   IF PT<&ALPHA THEN SIG=1;
      ELSE SIG=0;
   IF &A=1 THEN EQ_VAR='  EQUAL';
      ELSE EQ_VAR='UNEQUAL';
    IF &B=1 THEN EQ_N='  EQUAL';
      ELSE EQ_N='UNEQUAL';
   OUTPUT;
   KEEP T DF PT SIG EQ_VAR EQ_N;
END;
```

This SAS code not only reads in the t statistic (T), the degrees of freedom (DF), and the probability value of the t statistic (PT) from the PROC TTEST output file, but also adds the Monte Carlo study design information to the data for later analyses. Note that the SAS statements "INPUT WORD $ @@; IF WORD='Equal' THEN DO; ..." allow the program to keep reading the output file until it locates the word "Equal", regardless of where the word "Equal" is in the SAS output file. Once the word "Equal" is located, the three pieces of information following the word "Equal" are read into the temporary SAS data set named READIN.

As the program repeats the replications, each later output file replaces the previous output file on the disk, so it is always the current PROC TTEST output file that is being read. The relevant information from each replication of PROC TTEST is appended to a SAS permanent data set on disk (again, note the two-level name for this purpose) by using PROC APPEND. Finally, after all the results have been accumulated, PROC FREQ is used to check the actual Type I error rate of the t-test under each of the four conditions.

Based on one execution of Program 6.2, the output of PROC FREQ is presented in Output 6.2. It is obvious that these results are very similar to those from Program 6.1. This should not be surprising, because the two programs are fundamentally the same except for some programming variations.

Output 6.2
T-Test
Simulation
Results
(Program
6.2)

```
                                The SAS System

----------------------- EQ_VAR='  EQUAL' EQ_N='  EQUAL' -----------------------

                                       Cumulative   Cumulative
         SIG    Frequency    Percent    Frequency     Percent
         -----------------------------------------------------
          0       9516        95.2        9516         95.2
          1        484         4.8       10000        100.0

----------------------- EQ_VAR='  EQUAL' EQ_N=UNEQUAL -----------------------

                                       Cumulative   Cumulative
         SIG    Frequency    Percent    Frequency     Percent
         -----------------------------------------------------
          0       9488        94.9        9488         94.9
          1        512         5.1       10000        100.0

----------------------- EQ_VAR=UNEQUAL EQ_N='  EQUAL' -----------------------

                                       Cumulative   Cumulative
         SIG    Frequency    Percent    Frequency     Percent
         -----------------------------------------------------
          0       9505        95.1        9505         95.1
          1        495         5.0       10000        100.0

----------------------- EQ_VAR=UNEQUAL EQ_N=UNEQUAL -----------------------

                                       Cumulative   Cumulative
         SIG    Frequency    Percent    Frequency     Percent
         -----------------------------------------------------
          0       9733        97.3        9478         94.8
          1        267         2.7       10000        100.0
```

6.3 Example 2: Assessing the Effect of Data Non-Normality on the Type I Error Rate in ANOVA

Analysis of variance (ANOVA) is also a statistical technique widely used in a variety of disciplines, including, but not limited to, agriculture, sociology, psychology, education, range science, etc. Like many other parametric statistical techniques, one fundamental assumption for ANOVA is that the dependent variable is normally distributed. Another important assumption for ANOVA is that the groups come from populations with equal variances. But how serious are the consequences if the assumption about data normality is violated, or if the assumption of equal population variances is violated? Monte Carlo simulation is very useful in this situation if we are interested in answering these questions. In this example, we will present a SAS program example that implements a Monte Carlo study for assessing the consequences of data non-normality and unequal population variances on the Type I error rate of ANOVA analysis.

6.3.1 Design Considerations

In a real Monte Carlo simulation study, the design may be complex and may include a range of different degrees of data non-normality conditions, as well as a range of different degrees of population variance inequality. Furthermore, the design may also combine these two factors with a range of different sample sizes for the groups. In our example of ANOVA, we conduct a three-group ANOVA analysis under the true null hypothesis of $\mu_1 = \mu_2 = \mu_3 = 50$, i.e., all three groups are drawn from populations with the same mean of 50.

In order to keep our example reasonably straightforward, we only use one sample size condition—an equal sample size of 30 for all three groups. Also, we will only consider two data normality conditions: when data are normally distributed, and when data are non-normal with both moderate skewness (skewness=1.75) and kurtosis (kurtosis=3.75). For the assumption of equal population variances, we only include two conditions: when all three populations have equal variances ($\sigma^2_1 = \sigma^2_2 = \sigma^2_3 = 10$), and when the three populations have unequal variances ($\sigma^2_1 = 10$, $\sigma^2_2 = 20$, and $\sigma^2_3 = 40$). The two factors (data normality and equal variances) are fully crossed to give us a 2×2 design with four cells. Within each cell, we want 5,000 replications of ANOVA analysis so that reasonable accuracy can be achieved in estimating the actual Type I error rate in each cell. This design requires conducting ANOVA analysis for 20,000 samples (2×2×5000). This ANOVA Monte Carlo study design has the same schematic representation as the previous t-test shown in Table 6.1.

6.3.2 ANOVA Example Program

Program 6.3 presents a complete SAS program for the Monte Carlo study with the design described above. This program has many familiar elements discussed for the two t-test program examples. At the same time, it also contains some new elements for which some explanations may be warranted. Some detailed explanation is provided for some selected components following Program 6.3.

Program 6.3 *SAS Program for ANOVA Example*

```
LIBNAME ANOVA 'C:\ANOVA\TRIALS';

    * -- to avoid the problem of SAS Log Window becoming full;
PROC PRINTTO LOG='C:\ANOVA\TRIALS\LOGFILE.TMP';
RUN;

%MACRO ANOVA;

%DO A=1 %TO 2;        * A=1: normal data,  A=2: non-normal data;
%DO B=1 %TO 2;        * B=1: equal variance,  B=2: unequal variance;
%DO REP=1 %TO 5000;   * 5,000 replications in each cell;

%LET ALPHA=0.05;   * nominal Type I error rate;

PROC IML;

MEAN=50;           * common mean for 3 groups;
N=30;              * common sample size for 3 groups;
```

```
                          * Fleishman coefficients for data shapes
                            1st row: normal data, 2nd row: non-normal data;
DIST={1 0 0,
      .92966052480111 .39949667453766 -.03646699281275};

                          * variances of 3 groups
                            1st row: equal variances, 2nd row: unequal;
VAR={10 10 10,
     10 20 40};
                          * generate data for group 1;
X=RANNOR(J(N,1,0));
X=-DIST[&A,2] + DIST[&A,1]*X + DIST[&A,2]*X##2 + DIST[&A,3]*X##3;
X=X*SQRT(VAR[&B,1]) + MEAN;
GRP=J(N,1,1);                  * assign group number: group=1;
GROUP1=X||GRP;

                          * generate data for group 2;
X=RANNOR(J(N,1,0));
X=-DIST[&A,2] + DIST[&A,1]*X + DIST[&A,2]*X##2 + DIST[&A,3]*X##3;
X=X*SQRT(VAR[&B,2]) + MEAN;
GRP=J(N,1,2);                  * assign group number: group=2;
GROUP2=X||GRP;

                          * generate data for group 3;
X=RANNOR(J(N,1,0));
X=-DIST[&A,2] + DIST[&A,1]*X + DIST[&A,2]*X##2 + DIST[&A,3]*X##3;
X=X*SQRT(VAR[&B,3]) + MEAN;
GRP=J(N,1,3);                  * assign group number: group=3;
GROUP3=X||GRP;

                          * combine 3 groups data, vertical concatenation;
DATA=GROUP1//GROUP2//GROUP3;

                              * create SAS working data;
CREATE DATAALL FROM DATA[COLNAME={X GROUP}];
APPEND FROM DATA;

                          * run ANOVA analysis, and output ANOVA results
                            to a temporary SAS data set, 'ANOVAOUT';

PROC ANOVA DATA=DATAALL NOPRINT OUTSTAT=ANOVAOUT;
  CLASS GROUP;
  MODEL X=GROUP;
RUN;
                          * use 'ANOVAOUT' data;
                          * extract relevant ANOVA results;

DATA AA; SET ANOVAOUT;
  IF _TYPE_='ANOVA';
  DF_MOD=DF; SS_MOD=SS;

                          * add a variable indicating statistical
                            significance;
  IF PROB<&ALPHA THEN SIG='YES';
    ELSE SIG=' NO';

  KEEP DF_MOD SS_MOD F PROB SIG;    * keep relevant variables;

                          * extract error df, error sum-of-squares;

DATA BB; SET ANOVAOUT;
  IF _TYPE_='ERROR';
  DF_ERR=DF; SS_ERR=SS;
  KEEP DF_ERR SS_ERR;
```

```
                               * merge two data sets, add study design information;
DATA AB; MERGE AA BB;
   IF &A=1 THEN NORMAL='YES';
      ELSE IF &A=2 THEN NORMAL=' NO';
   IF &B=1 THEN EQ_VAR='YES';
      ELSE IF &B=2 THEN EQ_VAR=' NO';
                           * append each replication result to a permanent
                             SAS data set;
PROC APPEND BASE=ANOVA.ANOVA;

%END;          * close replication do loop;
%END;          * close B do loop;
%END;          * close A do loop;
%MEND ANOVA;   * macro 'ANOVA';
%ANOVA;        * run macro 'ANOVA';
RUN;


                     * obtain descriptive statistics for the simulation
                       results;
DATA A; SET ANOVA.ANOVA;
PROC SORT; BY NORMAL EQ_VAR;
PROC FREQ; BY NORMAL EQ_VAR;
   TABLES SIG;
RUN;
```

The first new element is probably the matrix DIST, as repeated below. This matrix contains the Fleishman coefficients for generating non-normal data, as discussed in Chapter 4. The first row of this matrix contains the coefficients for normally distributed data, and the second row contains the coefficients for generating non-normal data with skewness=1.75 and kurtosis=3.75. Those coefficients can either be obtained by using Program 4.4 in Chapter 4, or they can be found in the original article by Fleishman (1978). When the macro variable &A has value of 1 (&A=1), the first row is used for generating data. When &A=2, the second row is used in data generation, thus generating non-normal data drawn from a population with skewness=1.75 and kurosis=3.75.

```
        * Fleishman coefficients for data shapes
          1st row: normal data, 2nd row: non-normal data;

DIST={1 0 0,
92966052480111 .39949667453766 -.03646699281275};
```

The matrix VAR, as repeated below, contains the population variances of the three groups. The first row represents the equal variance condition, with all three groups drawn from populations of the same variance (10). The second row represents the unequal variance condition, with the first group having a population variance of 10, the second group of 20, and the third group of 40. When the macro variable &B=1, the first row is used to generate data for the three groups. When &B=2, the second row is used to generate data for the three groups.

```
        * VARIANCES OF 3 GROUPS
          1ST ROW: EQUAL VARIANCES, 2ND ROW: UNEQUAL;
     VAR={10 10 10,
          10 20 40};
```

The readers are reminded here that an element in a matrix is identified by row number and column number. For example, when the macro variable &A=1, the statement that generates Group 1 data in the program

```
X=-DIST[&A,2] + DIST[&A,1]*X + DIST[&A,2]*X##2 + DIST[&A,3]*X##3;
```

actually equals the following statement (rounded to six decimal places):

```
X=-.399497 + .929660*X + .399497*X##2 + (-.036467)*X##3;
```

In the same vein, when the macro variable &B=1, the statement

```
X=X*SQRT(VAR[&B,1]) + MEAN;
```

is equivalent to

```
X=X*SQRT(10) + MEAN;
```

because, when &B=1, the element as identified by VAR[&B,1] is 10, the element of the first row and first column of the matrix VAR. Once this is understood, the programming for generating data for the three groups is relatively easy to follow.

In this example, again, we use the SAS/STAT ANOVA procedure to conduct an ANOVA analysis. This time, however, we do not want any SAS output. (Note the NOPRINT option in PROC ANOVA.) Instead, we use the OUTSTAT option in PROC ANOVA to output the relevant results of the ANOVA analysis to a temporary SAS data set named ANOVAOUT. Later, we will use this data set to get all the relevant results of the ANOVA analysis that we want to keep. But to understand how we can obtain relevant information from this temporary SAS data set, we must first take a look at the content and structure of the data set. The content and structure of this temporary SAS data set for a hypothetical ANOVA analysis are presented below. As a reminder, the content and structure of the ANOVAOUT data set can be viewed by using the PRINT procedure.

```
                              The SAS System

OBS    _NAME_    _SOURCE_    _TYPE_    DF    SS      F           PROB
1        X       ERROR       ERROR     27    19.8    .           .
2        X       GROUP       ANOVA      2    49.4    33.6818     .000000046084
```

It is seen that this SAS data set contains the sum of squares for error and for the model, the degrees of freedom for error and the model, the F value, and the probability value of this ANOVA analysis for testing the null hypothesis that the means of the groups are equal. Once the content and structure of this data set are known, extracting the information from the data set is relatively easy, as shown by the following SAS program code:

```
                    * use 'ANOVAOUT' data;
                    * extract relevant ANOVA results;

DATA AA; SET ANOVAOUT;
   IF _TYPE_='ANOVA';
   DF_MOD=DF; SS_MOD=SS;

                       * add a variable indicating statistical
                         significance;
   IF PROB<&ALPHA THEN SIG='YES';
      ELSE SIG=' NO';

   KEEP DF_MOD SS_MOD F PROB SIG;      * keep relevant variables;

                    * extract error df, error sum-of-squares;

DATA BB; SET ANOVAOUT;
   IF _TYPE_='ERROR';
   DF_ERR=DF; SS_ERR=SS;
   KEEP DF_ERR SS_ERR;

                       * merge two data sets, add study design information;
DATA AB; MERGE AA BB;
   IF &A=1 THEN NORMAL='YES';
      ELSE IF &A=2 THEN NORMAL=' NO';
   IF &B=1 THEN EQ_VAR='YES';
      ELSE IF &B=2 THEN EQ_VAR=' NO';
                       * append each replication results to a permanent
                         SAS data set;
PROC APPEND BASE=ANOVA.ANOVA;
```

In this ANOVA Monte Carlo program, we keep all the numerical information that was generated by the OUTSTAT option in PROC ANOVA. First, we extract the information from the second row (model DF, model SS, F statistic, P value), and add information about statistical significance for our given nominal Type I error rate (ALPHA=0.05). We then extract the information from the first row (error DF, error SS). The two temporary SAS data sets (AA and BB) are then merged into one (AB) so that for each replication of the ANOVA analysis, there will be one line of data to be appended (PROC APPEND BASE=ANOVA.ANOVA) to a permanent SAS data set (ANOVA.ANOVA) on disk. Before the data are appended, some study design information is added to the data so that they can be used in later analyses. Although it is possible to save only the probability value for the purpose of this study, in our opinion and experience, it is more advantageous to save as much information as possible, because it is not always possible to anticipate what secondary analyses will be performed on these data in the future. For example, we may want to obtain the R-square value of the ANOVA model in the future. Although the R-square value is not in the permanent SAS data set ANOVA.ANOVA, it can easily be obtained by using the following statement in a SAS DATA step:

```
R_SQUARE = 1 - (SS_ERR / (SS_ERR+SS_MOD));
```

Had we only saved the P value information, we would not be able to obtain the information about the R-square value for each replication of the ANOVA analysis.

Output 6.3 presents the proportions of samples for which the ANOVA analysis rejected the true null hypothesis for each of the four design conditions (i.e., the actual Type I error rate for each of the four design conditions), from one execution of Program 6.3. These were obtained through the FREQ procedure at the end of the SAS program. As is seen from these results, the actual Type I error rate for each of the four data conditions is very close to the nominal Type I error rate that we specified in the program ('ALPHA=0.05'), even when data were non-normal with the specified skewness and kurtosis (skewness=1.75, kurtosis=3.75). These results indicate that, at least for the data conditions simulated in this program, ANOVA is quite robust even when data normality conditions are violated.

Output 6.3
ANOVA
Simulation
Results
(Program
6.3)

```
                              The SAS System

------------------------ NORMAL=' NO' EQ_VAR=' NO' ------------------------

                                         Cumulative  Cumulative
           SIG   Frequency   Percent   Frequency    Percent
           ---------------------------------------------------
           NO      4727       94.5       4727        94.5
           YES      273        5.5       5000       100.0

------------------------ NORMAL=' NO' EQ_VAR=YES --------------------------

                                         Cumulative  Cumulative
           SIG   Frequency   Percent   Frequency    Percent
           ---------------------------------------------------
           NO      4748       95.0       4748        95.0
           YES      252        5.0       5000       100.0

------------------------ NORMAL=YES EQ_VAR=' NO' --------------------------

                                         Cumulative  Cumulative
           SIG   Frequency   Percent   Frequency    Percent
           ---------------------------------------------------
           NO      4717       94.3       4717        94.3
           YES      283        5.7       5000       100.0

------------------------ NORMAL=YES EQ_VAR=YES ----------------------------

                                         Cumulative  Cumulative
           SIG   Frequency   Percent   Frequency    Percent
           ---------------------------------------------------
           NO      4763       95.3       4763        95.3
           YES      237        4.7       5000       100.0
```

6.4 Example 3: Comparing Different R² Shrinkage Formulas in Regression Analysis

Regression analysis, which is based on the ordinary least squares principle, is a statistical technique that enjoys widespread popularity among quantitative researchers across a variety of disciplines. In regression analysis, one important indicator for the fit of the regression model is the R^2—that is, the percentage of variation in the dependent variable that has been accounted for by the regression model. In regression analysis based on a sample, the regression coefficients, commonly known as regression weights, associated with the independent variables are optimally derived based on least squares principles, such that the R^2 for the regression model is maximized for the sample. This process of optimizing the regression weights of the independent variables for the sample tends to capitalize on the chance or sampling error associated with the particular sample used, which, in turn, causes the sample R^2 to be a positively biased estimator for its corresponding population R^2. In other words, if we draw many samples from a specified statistical population with known population R^2, the average of the sample R^2's will be higher than the population R^2. This positive bias in regression analysis is well known and is discussed by many authors (e.g., Cohen & Cohen 1983; Glass & Hopkins 1996; Pedhazur 1997; Stevens 1996).

To correct for the positive bias of the sample R^2, researchers have proposed different formulas so that the corrected sample R^2 will be a better estimate of the population R^2 than the original uncorrected sample R^2. However, it is not entirely clear which of these formulas has the best performance in terms of correcting for the positive bias of the sample R^2. For a researcher who is interested in this issue, Monte Carlo simulation is a good tool for the investigation.

6.4.1 Different Formulas for Correcting Sample R² Bias

Several formulas have been proposed to correct for the positive bias of sample R^2. Typically, the smaller the sample size, and the more predictor variables in the regression model, the greater positive bias the sample R^2 contains. For this reason, the correction formulas penalize small sample size and more independent variables in a regression model. In our example, we will look at four different R^2 shrinkage formulas for correcting the sample R^2, as shown below. In all the following formulas, N is the sample size, P is the number of predictor variables, R^2 is the sample R^2, and $\hat{R}^2$ is the sample R^2 corrected for positive bias.

The first formula takes the following form:

$$\hat{R}^2 = 1 - \frac{N}{N-P}(1-R^2) \tag{6.4}$$

This formula is generally known as the "Smith formula," and it was developed in the 1920s (Wherry 1931).

The second formula takes the following form:

$$\hat{R}^2 = 1 - \frac{N}{N-P-1}(1-R^2) \tag{6.5}$$

This formula has been cited widely with different names (for example, the Wherry formula, the Ezekiel formula, the Wherry/McNemer formula, etc.), and it is also the sample R^2 shrinkage formula currently implemented in the SAS REG procedure for computing the "adjusted R^2".

The third formula takes the form:

$$\hat{R}^2 = 1 - \frac{N-1}{N-P}(1-R^2) \tag{6.6}$$

This formula is the actual formula presented by Wherry (1931), although it is often cited in the literature by other names and is often confused with Formula 6.5, above.

The fourth formula takes the form :

$$\hat{R}^2 = R^2 - \frac{P-2}{N-P-1}(1-R^2) - \frac{2(N-3)}{(N-P-1)(N-P+1)}(1-R^2)^2 \tag{6.7}$$

This formula is often known as the Olkin and Pratt formula, and it is the approximation of Olkin and Pratt's unbiased estimate of the population R^2 (Olkin & Pratt 1958).

The correction, or "shrinkage," based on the correction formulas for sample R^2 presented above is usually very small when the sample size is large and when the ratio of N/P (the ratio of sample size to the number of predictors in the regression model) is relatively large. It is when the sample size is small and the N/P ratio is small that the effect of correction based on these formulas is noticeable.

6.4.2 Design Considerations

Two factors obviously should come into play for correcting the positive bias of the sample R^2: sample size (N) and the number of predictor variables (P), because these two factors affect the shrinkage of the sample R^2 in all the correction formulas presented above. As pointed out before, the effect of bias correction will be more noticeable when the sample size is small and the N/P ratio is small. So, for our example, we will focus on such conditions. In addition to these two factors, there may be other relevant considerations, such as the magnitude of the population R^2 and the strength of relationship among the predictors (statistically known as the degree of multicollinearity).

To keep our Monte Carlo SAS program example relatively straightforward, we will only consider the sample size and the N/P ratio. For the population R^2, we will only use the condition of population R^2=0.5. For the factor of multicollinearity, we will only use r=0.3 as the strength of relationship among all the predictor variables. The design of this Monte Carlo study is represented by Table 6.6.

Table 6.3 *Study Design for Estimating Sample R^2 Positive Bias Correction*

(Population R^2 = 0.5, Multicollinearity r = 0.3)	Sample Size		
Number of Predictors \ N/P Ratio	20	40	80
4	5	10	20
8	2.5	5	10

6.4.3 Regression Analysis Sample Program

To avoid unnecessarily complicating the SAS program for this Monte Carlo study, we choose to write two SAS programs for the study design presented above: one program for the 4-predictor condition, and the other for the 8-predictor condition. Because the two programs are essentially the same, we only present the SAS program for the 8-predictor condition as the example. Program 6.4 below presents the complete SAS program with detailed notes for the 8-predictor condition simulation.

Program 6.4 *Simulating Correction Formulas for Regression Sample R^2 Bias*

```
LIBNAME REG 'C:\REG\TRIALS';

      * -- to avoid the problem of SAS Log Window becoming full;
PROC PRINTTO LOG='C:\REG\TRIALS\LOGFILE.TMP';
RUN;
                        * population correlation matrix, with population R_square=0.50;
                        * multicollinearity r=0.30, 8 predictors;
DATA A (TYPE=CORR);
_TYPE_='CORR';
INPUT X1 X2 X3 X4 X5 X6 X7 X8 Y;
CARDS;
1.00 . . . . . . . .
0.30 1.00 . . . . . . .
0.30 0.30 1.00 . . . . . .
0.30 0.30 0.30 1.00 . . . . .
0.30 0.30 0.30 0.30 1.00 . . . .
0.30 0.30 0.30 0.30 0.30 1.00 . . .
0.30 0.30 0.30 0.30 0.30 0.30 1.00 . .
0.30 0.30 0.30 0.30 0.30 0.30 0.30 1.00 .
.44019 .44019 .44019 .44019 .44019 .44019 .44019 .44019 1.00
;
        * obtain factor pattern matrix for later data generation;
PROC FACTOR N=9 OUTSTAT=FACOUT;
DATA PATTERN; SET FACOUT;
  IF _TYPE_='PATTERN';
  DROP _TYPE_ _NAME_;
RUN;

%MACRO REG;           * starts the macro program 'reg';

                      * 3 sample size conditions: A=1:N=20, A=2:N=40, A=3:N=80;
%DO A=1 %TO 3;
    %IF &A=1 %THEN %DO; %LET N=20; %END;
    %IF &A=2 %THEN %DO; %LET N=40; %END;
    %IF &A=3 %THEN %DO; %LET N=80; %END;
%DO REP=1 %TO 2000;                  * number of replications in each cell;
                                     * generate correlated sample data of 9 variables;
PROC IML;
```

```
   USE PATTERN;                        * read in the factor pattern as a matrix 'F';
   READ ALL VAR _NUM_ INTO F;
  F=F`;                                * transpose 'F' for later premultiplication;

DAT=RANNOR(J(&N,9,0));                 * generate 9 random variables (&Nx9 dimension);
DAT=DAT`;                              * transpose the random data matrix (9x&N dimension);
DAT=F*DAT;                             * premultiply 'F' to 'DAT', variables become
                                         correlated;
DAT=DAT`;                              * transpose the data matrix back (&Nx9 dimension);

                                       * create a temporary SAS data set 'REGDATA';

CREATE REGDATA FROM DAT[COLNAME={X1 X2 X3 X4 X5 X6 X7 X8 Y}];
APPEND FROM DAT;

                                       * use SAS PROC REG to obtain sample r-square;
                                       * output the results to temporary SAS data
                                         'REGOUT';

PROC REG DATA=REGDATA NOPRINT OUTEST=REGOUT;
  MODEL Y =X1 X2 X3 X4 X5 X6 X7 X8 / SELECTION=RSQUARE;
RUN;
                                       * use 'REGOUT' data;
DATA A; SET REGOUT;
  IF _IN_=8;                           * select the row of data that contains sample r-square;
  P=8; N=&N; NP_RATIO=N/P;             * add study design features: N, P N/P RATIO;
  RSQ=_RSQ_;
  RSQ_ADJ1=1-(N/(N-P))*(1-RSQ);        * apply four correction formulas;
  RSQ_ADJ2=1-((N-1)/(N-P-1))*(1-RSQ);
  RSQ_ADJ3=1-((N-1)/(N-P))*(1-RSQ);
  RSQ_ADJ4=RSQ-((P-2)/(N-P-1))*(1-RSQ)-(2*(N-3))/((N-P-1)*(N-P+1))*(1-RSQ)**2;

 * obtain bias: deviation of r-square and adjusted r-squares from population r-square;

  BIAS_RSQ=RSQ-0.50;
  BIAS1=RSQ_ADJ1-0.50;
  BIAS2=RSQ_ADJ2-0.50;
  BIAS3=RSQ_ADJ3-0.50;
  BIAS4=RSQ_ADJ4-0.50;
                                   * only keep the relevant information for the study;
KEEP N P NP_RATIO RSQ RSQ_ADJ1 RSQ_ADJ2 RSQ_ADJ3 RSQ_ADJ4 BIAS_RSQ BIAS1 BIAS2 BIAS3
BIAS4;

                     * append the results from each replication to permanent SAS data set;

PROC APPEND BASE=REG.REG8_RSQ;

%END;              * close &A do loop;
%END;              * close &REP do loop;
%MEND REG;         * end the macro program 'REG';
%REG;              * run the macro 'REG' program;
RUN;

DATA A; SET REG.REG8_RSQ;
PROC SORT; BY NP_RATIO;              * analyze the results, obtain the average bias;
PROC MEANS; BY NP_RATIO;
  VAR BIAS_RSQ BIAS1 BIAS2 BIAS3 BIAS4;
RUN;
```

The first section of the program that may be new to the readers is the following:

```
* obtain factor pattern matrix for later data generation;

PROC FACTOR N=9 OUTSTAT=FACOUT;
DATA PATTERN; SET FACOUT;
  IF _TYPE_='PATTERN';
  DROP _TYPE_ _NAME_;
RUN;
```

In this section of the program, PROC FACTOR generates the factor pattern matrix based on the population correlation matrix of the nine variables (Y, and X1 to X8). The results of PROC FACTOR are output into a temporary SAS data set named FACOUT. Then the temporary SAS data set named PATTERN is constructed based on FACOUT, but only the relevant information is kept. To understand how this is achieved, we need to take a look at the data structure of the FACOUT data set.

Output 6.4a *Structure of the FACOUT Data Set*

OBS	_TYPE_	_NAME_	X1	X2	X3	X4	X5	X6	X7	X8	Y
						The SAS System					
1	MEAN		0.00	0.00	0.00	0.00	0.00	0.00	0.00	0.00	0.00
2	STD		1.00	1.00	1.00	1.00	1.00	1.00	1.00	1.00	1.00
3	N		10000	10000	10000	10000	10000	10000	10000	10000	10000
4	CORR	X1	1.00	0.30	0.30	0.30	0.30	0.30	0.30	0.30	0.44
5	CORR	X2	0.30	1.00	0.30	0.30	0.30	0.30	0.30	0.30	0.44
6	CORR	X3	0.30	0.30	1.00	0.30	0.30	0.30	0.30	0.30	0.44
7	CORR	X4	0.30	0.30	0.30	1.00	0.30	0.30	0.30	0.30	0.44
8	CORR	X5	0.30	0.30	0.30	0.30	1.00	0.30	0.30	0.30	0.44
9	CORR	X6	0.30	0.30	0.30	0.30	0.30	1.00	0.30	0.30	0.44
10	CORR	X7	0.30	0.30	0.30	0.30	0.30	0.30	1.00	0.30	0.44
11	CORR	X8	0.30	0.30	0.30	0.30	0.30	0.30	0.30	1.00	0.44
12	CORR	Y	0.44	0.44	0.44	0.44	0.44	0.44	0.44	0.44	1.00
13	COMMUNAL		1.00	1.00	1.00	1.00	1.00	1.00	1.00	1.00	1.00
14	PRIORS		1.00	1.00	1.00	1.00	1.00	1.00	1.00	1.00	1.00
15	EIGENVAL		3.68	0.70	0.70	0.70	0.70	0.70	0.70	0.70	0.42
16	PATTERN	FACTOR1	0.61	0.61	0.61	0.61	0.61	0.61	0.61	0.61	0.81
17	PATTERN	FACTOR2	-0.06	-0.06	-0.06	-0.06	-0.06	-0.06	-0.39	0.73	0.00
18	PATTERN	FACTOR3	-0.24	-0.24	-0.24	0.72	0.00	0.00	0.00	0.00	0.00
19	PATTERN	FACTOR4	-0.19	-0.19	-0.19	-0.19	0.75	0.00	0.00	0.00	0.00
20	PATTERN	FACTOR5	-0.16	-0.16	-0.16	-0.16	-0.16	-0.16	0.68	0.29	0.00
21	PATTERN	FACTOR6	0.59	-0.59	0.00	0.00	0.00	0.00	0.00	0.00	0.00
22	PATTERN	FACTOR7	-0.34	-0.34	0.68	0.00	0.00	0.00	0.00	0.00	0.00
23	PATTERN	FACTOR8	-0.15	-0.15	-0.15	-0.15	-0.15	0.76	0.00	0.00	0.00
24	PATTERN	FACTOR9	0.10	0.10	0.10	0.10	0.10	0.10	0.10	0.10	-0.50

In the output above, the underlined section contains the factor pattern matrix that we need to use. By using the SAS statements IF _TYPE_='PATTERN'; DROP _TYPE_ _NAME_, we are able to keep the underlined section of this temporary SAS data set, which will be used later as a matrix. Once the factor pattern matrix is obtained, it is then read into PROC IML as a matrix of 9×9 dimension. This matrix **F** is then transposed so that the columns become the factors (FACTOR1 to FACTOR9), and the rows become the variables (X1 to X8, Y), as required for later pre-multiplication with a random variable data matrix. The SAS code for accomplishing this is presented below.

```
PROC IML;
    USE PATTERN;              * read in the factor pattern as a matrix 'F';
    READ ALL VAR _NUM_ INTO F;
    F=F`;                     * transpose 'F' for later
                                premultiplication;
```

The next section that warrants some explanation is probably the following section. This section uses the SAS REG procedure to run regression analysis, then outputs the results to a temporary SAS data set named REGOUT by using the option OUTEST=REGOUT. The program then uses the REGOUT data set to obtain the sample R^2.

```
                        * use SAS PROC REG to obtain sample r-square;
                        * output the results to temporary SAS data set
                          'REGOUT';
PROC REG DATA=REGDATA NOPRINT OUTEST=REGOUT;
   MODEL Y =X1 X2 X3 X4 X5 X6 X7 X8 / SELECTION=RSQUARE;
RUN;
                        * USE 'REGOUT' DATA;
DATA A; SET REGOUT;
   IF _IN_=8;            * SELECT THE ROW OF DATA CONTAINS SAMPLE R-SQUARE;
```

To understand how the sample R^2 is selected from the temporary SAS data set REGOUT, it helps to take a look at the structure of REGOUT. For the sake of simplicity, we present a hypothetical regression analysis for a *3-predictor* model (Y=X1 X2 X3) as an example. The OUTEST='REGOUT' option in PROC REG generates the following temporary SAS data set.

Output 6.4b *Structure of the REGOUT Data Set*

					The SAS System								
OBS	_MODEL_	_TYPE_	_DEPVAR_	_RMSE_	INTERCEP	X1	X2	X3	Y	_IN_	_P_	_EDF_	_RSQ_
1	MODEL1	PARMS	Y	.90364	0	.4402	.	.	-1	1	2	78	.1938
2	MODEL1	PARMS	Y	.90364	0	.	.4402	.	-1	1	2	78	.1938
3	MODEL1	PARMS	Y	.90364	0	.	.	.4402	-1	1	2	78	.1938
4	MODEL1	PARMS	Y	.84860	0	.3386	.3386	.	-1	2	3	77	.2981
5	MODEL1	PARMS	Y	.84860	0	.3386	.	.3386	-1	2	3	77	.2981
6	MODEL1	PARMS	Y	.84860	0	.	.3386	.3386	-1	2	3	77	.2981
7	MODEL1	PARMS	Y	.81352	0	.2751	.2751	.2751	-1	**3**	4	76	**.3633**

The sample R^2 is underlined in the box. To select this sample R^2, we need to select the last line by specifying the maximum number of predictors in the model. In this case, the SAS command IF _IN_=3 accomplishes the task for this 3-predictor regression model. In Program 6.4, we have eight predictors in the regression model, so we specify IF _IN_=8. Later, we will drop all irrelevant variables by using the KEEP statement to keep only the variables of our choice. Once the sample R^2 is selected, the adjusted R^2s based on the four formulas are obtained, and the deviations of the sample R^2 and the four adjusted R^2s from the true population R^2 are computed as bias. All these results from each of the 6,000 replications of the simulation (2,000 replications for each sample size condition) are then appended (PROC APPEND BASE=*libref.data-set-name*) to a SAS permanent data set on disk by specifying the two-level name REG.REG8_RSQ ("*libref.data-set-name*") for future analyses.

Once the simulation is complete, the results saved in the file REG.REG8_RSQ can be used for a variety of analyses. Output 6.4c presents the results from the simple analysis of PROC MEANS. The variables used for this analysis are the deviation scores of the unadjusted sample R^2 and the four adjusted R^2s from the true population R^2 Ideally, the average deviation should be zero, which indicates that the sample statistic is not a biased estimator for the population parameter. As is seen in Output 6.4c, the unadjusted sample R^2 has obvious upward bias, as reasoned previously. When the N/P ratio is small (e.g., N/P=2.5), such upward bias is substantial. For the three N/P ratio conditions examined here, the upward bias is reduced by approximately half (.1983, .0963, .0453) when the N/P ratio is doubled (2.5, 5, 10).

For the N/P ratio conditions examined here, the first two R^2 shrinkage formulas tend to produce downward bias, i.e., the adjusted R^2 tends to be smaller than the true population R^2. The last two R^2 shrinkage formulas tend to be slightly biased positively, i.e., larger than the true population R^2. It appears that, among the four formulas, the fourth formula contains the least amount of bias. Of course, in order to draw any definite conclusions, a much more comprehensive Monte Carlo study must be conducted that should consider a variety of different regression models and data conditions (in terms of number of predictors, correlation patterns among the variables, strength of population R^2, degree of multicollinearity among the predictors, sample size, N/P ratio, etc.). So what has been presented here is simply an example and should not be construed as representing the general performance of the different R^2 shrinkage formulas.

Output 6.4c
Sample R^2
Bias
Simulation
Results
Comparing
Correction
Formulas for
(Program
6.4)

```
                              The SAS System
------------------------------------- NP_RATIO=2.5 -----------------------------------

     Variable    N        Mean        Std Dev      Minimum       Maximum
     ------------------------------------------------------------------------
     BIAS_RSQ   2000    0.1983442    0.1227444    -0.2524870    0.4685524
     BIAS1      2000   -0.0027596    0.2045740    -0.7541449    0.4475873
     BIAS2      2000   -0.0210418    0.2120130    -0.7997502    0.4456814
     BIAS3      2000    0.0223784    0.1943453    -0.6914377    0.4502080
     BIAS4      2000    0.0085889    0.2096738    -0.7975641    0.4511640
     ------------------------------------------------------------------------


------------------------------------- NP_RATIO=5 -------------------------------------

     Variable    N        Mean        Std Dev      Minimum       Maximum
     ------------------------------------------------------------------------
     BIAS_RSQ   2000    0.0962798    0.1002139    -0.2485962    0.3462413
     BIAS1      2000   -0.0046503    0.1252674    -0.4357453    0.3078016
     BIAS2      2000   -0.0079061    0.1260756    -0.4417824    0.3065616
     BIAS3      2000    0.0079659    0.1221357    -0.4123517    0.3126066
     BIAS4      2000    0.0056242    0.1257438    -0.4340228    0.3147714
     ------------------------------------------------------------------------


------------------------------------- NP_RATIO=10 ------------------------------------

     Variable    N        Mean        Std Dev      Minimum       Maximum
     ------------------------------------------------------------------------
     BIAS_RSQ   2000    0.0452773    0.0762414    -0.2206793    0.2722575
     BIAS1      2000   -0.0052474    0.0847126    -0.3007548    0.2469528
     BIAS2      2000   -0.0059590    0.0848320    -0.3018826    0.2465964
     BIAS3      2000    0.0010682    0.0836537    -0.2907453    0.2501159
     BIAS4      2000    0.0005336    0.0847887    -0.2970138    0.2514706
```

6.5 Summary

The several SAS Monte Carlo programming examples presented in this chapter have probably given readers some indication that the SAS System offers a high degree of flexibility for conducting Monte Carlo studies involving statistical techniques. The researcher can do the programming for the statistical technique in question (as in the first t-test example); can use SAS statistical procedures for analysis and save the output in a file on disk, and then obtain the relevant information from this file (the 2nd t-test example); or can use SAS statistical procedures for analysis and output the results to a temporary SAS data set from which the relevant information is obtained (the ANOVA example and the regression analysis example). This high degree of flexibility of the SAS System allows almost any analysis results to be obtained and saved in a Monte Carlo study.

When computationally complicated statistical procedures are involved, it is preferable to take full advantage of SAS/STAT procedures for the statistical computation and analysis instead of doing the programming ourselves. This not only results in less programming, and sometimes substantially so, it also ensures the accuracy of the statistical analysis. For many difficult statistical procedures, this is also probably the only feasible approach for conducting Monte Carlo studies for many quantitative researchers. Our experience also suggests that it is advantageous to save all potentially relevant information in a permanent data set instead of outputting all the results at the end of program without saving them. In a Monte Carlo study, especially a study that involves complicated design and statistical techniques, it is not always easy to anticipate what secondary analyses are needed for the results of the Monte Carlo study. For this reason, it is safer to save the results first, and worry about secondary analyses of the Monte Carlo results later. This especially makes sense for a SAS Monte Carlo program that may take a long time to finish.

6.6 References

Cohen, J., and P. Cohen. 1983. *Applied Multiple Regression/Correlation Analysis for the Behavioral Sciences.* 2d ed. Hillsdale, NJ: Lawrence Erlbaum Associates.

Fleishman, A. I. 1978. "A Method for Simulating Non-Normal Distributions." *Psychometrika* 43:521-531.

Glass, G. V., and K. D. Hopkins. 1996. *Statistical Methods in Education and Psychology.* 3d ed. Boston: Allyn and Bacon.

Olkin, E., and J. W. Pratt. 1958. "Unbiased Estimation of Certain Correlation Coefficients." *Annals of Mathematical Statistics* 29:201-211.

Pedhazur, E. J. 1997. *Multiple Regression in Behavioral Research: Explanation and Prediction.* 3d ed. Fort Worth, TX: Harcourt Brace College Publishers.

SAS Institute Inc. 1990. *SAS/STAT User's Guide,Vol. 2.* Cary, NC: SAS Institute Inc.

Stevens, J. 1996. *Applied Multivariate Statistics for the Social Sciences.* Hillsdale, NJ: Lawrence Erlbaum Associates.

Therry, R. J. 1931. "A New Formula for Predicting the Shrinkage of the Coefficient of Multiple Correlation." *Annals of Mathematical Statistics* 2:440-457.

Chapter 7 Conducting Monte Carlo Studies for Multivariate Techniques

7.1 Introduction

Chapters 1 to 5 have covered the basic concepts and procedures for conducting a Monte Carlo study. At the same time, the basic components of SAS programs necessary for implementing a Monte Carlo study have also been explained. In Chapter 6, we presented and discussed some complete examples of using SAS for conducting Monte Carlo simulation for some widely used univariate statistical techniques, such as t-tests, analysis of variance (ANOVA), and regression analysis. In this chapter, we present and discuss two complete Monte Carlo simulation study examples for more complicated multivariate statistical techniques. Specifically, we will present the following Monte Carlo study examples involving different statistical techniques:

- a structural equation modeling example for assessing the effects of sample size and estimation methods on a group of widely known descriptive model fit indices

- an example for comparing logistic regression with linear discriminant analysis in classification accuracy in a two-group situation.

For each of the above examples, we will present a) the theoretical rationale for conducting the study, and the major issues involved; b) the annotated SAS program for implementing the Monte Carlo study, with detailed explanations of the SAS code; c) the selected and relevant results from the actual simulation based on the SAS program provided. We want to point out that, when Monte Carlo studies involve these complicated statistical techniques, it is important to use SAS/STAT procedures, rather than to do statistical programming ourselves, because the latter is often beyond the reach of many research practitioners. Even for those who may have the technical expertise for the required statistical programming, the accuracy and validity of such statistical programming may often be in question.

7.2 Example 1: A Structural Equation Modeling Example

Structural equation modeling (SEM) has increasingly been seen as a useful quantitative technique for specifying, estimating, and testing hypothesized models describing relationships among a set of substantively meaningful variables. Much of SEM's attractiveness is due to the method's applicability in a wide variety of research situations (e.g., Baldwin 1989; Bollen & Long 1993; Byrne 1994; Jöreskog & Sörbom 1989; Loehlin 1992; Pedhazur & Schmelkin 1991; SAS Institute 1997). Furthermore, many widely used statistical techniques may also be considered as special cases of SEM, including regression analysis, canonical correlation analysis, confirmatory factor analysis, and path analysis (Bagozzi, Fornell & Larcker 1981; Bentler 1992; Fan 1996; Jöreskog & Sörbom 1989). Because of such generality, SEM has been heralded as a unified model that joins methods from econometrics, psychometrics, sociometrics, and multivariate statistics (Bentler 1994).

Despite SEM's popularity in the research of social and behavioral sciences, there are some thorny issues in SEM applications, one of which is SEM model fit assessment. In SEM, initially, the assessment of model fit was conceptualized as a dichotomous decision process of either retaining the null hypothesis that the model fits the data, or rejecting it. The empirical basis for such a dichotomous decision is a χ^2 test assessing the degree of discrepancy between two covariance matrices: the original sample covariance matrix, and the reconstructed covariance matrix based on the specified model and the resultant model parameter estimates. In practice, considerable uncertainty regarding model fit often arises. The χ^2 test approach to model fit assessment is confounded with sample size: the power of the test increases with an increase of sample size in the analysis (i.e., χ^2 tends to increase as sample size increases). As a result, model fit assessment using this approach becomes stringent when sample size is large, and lenient when sample size is small.

7.2.1 Descriptive Indices for Assessing Model Fit

Because of the concerns related to the χ^2 test for model fit assessment in SEM (Thompson & Daniel 1996), a variety of indices for assessing model fit have been developed for assessing the fit between a theoretical model and empirical data. Unlike the χ^2 test, which can often be used for the inferential purpose of rejecting or retaining a model, these alternative fit indices are descriptive in nature, and typically, no inferential decision is made based on these indices. In other words, these fit indices are used to describe the fit, rather than to test fit statistically. The relative performance characteristics of these different fit indices, and their comparability under different data conditions, however, are not well understood. For many practitioners who use SEM in their research, there is often confusion with regard to which indices to use under what data conditions.

Descriptive SEM fit indices were developed with different rationales and with different motivations (Gerbing & Anderson 1993). As Fan and Wang (1998) discussed, there are several major categories of SEM descriptive fit indices. The first category may be described as being based on *covariance matrix reproduction*. These indices assess the degree to which the reproduced covariance matrix based on the specified model has accounted for the original sample covariance matrix. Examples of this type of fit indices are the Goodness-of-Fit Index (GFI) and the Adjusted Goodness-of-Fit Index (AGFI) (Jöreskog & Sörbom 1989).

The second major category of fit indices can be described as *relative model fit* indices, also known as "incremental fit" indices in the literature. They assess model fit by evaluating the improvement of fit of a given model over that of a more restricted *null* model, which usually assumes no relationships among the measured variables. Examples of this type of fit indices are Bentler and Bonnet's normed and non-normed fit indices (NFI and N_NFI), Bentler's Comparative Fit Index (CFI), and Bollen's incremental fit index (DELTA2).

The third category of model fit indices can be called *parsimony weighted* indices. These indices take model parsimony into consideration by imposing penalties for specifying more elaborate models. Examples are the fit index by James, Mulaik and Brett (1982) and that by Mulaik et al. (1989). These fit indices are most useful for assessing competing theoretical models, but are less informative in situations where only one model is being fitted to data. In addition to those discussed above, there are some others, such as McDonald's index of noncentrality (McDonald 1989), and the root mean squared error of approximation (RMSEA, Steiger & Lind 1980) as an index to quantify the amount of model *misfit*.

7.2.2 Design Considerations

There are several major factors that have the potential to influence the performance of SEM descriptive model fit indices. Obviously, model specification, i.e., the extent to which a model is correctly specified, should be the primary determinant for model fit assessment. In other words, model fit indices should be sensitive enough to the degree of model misspecification, and model misspecification should be the major contributor to the variation of sample model fit indices. In reality, there exist a few confounding factors that may affect model fit assessment, such as estimation methods (e.g., maximum likelihood vs. generalized least squares) used in SEM analysis, and sample size. Ideally, model fit indices should not be sensitive to the estimation method used for model fitting, and this factor should contribute minimally to the variation of sample model fit indices. Furthermore, because descriptive model fit indices were designed to overcome the shortcoming of the χ^2 test, i.e., its over-reliance on sample size, it makes sense to expect that the descriptive model fit indices should be minimally affected by sample size.

7.2.3 SEM Fit Indices Studied

Based on the consideration of comparability, nine widely known SEM fit indices were chosen for investigation in the present example: goodness-of-fit index (GFI), adjusted goodness-of-fit index (AGFI), Bentler's comparative fit index (CFI), McDonald's centrality index (CENTRA), Bentler and Bonnett's non-normed fit index (N_NFI) and normed fit index (NFI), Bollen's normed fit index rho1 (RHO1), Bollen's non-normed index delta2 (DELTA2), and RMSEA (root mean squared error of approximation) (Steiger 1990; Steiger & Lind 1980). The GFI, AGFI, and CFI are normed fit indices ranging from 0 to 1 in value, while non-normed indices can have values from 0 to slightly over 1. Of these nine fit indices, five of them belong to the category of *relative model fit* indices (CFI, N_NFI, NFI, RHO1, and DELTA2) discussed previously. RMSEA is an index for model *misfit*, and a small RMSEA value (close to 0) indicates little misfit, while a relatively large RMSEA value (e.g., >.10) indicates more severe model misfit.

7.2.4 Design of Monte Carlo Simulation

Three factors were incorporated into the design of this example: model specification (two levels: true, and misspecified models), estimation methods (two levels: maximum likelihood and generalized least squares), and sample size (four levels: 100, 200, 500, and 1000). The three factors were fully crossed with each other, creating 16 (2×2×4) different cell conditions. Within each cell condition, 200 replications were implemented (more replications may be implemented easily if time is not a concern). This balanced experimental design allows for a systematic assessment of the effects of the three factors on the SEM fit indices. The design required the generation of 3,200 random samples (2×2×4×200) for model fitting.

A widely-known model from substantive research (Wheaton et al. 1977), with six observed and three latent variables, is used in the simulation (Figure 7.1).

Figure 7.1 *True Model with Population Parameters (Presented in LISREL Matrices) and Model Misspecification Conditions*

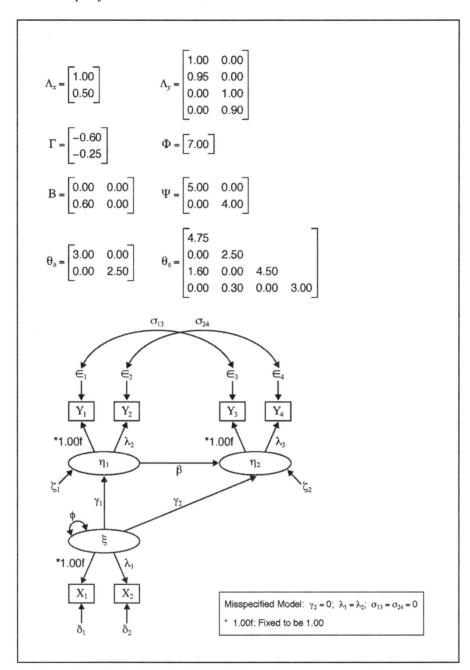

This model has been discussed extensively in SEM literature (e.g., Bentler 1992; Jöreskog & Sörbom 1989). The true model with *population* parameters (presented in LISREL convention matrices) and the misspecified model conditions are also presented in Figure 7.1.

7.2.4.1 Deriving the Population Covariance Matrix

Once the model population parameters are fully specified, the population covariance matrix (Σ) is obtained through the following formula (Jöreskog & Sörbom 1989, p. 5). This covariance matrix (Σ) serves as the target population covariance matrix in generating random data samples:

$$\Sigma = \begin{bmatrix} Cov_y & Cov_{yx} \\ Cov_{xy} & Cov_x \end{bmatrix}$$

$$= \begin{bmatrix} \Lambda_y (I-B)^{-1}(\Gamma\Phi\Gamma'+\Psi)(I-B')^{-1}\Lambda'_y+\theta_\varepsilon & \Lambda_y(I-B)^{-1}\Gamma\Phi\Gamma\Lambda'_x \\ \Lambda_x\Phi\Gamma'(I-B')^{-1}\Lambda'_y & \Lambda_x\Phi\Lambda'_x+\theta_\delta \end{bmatrix} \tag{7.1}$$

Based on (7.1), and by using the eight matrices defined in Figure 7.1, the population covariance matrix for the specified true model in Figure 7.1 can be derived by using PROC IML, as shown in Program 7.1, below:

Program 7.1 *Deriving the Population Covariance Matrix from Model Parameters*

```
*** Program 7.1 ***;
*** Deriving population covariance matrix from model parameters;

PROC IML;

LX = {1.00, 0.50};
LY = {1.00 0.00, 0.95 0.00, 0.00 1.00, 0.00 0.90};
GA = {-0.60, -0.25};
PH = {7.00};
PS = {5.00 0.00, 0.00 4.00};
TD = {3.00 0.00,
      0.00 2.50};
TE = {4.75 0.00 1.60 0.00,
      0.00 2.50 0.00 0.30,
      1.60 0.00 4.50 0.00,
      0.00 0.30 0.00 3.00};
B  = {0.00 0.00, 0.60 0.00};
I = {1 0, 0 1};

COVY = LY*(INV(I-B))*(GA*PH*GA'+PS)*(INV(I-B'))*LY'+TE;
COVX = LX*PH*LX' + TD;
COVYX = LY*(INV(I-B))*GA*PH*LX';
COVXY = LX*PH*GA'*(INV(I-B'))*LY';

UPPER = COVX || COVXY;
LOWER = COVYX || COVY;

COV = UPPER // LOWER;

PRINT COV;
RUN;
```

The output from running Program 7.1 is the population covariance matrix as shown in Output 7.1.

Output 7.1
Population
Covariance
Matrix
Derived
from Model
Parameters

```
      COV

10         3.5       -4.2      -3.99      -4.27      -3.843
 3.5       4.25      -2.1      -1.995     -2.135     -1.9215
-4.2      -2.1       12.27      7.144      7.162      5.0058
-3.99     -1.995      7.144     9.2868     5.2839     5.05551
-4.27     -2.135      7.162     5.2839    12.9047     7.56423
-3.843    -1.9215     5.0058    5.05551    7.56423    9.807807
```

Once this population covariance matrix is derived, Program 4.10 can be used to obtain the population correlation matrix and variable standard deviations for data generation. By using the covariance matrix above in Part II of Program 4.10, we obtain the population correlation matrix and population standard deviations. Table 7.1 presents the resultant population correlation matrix, plus variable means and variances, used for data generation. Because the means of the variables do not affect SEM model fitting (unless a mean structure model is tested), all the measured variables were centered with means being zeros.

Table 7.1 *Model Population Correlations, Means, and Variances*

σ^2	10.000000	4.250000	12.270000	9.286800	12.904700	9.807807
μ	0	0	0	0	0	0
X_1	1.000000					
X_2	.536875	1.000000				
Y_1	-.379164	-.290805	1.000000			
Y_2	-.414038	-.317552	.669246	1.000000		
Y_3	-.375884	-.288290	.569164	.482667	1.000000	
Y_4	-.388047	-.297619	.456315	.529719	.672364	1.000000

7.2.4.2 Dealing with Model Misspecification

Although a true model is relatively easy to specify in simulation research, model misspecification is difficult to handle for at least two reasons: (1) model misspecification can take a variety of forms; and (2) the degree of model misspecification is not easily quantified. In other words, it is difficult to make *a priori* predictions about the *severity* of model misspecification (Gerbing & Anderson 1993). In the present study, model misspecification was achieved by fixing/constraining certain parameters in the model which should be set free for estimation. The degree of model misspecification was empirically determined by fitting the misspecified model to the population covariance matrix Σ, and the resultant values of fit indices were used as indicators of severity of model misfit. The "misspecified" model was defined as producing fit indices between .93 and .95 when it was fitted to the *population* covariance matrix, and a χ^2 test would reach statistical significance of rejecting the model for sample size around 150.

Table 7.2 schematically represents the design for this simulation study example.

Table 7.2 *Schematic Representation of the Design for SEM Monte Carlo Study Example*

		Sample N	Model Specification	
			True	**Misspecified**
Estimation Method	**Maximum Likelihood**	100	200 Replications	200 Replications
		200	200 Replications	200 Replications
		500	200 Replications	200 Replications
		1000	200 Replications	200 Replications
	Generalized Least Squares	100	200 Replications	200 Replications
		200	200 Replications	200 Replications
		500	200 Replications	200 Replications
		1000	200 Replications	200 Replications

7.2.5 SEM Example Program

Program 7.2 presents the complete SAS macro program for this Monte Carlo study example, with annotated notes for the functions of different components in this complete SAS program. This program implements the design discussed previously and saves all the desired analysis results (sample model fit indices) to an external SAS system file that can be accessed easily in later analyses. Program 7.2 appears to be long, but a careful look reveals that it consists of many components that have been discussed in previous chapters. There are, however, several features in this program that require some more detailed discussion.

Program 7.2 *Simulating Structural Equation Models*

```
/*****************************************************************/
/* this program conducts Monte Carlo simulation of SEM, and outputs*/
/* parameter estimates and fit indices to a SAS system file named  */
/* 'SEM_FITS'.  2 models are simulated in this program: true,      */
/* & misspecified models.                                          */
/*****************************************************************/

/*****************************************************************/
%LET MC=200;   * # of Monte Carlo replications for each cell condition;
/*****************************************************************/

LIBNAME SEM 'C:\SEM\SAS\';

     * -- to direct the SAS log to a disk file;
PROC PRINTTO LOG='C:\SEM\SAS\LOGFILE.TMP';

DATA A (TYPE=CORR);
_TYPE_='CORR';
INPUT X1 X2 Y1 Y2 Y3 Y4;
CARDS;
1.000000 . . . . .
```

```
    .536875 1.000000 . . . .
  -.379164 -.290805 1.000000 . . .
  -.414038 -.317552  .669246 1.000000 . .
  -.375884 -.288290  .569164  .482667 1.000000 .
  -.388047 -.297619  .456315  .529719  .672364 1.000000
  ;
                    * obtain factor pattern matrix for later data generation;
PROC FACTOR N=6 OUTSTAT=FACOUT;
DATA PATTERN; SET FACOUT;
  IF _TYPE_='PATTERN';
  DROP _TYPE_ _NAME_;
RUN;

%MACRO SEM_MC;  * start of monte carlo simulation macro 'SEM_MC';

                  * do-loop for 2 conditions for true and misspecified models;
%DO MODEL = 1 %TO 2;
  %IF &MODEL=1 %THEN %DO; %LET MODL=TRU; %END;
  %IF &MODEL=2 %THEN %DO; %LET MODL=MIS; %END;

                  * do-loop for 2 estimation procedures;
%DO A = 1 %TO 2;
  %IF &A=1 %THEN %DO; %LET METHOD=MAX;  %END;
  %IF &A=2 %THEN %DO; %LET METHOD=GLS;  %END;

                  * do-loop for 4 sample size conditions;
%DO B = 1 %TO 4;
  %IF &B=1 %THEN %DO; %LET SMPLN=100;  %END;
  %IF &B=2 %THEN %DO; %LET SMPLN=200;  %END;
  %IF &B=3 %THEN %DO; %LET SMPLN=500;  %END;
  %IF &B=4 %THEN %DO; %LET SMPLN=1000; %END;

%DO C=1 %TO &MC;    * do-loop for the number of replications in each cell;

PROC IML;                    * use SAS PROC IML for data generation;
  USE PATTERN;               * use the factor pattern matrix;
  READ ALL VAR _NUM_ INTO F;
  F=F';

              * diagonal matrix containing variances for 6 variables;

  VAR={10    0      0      0       0       0,
        0  4.25    0      0       0       0,
        0    0  12.27    0       0       0,
        0    0      0  9.2868    0       0,
        0    0      0      0  12.9047    0,
        0    0      0      0       0  9.807807};

STD=SQRT(VAR);            * matrix containing stds for the 6 variables;
X=RANNOR(J(&SMPLN,6,0)); * generate 6 random normal variables;
XT=X';                   * transpose the data matrix for multiplication;

              * transform uncorrelated variables to correlated ones;
XTCORR=F*XT;

        *transform the scale of the variables
          (from std=1 to std=specified above);

XTSTD=STD*XTCORR;

              * transpose the data matrix back;
XY=XTSTD';
RUN;
```

```
                        * create SAS data set 'DAT';
CREATE DAT FROM XY[COLNAME={X1 X2 Y1 Y2 Y3 Y4}];
APPEND FROM XY;
                            * implement the true model;
                            * output the model fitting results to
                              data set 'SEMOUT';
%IF &MODEL=1 %THEN %DO;

PROC CALIS DATA=DAT METHOD=&METHOD COV OUTRAM=SEMOUT NOPRINT;
  LINEQS
     X1 =       FK  +   EX1,
     X2 = LX2 FK  +   EX2,
     Y1 =       FE1 +   EY1,
     Y2 = LY2 FE1 +   EY2,
     Y3 =       FE2 +   EY3,
     Y4 = LY4 FE2 +   EY4,
     FE1= GA1 FK  +   DE1,
     FE2= GA2 FK  +  BE1 FE1 + DE2;
STD
 FK EX1 EX2 EY1 EY2 EY3 EY4 DE1 DE2 =
 VFK VEX1 VEX2 VEY1 VEY2 VEY3 VEY4 VDE1 VDE2;
COV
  EY1 EY3 = C_EY13,  EY2 EY4 = C_EY24;
RUN;

DATA SEMOUT; SET SEMOUT;   * keep only the relevant results;
   KEEP _NAME_ _ESTIM_;
RUN;

                            * transpose the SAS data set 'SEMOUT' to 'NEWFITS';
PROC TRANSPOSE DATA=SEMOUT OUT=NEWFITS LET;

   DATA NEWFITS;  SET NEWFITS;    * add simulation design information;
   MTHD="&METHOD"; MODEL="&MODL";

                            * keep the desired model fit indices;

   KEEP MODEL MTHD N FIT NPARM DF CHISQUAR P_CHISQ CHISQNUL GFI AGFI
        RMSEAEST COMPFITI BB_NONOR BB_NORMD BOL_RHO1 BOL_DEL2 CENTRALI;

                            * append results of each run to a SAS system file;

PROC APPEND BASE=SEM.SEM_FITS FORCE;

%END;        * end of implementing the true model;

                            * implement misspecified model;
%IF &MODEL=2 %THEN %DO;

PROC CALIS DATA=DAT METHOD=&METHOD COV OUTRAM=SEMOUT NOPRINT;
  LINEQS
     X1 =       FK  +   EX1,
     X2 = LX2 FK  +   EX2,
     Y1 =       FE1 +   EY1,
     Y2 = LX2 FE1 +   EY2,
     Y3 =       FE2 +   EY3,
     Y4 = LY4 FE2 +   EY4,
     FE1= GA1 FK  +   DE1,
     FE2= 0   FK  +  BE1 FE1 + DE2;    * misspecification: GA2 fixed;
                                        * constrained: LY2=LX2;
STD
 FK EX1 EX2 EY1 EY2 EY3 EY4 DE1 DE2 =
 VFK VEX1 VEX2 VEY1 VEY2 VEY3 VEY4 VDE1 VDE2;
```

```
         * misspecification: error covariances fixed to zeros;
*COV
  EY2 EY4 = C_EY24, EY1 EY3 = C_EY13;
RUN;


DATA SEMOUT; SET SEMOUT;
   KEEP _NAME_ _ESTIM_;
RUN;

PROC TRANSPOSE DATA=SEMOUT OUT=NEWFITS LET;
   DATA NEWFITS;   SET NEWFITS;   * add simulation design information;
   MTHD="&METHOD"; MODEL="&MODL";
   KEEP MODEL MTHD N FIT NPARM DF CHISQUAR P_CHISQ CHISQNUL GFI AGFI
        RMSEAEST COMPFITI BB_NONOR BB_NORMD BOL_RHO1 BOL_DEL2 CENTRALI;

PROC APPEND BASE=SEM.SEM_FITS FORCE;

%END;              * end of implementing the misspecified model;

%END;              * close the do-loop for replications in each cell;
%END;              * close the do-loop for sample size conditions;
%END;              * close the do-loop for estimation procedure;
%END;              * close the do-loop for model specification conditions;
%MEND SEM_MC;      * end of simulation macro 'SEM_MC';
%SEM_MC;           * running the macro 'SEM_MC';
RUN;

PROC PRINTTO PRINT=PRINT;  * direct output to SAS Output window;
RUN;

/*        * descriptive analysis for the 9 descriptive model fit indices;
DATA D2; SET SEM.SEM_FITS;
PROC SORT; BY MODEL MTHD N;
PROC MEANS MEAN STD MAX MIN;
   BY MODEL MTHD N;
   VAR GFI AGFI RMSEAEST COMPFITI BB_NONOR BB_NORMD BOL_RHO1 BOL_DEL2
CENTRALI;
RUN;
*/
```

7.2.6 Some Explanations of Program 7.2

First of all, the program directs the SAS log to an external file (LOGFILE.TMP) on the hard drive by using the PRINTTO procedure:

```
        * -- to direct the SAS log to a disk file;
   PROC PRINTTO LOG='C:\SEM\SAS\LOGFILE.TMP';
```

As discussed in Chapter 6, when hundreds and thousands of replications need to be run, the SAS log can overwhelm the SAS Log window capacity. Thus, it is important to direct the SAS log to an external file to prevent SAS from stopping the operation and asking you what to do.

One important feature in this program is that we use the SAS CALIS procedure for fitting the structural equation models, and we use the statistical output from PROC CALIS to obtain all the fit indices of interest. Because structural equation modeling is mathematically sophisticated and computationally intensive, it is only feasible to conduct a Monte Carlo study in SEM if we do not have to worry about doing statistical programming ourselves. Once a random sample of data drawn from a pre-specified statistical population (see Table 7.1 for the specifications of the statistical population) is generated, a particular SEM model (true or misspecified) is fitted to the sample data. For fitting the true model, we have the following commands:

```
                              * implement the true model;
                              * output the model fitting results to
                                data set 'SEMOUT';
%IF &MODEL=1 %THEN %DO;

PROC CALIS DATA=DAT METHOD=&METHOD COV OUTRAM=SEMOUT NOPRINT;
   LINEQS
      X1 =      FK   +    EX1,
      X2 = LX2 FK   +    EX2,
      Y1 =      FE1 +    EY1,
      Y2 = LY2 FE1 +    EY2,
      Y3 =      FE2 +    EY3,
      Y4 = LY4 FE2 +    EY4,
      FE1= GA1 FK   +    DE1,
      FE2= GA2 FK   +    BE1 FE1 + DE2;
   STD
    FK EX1 EX2 EY1 EY2 EY3 EY4 DE1 DE2 =
    VFK VEX1 VEX2 VEY1 VEY2 VEY3 VEY4 VDE1 VDE2;
   COV
      EY1 EY3 = C_EY13, EY2 EY4 = C_EY24;
   RUN;
```

In this group of PROC CALIS options and statements, the method for estimation is varied (METHOD=&METHOD) between "maximum likelihood" and "generalized least squares," as one DO loop specifies. For obtaining the model fitting results, the option OUTRAM=SEMOUT accomplishes the task. Here, OUTRAM is a keyword in PROC CALIS requesting the model fitting results to be output to a temporary SAS data set. This SAS data set is named SEMOUT here and will be used later.

The SEMOUT data set contains all the model fit indices, model parameter estimates, and more. To understand how model fit indices are obtained, we need to take a look at the structure of the SEMOUT data set by using a simple command:

```
PROC PRINT DATA=SEMOUT;
RUN;
```

When the true model in Figure 7.1 is fitted to the population covariance matrix (correlation matrix and variable variances) in Table 7.1, the temporary SAS data set SEMOUT has the following structure and analysis results:

Output 7.2 *Contents of the SEMOUT Data Set*

Obs	_TYPE_	_NAME_	_MATNR_	_ROW_	_COL_	_ESTIM_	_STDERR_
1	MODEL	_SEL_	1	6	17	12.00	0.00000
2	MODEL	_BETA_	2	17	17	13.00	2.00000
3	MODEL	_GAMMA_	3	17	9	14.00	0.00000
4	MODEL	_PHI_	4	9	9	8.00	0.00000
5	VARNAME	X1	1	.	1	.	.
6	VARNAME	X2	1	.	2	.	.
7	VARNAME	Y1	1	.	3	.	.
8	VARNAME	Y2	1	.	4	.	.
9	VARNAME	Y3	1	.	5	.	.
10	VARNAME	Y4	1	.	6	.	.
11	VARNAME	FE1	1	.	7	.	.
12	VARNAME	FE2	1	.	8	.	.
13	VARNAME	FK	1	.	9	.	.
14	VARNAME	EX1	1	.	10	.	.
15	VARNAME	EX2	1	.	11	.	.
16	VARNAME	EY1	1	.	12	.	.
17	VARNAME	EY2	1	.	13	.	.
18	VARNAME	EY3	1	.	14	.	.
19	VARNAME	EY4	1	.	15	.	.
20	VARNAME	DE1	1	.	16	.	.
21	VARNAME	DE2	1	.	17	.	.
22	METHOD	ML	.	.	.	.	.
23	STAT	N	.	.	.	150.00	.
24	STAT	FIT	.	.	.	0.00	.
25	STAT	GFI	.	.	.	1.00	.
26	STAT	AGFI	.	.	.	1.00	.
27	STAT	RMR	.	.	.	0.00	.
28	STAT	PGFI	.	.	.	0.27	.
29	STAT	NPARM	.	.	.	17.00	.
30	STAT	DF	.	.	.	4.00	.
31	STAT	N_ACT	.	.	.	0.00	.
32	STAT	CHISQUAR	.	.	.	0.00	.
33	STAT	P_CHISQ	.	.	.	1.00	.
34	STAT	CHISQNUL	.	.	.	349.59	.
35	STAT	RMSEAEST	.	.	.	0.00	.
36	STAT	RMSEALOB	.	.	.	.	.
37	STAT	RMSEAUPB	.	.	.	.	.
38	STAT	P_CLOSFT	.	.	.	1.00	.
39	STAT	ECVI_EST	.	.	.	0.24	.
40	STAT	ECVI_LOB	.	.	.	.	.
41	STAT	ECVI_UPB	.	.	.	.	.
42	STAT	COMPFITI	.	.	.	1.00	.
43	STAT	ADJCHISQ	.	.	.	.	.
44	STAT	P_ACHISQ	.	.	.	.	.
45	STAT	RLSCHISQ	.	.	.	0.00	.
46	STAT	AIC	.	.	.	-8.00	.
47	STAT	CAIC	.	.	.	-24.04	.
48	STAT	SBC	.	.	.	-20.04	.
49	STAT	CENTRALI	.	.	.	1.01	.
50	STAT	BB_NONOR	.	.	.	1.04	.
51	STAT	BB_NORMD	.	.	.	1.00	.
52	STAT	PARSIMON	.	.	.	0.27	.
53	STAT	ZTESTWH	.	.	.	-4.00	.
54	STAT	BOL_RHO1	.	.	.	1.00	.
55	STAT	BOL_DEL2	.	.	.	1.01	.
56	STAT	CNHOELT	.	.	.	543658928584.00	.
57	ESTIM		2	3	7	1.00	0.00000
58	ESTIM	LY2	2	4	7	0.95	0.14270
59	ESTIM		2	5	8	1.00	0.00000
60	ESTIM	LY4	2	6	8	0.90	0.13770
61	ESTIM	BE1	2	8	7	0.60	0.12628
62	ESTIM		3	1	1	1.00	0.00000
63	ESTIM		3	1	2	1.00	0.00000
64	ESTIM	LX2	3	2	1	0.50	0.09780
65	ESTIM		3	2	3	1.00	0.00000

Output 7.2 *Contents of the SEMOUT Data Set (continued)*

66	ESTIM		3	3	4	1.00	0.00000
67	ESTIM		3	4	5	1.00	0.00000
68	ESTIM		3	5	6	1.00	0.00000
69	ESTIM		3	6	7	1.00	0.00000
70	ESTIM	GA1	3	7	1	-0.60	0.14131
71	ESTIM		3	7	8	1.00	0.00000
72	ESTIM	GA2	3	8	1	-0.25	0.13331
73	ESTIM		3	8	9	1.00	0.00000
74	ESTIM	VFK	4	1	1	7.00	1.63916
75	ESTIM	VEX1	4	2	2	3.00	1.25943
76	ESTIM	VEX2	4	3	3	2.50	0.41890
77	ESTIM	VEY1	4	4	4	4.75	1.13774
78	ESTIM	VEY2	4	5	5	2.50	0.95706
79	ESTIM	C_EY13	4	6	4	1.60	0.78801
80	ESTIM	VEY3	4	6	6	4.50	1.25757
81	ESTIM	C_EY24	4	7	5	0.30	0.62251
82	ESTIM	VEY4	4	7	7	3.00	1.00843
83	ESTIM	VDE1	4	8	8	5.00	1.19037
84	ESTIM	VDE2	4	9	9	4.00	0.98312

Of the eight columns in this SAS data set, only two columns (column heading _NAME_, and _ESTIM_) contain what we need, and for our purposes, the rest can be discarded. The column with the heading _NAME_ contains the names of the model fit indices or names of model parameters. The column with the heading _ESTIM_ contains the sample estimates of the model fit indices and model parameters. So the next group of SAS statements in Program 7.2 only keeps the two columns _NAME_ and _ESTIM_:

```
DATA SEMOUT; SET SEMOUT;  * only keep the relevant results;
   KEEP _NAME_ _ESTIM_;
RUN;
```

After the unnecessary columns are dropped from the temporary SEMOUT data set by the SAS statements above, the data set is then transposed from two columns and 84 rows (84 rows for this model only; different models have different numbers of rows, due to the different numbers of model parameters) to two rows and 84 columns by using the TRANSPOSE procedure:

```
             * transpose the SAS data set 'SEMOUT' to 'NEWFITS';
PROC TRANSPOSE DATA=SEMOUT OUT=NEWFITS LET;
```

In the new data set, NEWFITS, the first row represents the variable names, and the second row contains the sample model fit indices and parameter estimates. Because we do not need all the variables from each model fitting analysis, we only keep what we need. In addition, our Monte Carlo simulation design information (i.e., what estimation method is used for this sample, and which model is fitted to the sample data) for each model fitting analysis needs to be added to the data for later analyses. The following group of SAS commands accomplish these tasks:

```
DATA NEWFITS;  SET NEWFITS;   * add simulation design information;
MTHD="&METHOD"; MODEL="&MODL";


                   * keep the desired model fit indices;
KEEP MODEL MTHD N FIT NPARM DF CHISQUAR P_CHISQ CHISQNUL GFI AGFI
    RMSEAEST COMPFITI BB_NONOR BB_NORMD BOL_RHO1 BOL_DEL2 CENTRALI;
```

In the KEEP statement, the last nine variables are the model fit indices we are interested in studying, and they are as follows:

GFI: goodness-of-fit index

AGFI: Adjusted goodness-of-fit index

RMSEAEST: root mean square of approximation

COMPFITI: comparative fit index

BB_NONOR: Bentler-Bonnet non-normed fit index

BB_NORMD: Bentler-Bonnet normed fit index

BOL_RHO1:   Bollen's RHO1

BOL_DEL2:   Bollen's delta 2

CENTRALI: McDonald's index of non-centrality

Finally, the results from each sample need to be accumulated in an external SAS file for later analyses. The SAS APPEND procedure appends the results from each sample to the SAS file named SEM_FITS.

```
                    * append results of each run to a SAS system file;
PROC APPEND BASE=SEM.SEM_FITS FORCE;

%END;       * end of implementing the true model;
```

By this time, the first sample in the first cell (true model, estimation method of maximum likelihood, and sample size of 100) is complete, and the results are saved. For the misspecified model, the SAS programming code has almost the same structure, but with a slightly modified model implemented. By the time SAS Program 7.2 is completed, the SAS file SEM_FITS will contain 18 variables and 3,200 cases, with each case representing the model fitting results for each random sample drawn from the statistical population specified in Table 7.1. All the design information is contained in the SAS file for later analyses. One example descriptive analysis will be to obtain the means, standard deviations, maximum value, and minimum value of each model fit index, broken down by sample size, estimation method, and model specification, similar to the following:

```
         * descriptive analysis for the 9 descriptive model fit indices;
DATA D2; SET SEM.SEM_FITS;
PROC SORT; BY MODEL MTHD N;
PROC MEANS MEAN STD MAX MIN;
   BY MODEL MTHD N;
   VAR GFI AGFI RMSEAEST COMPFITI BB_NONOR BB_NORMD
       BOL_RHO1 BOL_DEL2 CENTRALI;
RUN;
```

7.2.7 Selected Results from Program 7.2

As an example of the results obtained from this simulation program, Table 7.3 presents the means of the nine fit indices for the misspecified model based on the execution of Program 7.2. For each sample size condition, the values in the upper row are the means of the fit indices based on the maximum likelihood estimation method for model fitting, and the values in the lower row are the means of the fit indices based on the generalized least squares estimation method for model fitting. Notice that for the relative fit indices (CFI, N_NFI, NFI, RHO1, DELTA2), the difference between model fit index values based on the estimation method (maximum likelihood vs. generalized least squares) is very obvious. In other words, for this group of fit indices, the estimation method used in model fitting appears to be influential for the fit index value obtained. For the other four fit indices (GFI, AGFI, RMSEA, CENTRA), however, the estimation method does not appear to affect the sample model fit index value to the same degree as it does for the relative fit indices. Of course, more detailed or more sophisticated analyses could be conducted for the obtained sample fit indices from this simulation study. For an example of such analyses in real research situations, see Fan and Wang (1998).

Table 7.3 *Means of Fit Indices from Two Estimation Methods for the Misspecified Model*

Sample N	Model Fit Indices								
	GFI	AGFI	CFI	N_NFI	NFI	RHO1	DELTA2	RMSEA	CENTRA
100	.94	.84	.95	.90	.92	.85	.95	.12	.94
	.94	.85	.86	.74	.79	.60	.88	.10	.96
200	.95	.87	.95	.90	.93	.87	.95	.12	.94
	.95	.87	.85	.73	.82	.66	.86	.11	.95
500	.96	.89	.95	.90	.94	.89	.95	.12	.94
	.96	.89	.85	.72	.83	.69	.85	.11	.95
1000	.96	.89	.95	.90	.94	.90	.95	.12	.94
	.96	.90	.85	.72	.84	.71	.85	.12	.95

Note: For each sample size condition, the means in the upper row are based on the maximum likelihood estimation method for model fitting, and the means in the lower row are based on the generalized least squares estimation method for model fitting.

7.3 Example 2: Linear Discriminant Analysis and Logistic Regression for Classification

In many different disciplines, there is often a need to predict an individual's group membership based on a battery of measurements. Both predictive discriminant analysis (PDA) and logistic regression (LR) have been the popular statistical tools for this purpose (Yarnold, Hart & Soltysik 1994). The relative efficacy of these two statistical methods under different data conditions, however, has been an issue of debate (e.g., Barón 1991; Dattalo 1994; Dey & Astin 1993). In our example here, we only examine the performance of logistic regression and linear discriminant analysis for classification in two-group situations. In the following discussion, PDA is used only for predictive discriminant analysis based on a linear discriminant function.

7.3.1 Major Issues Involved

Since both PDA and LR can be used for predicting or classifying individuals into different groups based on a set of measurements, a logical question often asked is: how do the two techniques compare with each other? In the literature, there has been some discussion about the relative merits of these two different techniques (e.g., Dattalo 1994; Fraser et al. 1994; Wilson & Hardgrave 1995).

Theoretically, PDA is considered as having more stringent data assumptions. Two prominent assumptions for PDA are multivariate data normality, and homogeneity of the covariance matrices of the groups (Johnson & Wichern 1988; Stevens 1996). However, it is not entirely clear what consequences the violation of these assumptions may have on PDA results. LR, on the other hand, is considered relatively free of these stringent data assumptions (Cox & Snell 1989; Neter, Wasserman, & Kutner 1989; Tabachnick & Fidell 1996). Although there is no strong logical reason to expect the superiority of one technique over the other in classification accuracy when the assumptions for PDA hold, it would be reasonable to expect that LR should have the upper hand when some of these assumptions for PDA are not tenable (Neter et al. 1989; Tabachnick & Fidell 1996).

Research findings about the relative performance of these two methods appear to be inconsistent. With regard to data normality, Efron (1975) showed that under the optimal data condition of multivariate normality and equal covariance matrices for the groups, a linear discriminant function is more economical and more efficient than logistic regression. When the data are not multivariate normal, results from some simulation studies (e.g., Barón 1991; Bayne et al. 1984) indicated that LR performed better than PDA. This finding, however, has not been unequivocally supported by the studies that compared the two techniques by using extant data sets, because quite a few studies involving actual non-normal data sets suggested very little practical difference between the two techniques (e.g., Cleary & Angel 1984; Dey & Astin 1993; Meshbane & Morris 1996).

With regard to the assumption of equal covariance matrices for PDA, there appears to be a lack of empirical studies to compare the relative performance of PDA and LR when this assumption does not hold. Researchers seem to assume that LR should be the method of choice when the two groups do not have equal covariance matrices (Harrell & Lee 1985; Press & Wilson 1978). Several studies that involved extant data sets did not suggest that PDA's performance would suffer appreciably because the assumption was violated (Knoke 1982; Meshbane & Morris 1996). No one seems to have specifically manipulated this condition in simulation studies to examine its effect on the performance of PDA and LR.

Relative performance of PDA and LR under different sample size conditions is also an issue of interest. Viewed from the perspective of statistical estimation in general, maximum likelihood estimators (as in LR) tend to require larger samples to achieve stable results than ordinary least square estimators (as in PDA). Inconsistent results have been reported about the relative performance of the two techniques with regard to sample size conditions. For example, in a simulation study, Harrell and Lee (1985) implied that PDA performed better under small sample size conditions. Johnson and Seshia (1992) showed that, when the techniques were applied to real data sets, the findings did not clearly show that this was the case.

In addition to the three issues (data normality, equal covariance matrices, and sample size), another issue that has attracted relatively little attention in the literature is the situation where two groups have different population proportions, and what effect this condition has on the classification accuracy of PDA and LR. There has been some discussion in the literature that it may make very little practical difference whether PDA or LR is used for classification when two groups have approximately equal proportions. But when the two groups have very different proportions (e.g., 0.10 : 0.90), logistic regression may perform better than a linear discriminant function (Cleary & Angel 1984; Dey & Astin 1993; Neter et al. 1989; Press & Wilson 1978).

Our example has considered two issues discussed above: homogeneity of covariance matrices, and sample size. Although data normality conditions and group proportions are interesting issues, for the sake of keeping the programming example manageable, data normality is not examined in this example, and only the condition of equal group proportions (i.e., 0.50 : 0.50) is used in the example.

7.3.2 Design

A crossed two-factor experimental design was implemented for the data structure pattern described in Table 7.4. The data structure described here is arbitrarily specified. The degree of group separation in the multivariate space as measured by the Mahalanobis distance $[D^2 = (\mu_1 - \mu_2)' \Sigma^{-1}_{pooled} (\mu_1 - \mu_2)]$ is provided.

Table 7.4 *Data Structure Pattern Simulated in the Example*

Common Covariance Matrix $(\Sigma_{common})^a$:

X1	1.00		
X2	0.30	1.00	
X3	0.50	0.40	1.00
σ^2	4.00	4.00	4.00
μ_1^b	5.00	5.00	5.00
μ_2	9.00	9.00	9.00

Group Separation (Mahalanobis Distance: $D^2=(\mu_1-\mu_2)'\ \Sigma^{-1}_{pooled}(\mu_1-\mu_2)$:

Equal Σs: D^2 = 6.70
Unequal Σs: D^2 = 6.70 (Group Proportions: 0.50:0.50)

a: For the condition of <u>equal</u> Σs, this common covariance matrix is used for <u>both</u> groups. For the condition of <u>unequal</u> Σs, $2/5(\Sigma_{common})$ is used for Group 1 population, and $8/5(\Sigma_{common})$ is used for Group 2 population.

b: Mean row vectors for Group 1 and Group 2, respectively.

The two factors manipulated under each data pattern were sample size (4 levels: 60, 100, 200, 400) and equality of covariance matrices (2 levels: equal, unequal). The fully crossed design for the data structure pattern, with 1000 replications in each cell, required the generation and model-fitting of 8,000 (4×2×1000) samples. This design makes it possible to systematically assess the potential impact of the two factors on the classification accuracy of PDA and LR.

Although no theoretical guidelines are available about what is a small or a large sample size for the purpose of classification for the two methods, the review of Meshbane and Morris (1996) of 32 real research data sets used for two-group classification has sample sizes ranging from 100 to 285. Compared with these 32 data sets, the sample size conditions specified in this study (60, 100, 200, 400) could be considered as ranging from relatively small to moderately large.

The degree of inequality of covariance matrices between the two groups was specified a priori as one group having a covariance matrix 4 times larger than that of the other group. To avoid the confounding of group separation (as measured by Mahalanobis distance D^2) and heterogeneity of covariance matrices, the covariance matrices for the two populations were specified as follows:

1. Specify a common covariance matrix Σ_{common}, and this Σ_{common} is used for the two populations for the condition of equal covariance;

2. For the condition of unequal covariance matrices, the group with the smaller covariance matrix has $2/5(\Sigma_{common})$ as its population covariance matrix; the group with the larger covariance matrix has $8/5(\Sigma_{common})$ as its population covariance matrix.

As shown in Table 7.4, the specification for the condition of unequal covariance matrices for the two populations maintained the same population separation as measured by the Mahalanobis distance D^2, thus avoiding the confounding of heterogeneous covariance matrices with the degree of group separation.

7.3.3 Data Source and Model Fitting

For each sample, first a pseudo-population is generated that is 20 times larger than the size of the sample desired. This pseudo-population has the exact proportions of the two groups (0.50 : 0.50). Once this pseudo-population is generated, a simple random sample of a specified sample size (60, 100, 200, or 400) is drawn from this pseudo-population. In other words, although the population proportions of the groups are exact, the sample proportions may not be. This procedure models the research reality: sample proportion varies around the population proportion within the limits of sampling error.

Although statistical inference assumes an infinite population from which a sample is drawn, as Glass and Hopkins (1996, p. 224) pointed out, when the sampling fraction n/N =.05 or less (n: sample size; N: finite population size), the precision of statistical inferences would only be minimally and negligibly affected. This consideration motivated the decision to generate a pseudo-population 20 times larger than the sample size.

Once a sample was drawn, the sample data are fitted to both the linear discriminant analysis model and the logistic regression model, and the classification error rates from the two models are obtained. For PDA, the SAS DISCRIM procedure is used for model fitting, and the linear classification rule is used in the classification. For LR, the SAS LOGISTIC procedure is used for LR model fitting, and the maximum posterior probability rule, i.e., 0.5 on the modeled probability function for the modeled group, is specified for the classification. In this study, the modeled group is always the group with an equal or smaller covariance matrix. The classification error rates for the two groups and those for the total sample under both PDA and LR are collected and saved in a SAS data file for later analyses.

Because both PDA and LR classification contain upward bias due to the fact that the model estimation and classification are done on the same sample, bias-corrected classification error rates for the two methods were used in the present study. For PDA, the bias correction is achieved through the leave-one-out approach (Huberty 1994; Lachenbruch 1967), which is often known as "jackknifing" in the context of PDA (Johnson & Wichern 1988). For LR, although computing power has made the computational intensity of LR less of a concern, for a resampling technique like jackknifing, to repeatedly fit the model to the data for each observation left out could still be computationally expensive (SAS Institute 1997, p. 461). For this reason, instead of the leave-one-out strategy, the SAS LOGISTIC procedure implements a less expensive, one-step algebraic approximation for correcting the upward bias. Readers are referred to the original source for this bias correction (SAS Institute 1997, pp. 461-468).

7.3.4 Example Program Simulating Classification Error Rates of PDA and LR

Program 7.3 presents the complete SAS program for conducting the Monte Carlo study for comparing the classification accuracy of linear discriminant analysis and logistic regression for a two group problem described above. As discussed previously, from each random sample drawn from the defined statistical population, this program obtains the bias-corrected classification error rates (the error rate for each of the two groups and the overall error rate) from both linear discriminant analysis and logistic regression, and saves these error rates to a SAS file on disk for later analyses.

Program 7.3 *Simulating Classification Error Rates of PDA and LR*

```
/* This program conducts Monte Carlo simulation for comparing classification
   error rates from linear discriminant function and from logistic regression
   for a two-group situation. SAS PROC DISCRIM and SAS PROC LOGISTIC are used
   for group membership classification.  The results of classification error
   rates for the respective two groups and the overall error rate from both
   PROC DISCRIM and PROC LOGISTIC are saved in an external SAS file for
   future analyses.
*/

LIBNAME PDA_LR 'C:\PDA_LR\SAS';

     * -- to direct the SAS log to an external file;
PROC PRINTTO LOG='C:\PDA_LR\SAS\LOGFILE.TMP';
RUN;

DATA D1(TYPE=CORR);
  INPUT _TYPE_ $ _NAME_ $ X1-X3;
  CARDS;
CORR X1  1  .  .
CORR X2  0.30  1  .
CORR X3  0.50  0.40  1
;
              *obtain factor pattern matrix for later data generation;
PROC FACTOR N=3 OUTSTAT=FACTOUT;
DATA PATTERN;   SET FACTOUT;
     IF _TYPE_ = 'PATTERN';
     DROP _TYPE_ _NAME_;
RUN;

%MACRO PDA_LR;         * start of simulation macro;

%DO A = 1 %TO 2;       * A=1: equal group covariance, A=2: unequal;

                       * specify four pseudo-population sizes (N1+N2);
                       * specify sample size conditions (N);
%DO B = 1 %TO 4;
  %IF &B=1 %THEN %DO; %LET N1=600;  %LET N2=600;  %LET N=60;   %END;
  %IF &B=2 %THEN %DO; %LET N1=1000; %LET N2=1000; %LET N=100;  %END;
  %IF &B=3 %THEN %DO; %LET N1=2000; %LET N2=2000; %LET N=200;  %END;
  %IF &B=4 %THEN %DO; %LET N1=4000; %LET N2=4000; %LET N=400;  %END;

%DO NITER=1 %TO 1000;     * specify the # of replications within each cell;

PROC IML;
```

```
   USE PATTERN;                  * use the factor pattern matrix;
   READ ALL VAR _NUM_ INTO FT;
   F=FT`;
   MEAN1={5 5 5};                * specify two mean vectors for the two populations;
   MEAN2={9 9 9};

   VAR={4 0 0,
        0 4 0,
        0 0 4};                  * specify the common variances of the 3 variables;

                                 * specify equal (&A=1) and
                                   unequal (&A=2) covariance conditions;
IF &A=1 THEN VAR1=VAR;
  ELSE VAR1=(2/5)*VAR;
IF &A=1 THEN VAR2=VAR;
  ELSE VAR2=(8/5)*VAR;

************ GROUP 1 DATA **********;

G1DATA=RANNOR(J(&N1,3,0));   * generate 3 random normal variables;
G1DATAT=G1DATA`;             * transpose the data matrix for multiplication;
G1DATAT=F*G1DATAT;          * transform uncorrelated variables to correlated;

STD1=SQRT(VAR1);            * transform the variables to specified scales;
G1DATAT=(STD1*G1DATAT)`;
X1=G1DATAT[,1] + MEAN1[,1];
X2=G1DATAT[,2] + MEAN1[,2];
X3=G1DATAT[,3] + MEAN1[,3];
GROUP1=J(&N1,1,1);          * assigning group number;
G1DATA=GROUP1||X1||X2||X3;

******** GROUP 2 DATA *******************;

G2DATA=RANNOR(J(&N2,3,0));   * generate 3 random normal variables;
G2DATAT=G2DATA`;             * transpose the data matrix for multiplication;
G2DATAT=F*G2DATAT;          * transform uncorrelated variables to correlated;

STD2=SQRT(VAR2);            * transform variables to specified scales;
G2DATAT=(STD2*G2DATAT)`;
X1=G2DATAT[,1] + MEAN2[,1];
X2=G2DATAT[,2] + MEAN2[,2];
X3=G2DATAT[,3] + MEAN2[,3];
GROUP2=J(&N2,1,2);          * assigning group number;
G2DATA=GROUP2||X1||X2||X3;
RUN;

G12DATA=G1DATA//G2DATA;      * combine data of two groups;

CREATE DATA FROM G12DATA[COLNAME={GROUP X1 X2 X3}];
APPEND FROM G12DATA;

      * draw a random sample of size N from the pseudo-population;

DATA TEMP; SET DATA;
  RANNO=RANUNI(0);
PROC SORT; BY RANNO;
DATA SMPLDAT; SET TEMP(OBS=&N); DROP RANNO;

              * direct SAS PROC DISCRIM output to an external file;

FILENAME NEWOUT 'C:\PDA_LR\SAS\OUTFILE';
PROC PRINTTO PRINT=NEWOUT NEW;

      * PROC DISCRIM, requesting jackknife procedure (CROSSVALIDATE);
```

```
PROC DISCRIM CROSSVALIDATE DATA=SMPLDAT;
  CLASS GROUP;
  PRIORS PROPORTIONAL;
  VAR X1 X2 X3;
RUN;

PROC PRINTTO PRINT=PRINT;  * direct SAS output back to SAS Output window;
RUN;

  * read in the external file containing output from PROC DISCRIM;
  * read in jackknifed classification error rates for two groups and combined;

DATA PDAERROR; INFILE NEWOUT;
  INPUT WORD1 $ @;
    IF WORD1='Rate' THEN DO;
          INPUT DAG1_ERR DAG2_ERR DA_ERR;
          KEEP DAG1_ERR DAG2_ERR DA_ERR;
          OUTPUT;
    END;
RUN;

DATA PDAERROR; SET PDAERROR;      * keep the jackknifed errors only;
N=_N_;
IF N=2;  DROP N;
RUN;

        * direct PROC LOGISTIC output to an external file for later use;

FILENAME NEWOUT 'C:\PDA_LR\SAS\OUTFILE';
PROC PRINTTO PRINT=NEWOUT NEW;

        * conduct PROC LOGISTIC analysis for the sample data;
        * requesting classification table;
        * with probability = 0.5 as the cut-off point for classification;

PROC LOGISTIC DATA=SMPLDAT;
  MODEL GROUP=X1 X2 X3/CTABLE PPROB=.5;
RUN;

        * direct SAS output back to SAS Output window;
PROC PRINTTO PRINT=PRINT; RUN;

        * from the external file containing output from PROC LOGISTIC;
        * read in the following:
            (a) overall correct classification rate (LRRATE),
            (b) GROUP 1 correct classification rate (G1RATE),
            (c) GROUP 2 correct classification rate (G2RATE);
        * construct and keep the classification error rates for
            (i) GROUP 1, (ii) GROUP 2, and (iii) overall error rate;

DATA LRERROR; INFILE NEWOUT;
  INPUT PRIOR $ @;
    IF PRIOR='0.500' THEN DO;
       INPUT V1 V2 V3 V4 LRRATE G1RATE G2RATE;
              LRG1_ERR=1-G1RATE/100;
              LRG2_ERR=1-G2RATE/100;
              LR_ERR=1-LRRATE/100;
       KEEP LRG1_ERR LRG2_ERR LR_ERR;
       OUTPUT;
    END;

     * merge error rates from PDA and LR;
     * add simulation study design information;
     * append the results from each sample to a SAS file "RESULTS";
```

```
DATA PDA_LR;
  MERGE PDAERROR LRERROR;
  N=&N; IF &A=1 THEN COV='EQUAL'; ELSE IF &A=2 THEN COV='NO_EQ';
PROC APPEND BASE=PDA_LR.RESULTS FORCE;
RUN;

%END;            * end of do-loop for replications in each cell;
%END;            * end of do-loop for each sample size condition;
%END;            * end of do-loop for each covariance equality condition;
%MEND PDA_LR;    * end of simulation macro;
%PDA_LR;         * run the simulation macro;
RUN;


/*
PROC SORT; BY COV N;
PROC MEANS MEAN STD MIN MAX; BY COV N;
  VAR DAG1_ERR LRG1_ERR DAG2_ERR LRG2_ERR DA_ERR LR_ERR;
TITLE1 'Average Classification Error Rates';
TITLE2 'Comparison of Discriminant Analysis and Logistic Regression';
TITLE3 'For GROUP 1, GROUP 2, and Overall';
RUN;
*/
```

7.3.5 Some Explanations of Program 7.3

Although Program 7.3 contains many comments to remind the readers about the functions of different program components, some discussion is warranted here to illustrate some unique features in this program. The first feature that appears to be new is the following:

```
%DO B = 1 %TO 4;
  %IF &B=1 %THEN %DO; %LET N1=600;  %LET N2=600;  %LET N=60;  %END;
  %IF &B=2 %THEN %DO; %LET N1=1000; %LET N2=1000; %LET N=100; %END;
  %IF &B=3 %THEN %DO; %LET N1=2000; %LET N2=2000; %LET N=200; %END;
  %IF &B=4 %THEN %DO; %LET N1=4000; %LET N2=4000; %LET N=400; %END;
```

As discussed previously, in this program, we generate a finite pseudo-population first, and then draw a random sample from this pseudo-population. The pseudo-population has the exact 0.50:0.50 equal proportions for the two groups, but a random sample from such a pseudo-population may not have exact equal proportions due to random sampling error. The SAS statements above specify the pseudo-population size (N1+N2, for Group 1 and Group 2 pseudo-populations, respectively), and the sample size (N) for each sample size condition. For each of the four sample size conditions, the sample size (N) is 1/20 of the pseudo-population size, as discussed previously in the section on the study design.

To draw a random sample of size N from the pseudo-population of size N1+N2, we generate a random number (RANNO), sort the pseudo-population data by that random number, and then select the first N observations as our sample.   This is accomplished by the following SAS statements:

```
        * draw a random sample of size N from the pseudo-population;

DATA TEMP; SET DATA;
  RANNO=RANUNI(0);
PROC SORT; BY RANNO;
DATA SMPLDAT; SET TEMP(OBS=&N); DROP RANNO;
```

For both the PROC DISCRIM and PROC LOGISTIC analysis results, the information we desire is only available in the SAS output file. For this reason, we first direct the SAS output to an external file on disk, and then read in that external file and extract the information we need. For PROC DISCRIM results, this is accomplished by the following SAS statements:

```
    * read in the external file containing output from PROC DISCRIM;
    * read in jackknifed classification error rates for two groups and
      combined;

DATA PDAERROR; INFILE NEWOUT;
  INPUT WORD1 $ @;
    IF WORD1='Rate' THEN DO;
            INPUT DAG1_ERR DAG2_ERR DA_ERR;
            KEEP DAG1_ERR DAG2_ERR DA_ERR;
            OUTPUT;
    END;
RUN;

DATA PDAERROR; SET PDAERROR;      * keep the jackknifed errors only;
N=_N_;
IF N=2;   DROP N;
RUN;
```

To understand how the SAS statements above extract the jackknifed classification errors for two groups and the overall classification error, we have to know what PROC DISCRIM output looks like. Because we requested the jackknife procedure for PROC DISCRIM (by specifying the CROSSVALIDATE option), the output contains two sections, one for the original classification results (not corrected for bias), and the other for bias-corrected classification results. Relevant sections of the PROC DISCRIM output are reproduced below based on an artificially constructed data set of 50 cases for each of the two groups (Group A and Group B):

Output 7.3a *Partial Output from PROC DISCRIM*

```
                        The DISCRIM Procedure
             Resubstitution Summary using Linear Discriminant Function

             Number of Observations and Percent Classified into group

             From group              A            B          Total

                         A          48            2            50
                                  96.00         4.00       100.00

                         B           1           49            50
                                   2.00        98.00       100.00

                   Total           49           51           100
                                  49.00        51.00       100.00

             Priors              0.5          0.5

                        Error Count Estimates for group

                                    A            B          Total

             Rate                0.0400       0.0200       0.0300
             Priors              0.5000       0.5000


             Cross-validation Summary using Linear Discriminant Function

             Number of Observations and Percent Classified into group

             From group              A            B          Total

                         A          47            3            50
                                  96.00         4.00       100.00

                         B           2           48            50
                                   2.00        98.00       100.00

                   Total           49           51           100
                                  49.00        51.00       100.00

             Priors              0.5          0.5
                        Error Count Estimates for group

                                    A            B          Total

             Rate                0.0600       0.0400       0.0500
             Priors              0.5000       0.5000
```

The two highlighted rows contain classification errors for the two groups and the overall classification error. The first highlighted row is for errors not corrected for bias, and the second highlighted row contains bias-corrected classification errors based on the jackknife procedure (from the CROSSVALIDATE option). The following SAS statements keep reading the output file until SAS encounters the word Rate. Then it inputs the three numerical variables after the word Rate as the Group 1 error rate (DAG1_ERR), the Group 2 error rate (DAG2_ERR), and the overall error rate (DA_ERR).

```
        INPUT WORD1 $ @;
    IF WORD1='Rate' THEN DO;
            INPUT DAG1_ERR DAG2_ERR DA_ERR;
            KEEP DAG1_ERR DAG2_ERR DA_ERR;
            OUTPUT;
    END;
```

From the PROC DISCRIM output for each sample, two cases will be read in. The first case is for error rates not corrected for bias, and the second case is for error rates corrected for bias based on the jackknife procedure. We only want to keep the second case of bias-corrected error rates, and this is accomplished by the following SAS statements:

```
DATA PDAERROR; SET PDAERROR;      * keep the jackknifed errors only;
N=_N_;
IF N=2;   DROP N;
RUN;
```

Once the bias-corrected classification error rates from PROC DISCRIM are obtained, a similar programming sequence is used for obtaining the classification error rates from the PROC LOGISTIC analysis. First, the PROC LOGISTIC analysis is done, and the output is directed to an external file in ASCII format (i.e., text file). This external file is then read in to SAS to extract the classification error rates respectively for the two groups, as well as the overall classification error rate. The task is accomplished by the following SAS statements:

```
* from the external file containing output from PROC LOGISTIC;
 * read in the following:
        (a) overall correct classification rate (LRRATE),
        (b) GROUP 1 correct classification rate (G1RATE),
        (c) GROUP 2 correct classification rate (G2RATE);
 * construct and keep the classification error rates for
        (i) GROUP 1, (ii) GROUP 2, and (iii) overall error rate;

DATA LRERROR; INFILE NEWOUT;
  INPUT PRIOR $ @;
    IF PRIOR='0.500' THEN DO;
      INPUT V1 V2 V3 V4 LRRATE G1RATE G2RATE;
            LRG1_ERR=1-G1RATE/100;
            LRG2_ERR=1-G2RATE/100;
            LR_ERR=1-LRRATE/100;
      KEEP LRG1_ERR LRG2_ERR LR_ERR;
      OUTPUT;
    END;
```

To understand how the SAS statements extract the classification error rates of interest, we need to take a look at the structure of the relevant section of PROC LOGISTIC output, as follows:

Output 7.3b *Partial Output from PROC LOGISTIC*

	Classification Table								
	Correct		Incorrect			Percentages			
Prob		Non-		Non-		Sensi-	Speci-	False	False
Level	Event	Event	Event	Event	Correct	tivity	ficity	POS	NEG
0.500	47	48	2	3	**95.0**	**94.0**	**96.0**	4.1	5.9

In the above, the three highlighted numbers are i) the overall correct classification rate for the two groups combined, ii) the correct classification rate for Group 1 (the modeled group in PROC LOGISTIC, also referred to as EVENT), and iii) the correct classification rate for Group 2 (also referred to as NON-EVENT). In other words, SENSITIVITY represents the correct classification rate for the modeled group (EVENT), while SPECIFICITY represents the correct classification rate for the other group (NON-EVENT). All the correct classification rates are expressed as percentages. Classification error rates can easily be constructed based on these correct classification rates. The SAS statements above read in the three correct classification rates (LRRATE, G1RATE, G2RATE) from the external file containing PROC LOGISTIC output, and construct three classification error rates (LRG1_ERR, LRG2_ERR, LR_ERR).

Finally, for each sample, the classification error rates from linear discriminant function analysis (PDA) and logistic regression analysis (LR) are merged into one temporary SAS data set (PDA_LR), and the relevant Monte Carlo study design information is added to the data (sample size N, equal/unequal covariance matrices). The data are then appended to an external SAS file on disk for later use (PDA_LR.RESULTS), as accomplished by the following SAS statements:

```
* merge error rates from PDA and LR;
* add simulation study design information;
* append the results from each sample to SAS file "RESULTS";

DATA PDA_LR;
  MERGE PDAERROR LRERROR;
  N=&N; IF &A=1 THEN COV='EQUAL'; ELSE IF &A=2 THEN COV='NO_EQ';
PROC APPEND BASE=PDA_LR.RESULTS FORCE;
     RUN;
```

By this time, the simulation process for each random sample is complete, and all the DO loops in the program, as well as the PDA_LR macro, are brought to a close. Once the PDA_LR macro is run, the results can be analyzed by routine SAS procedures similar to the following:

```
DATA A; SET PDA_LR.RESULTS;
PROC SORT; BY COV N;
PROC MEANS MEAN STD MIN MAX; BY COV N;
  VAR DAG1_ERR LRG1_ERR DAG2_ERR LRG2_ERR DA_ERR LR_ERR;
TITLE1 'Average Classification Error Rates';
TITLE2 'Comparison of Discriminant Analysis and Logistic Regression';
TITLE3 'For GROUP 1, GROUP 2, and Overall';
RUN;
```

7.3.6 Selected Results from Program 7.3

Based on one execution of Program 7.3 with 1,000 replications in each cell condition, part of the results are presented in the following table. It is observed that when the two groups have equal covariance matrices, there is little difference between PDA and LR in their classification error rates. When the groups have unequal covariance matrices, PDA produces small classification error rates (range of .02-.03) for the group with the smaller covariance matrix, but substantially larger classification error rates (range of .16-.17) for the group with the larger covariance matrix. Although LR also has this tendency, its classification error rates are more evenly distributed between the two groups (ranges of .06-.08 and .11-.12, respectively, for two groups). Of course, in a real Monte Carlo study, more detailed and sophisticated analyses should be conducted, as seen in the article by Fan and Wang (1999) that focuses on similar issues.

Table 7.5 *PDA and LR Classification Error Rates for Group 1, Group 2, and Combined*

		Combined Sample Size			
	Method	60	100	200	400
Equal Σ					
Group 1 or 2	PDA	11 (06)	10 (04)	10 (03)	10 (02)
	LR	11 (05)	11 (04)	10 (03)	10 (02)
Overall	PDA	11 (04)	10 (03)	10 (02)	10 (02)
	LR	11 (04)	11 (03)	10 (02)	10 (02)
Unequal Σ					
Group 1 with	PDA	03 (03)	02 (02)	02 (02)	02 (01)
Smaller Σ	LR	08 (04)	07 (03)	06 (02)	06 (02)
Group 2 with	PDA	17 (07)	16 (05)	16 (03)	16 (02)
Larger Σ	LR	12 (05)	11 (04)	11 (03)	11 (02)
Overall	PDA	10 (04)	09 (03)	09 (02)	09 (01)
	LR	10 (04)	09 (03)	08 (02)	08 (01)

Note: Each entry is the mean classification error rate (standard deviation in parentheses) based on the classification error rates of 1,000 samples. The second place decimal point is omitted.

7.4 Summary

This chapter is a natural extension of Chapter 6. In Chapter 6, we presented Monte Carlo study examples involving some basic statistical techniques. In this chapter, we provided two complete Monte Carlo examples involving more complicated statistical techniques. These are real research examples involving real analytical issues. In these two examples, we provided the background for each Monte Carlo study, as well as detailed discussion about study designs and simulated data conditions. Further, these examples integrated the procedures presented in previous chapters. We hope that this chapter, together with Chapter 6, will provide the foundation for those interested in conducting Monte Carlo studies involving these and other statistical techniques.

7.5 References

Bagozzi, R. P., C. Fornell, and D. F. Larcker. 1981. "Canonical Correlation Analysis as a Special Case of Structural Relations Model." *Multivariate Behavioral Research* 16:437-454.

Baldwin, B. 1989. "A Primer in the Use and Interpretation of Structural Equation Models." *Measurement and Evaluation in Counseling and Development* 22:100-112.

Barón, A. E. 1991. "Misclassification among Methods Used for Multiple Group Discrimination: The Effects of Distributional Properties." *Statistics in Medicine* 10:757-766.

Bayne, C. K., J. J. Beauchamp, V. E. Kane, and G. P. McCabe. 1983. "Assessment of Fisher and Logistic Linear and Quadratic Discrimination Models." *Computational Statistics and Data Analysis* 1:257-273.

Bentler, P. M. 1992. *EQS Structural Equations Program Manual*. Los Angeles: BMDP Statistical Software.

Bentler, P. M. 1994. "Foreword." In B. M. Byrne, *Structural Equation Modeling with EQS and EQS/Windows*. Newbury Park, CA: Sage Publications.

Bollen, K. A., and J. S. Long. 1993. "Introduction." In *Testing Structural Equation Models*, ed. K. A. Bollen and J. S. Long. Newbury Park, CA: Sage Publications.

Byrne, B. M. 1994. Structural Equation Modeling with EQS and EQS/Windows: Basic Concepts, Applications, and Programming. Newbury Park, CA: Sage Publications.

Cleary, P. D., and R. Angel. 1984. "The Analysis of Relationships Involving Dichotomous Dependent Variables." *Journal of Health and Social Behavior* 25:334-348.

Cox, D. R., and E. J. Snell. 1989. *The Analysis of Binary Data*. 2d ed. London: Chapman and Hall.

Dattalo, P. 1994. "A Comparison of Discriminant Analysis and Logistic Regression." *Journal of Social Service Research* 19:121-144.

Dey, E. L., and A. W. Astin. 1993. "Statistical Alternatives for Studying College Student Retention: A Comparative Analysis of Logit, Probit, and Linear Regression." *Research in Higher Education* 34:569-581.

Efron, B. 1975. "The Efficiency of Logistic Regression Compared to Normal Discriminant Analysis." *Journal of the American Statistical Association* 70:892-898.

Fan, X. 1996. "Structural Equation Modeling and Canonical Correlation Analysis: What Do They Have in Common?" *Structural Equation Modeling: A Multidisciplinary Journal* 4:64-78.

Fan, X., and L. Wang. 1998. "Effects of Potential Confounding Factors on Fit Indices and Parameter Estimates for True and Misspecified SEM Models." *Educational and Psychological Measurement* 58:699-733.

Fan, X., and L. Wang. 1999. "Comparing Logistic Regression with Linear Discriminant Analysis in Their Classification Accuracy." *Journal of Experimental Education* 67:265-286.

Fraser, M. W., J. M. Jensen, D. Kiefer, and C. Popuang. 1994. "Statistical Methods for the Analysis of Critical Events." *Social Work Research* 18(3):163-177.

Gerbing, D. W., and J. C. Anderson. 1993. "Monte Carlo Evaluations of Goodness-of-Fit Indices for Structural Equation Models." In *Testing Structural Equation Models*, ed. K. A. Bollen and J. S. Long, 40-65. Newbury Park, CA: Sage Publications.

Glass, G. V., and K. D. Hopkins. 1996. *Statistical Methods in Education and Psychology.* 3d ed. Boston: Allyn and Bacon.

Harrell, F. E., Jr., and K. L. Lee. 1985. "A Comparison of the Discrimination of Discriminant Analysis and Logistic Regression under Multivariate Normality." In *Biostatistics: Statistics in Biomedical, Public Health and Environmental Sciences*, ed. P. K. Sen, 333-343. Amsterdam: North Holland.

Huberty, C. J. 1994. *Applied Discriminant Analysis.* New York: Wiley.

James, L. R., S. A. Mulaik, and J. M. Brett. 1982. *Causal Analysis: Models, Assumptions, and Data.* Beverly Hills, CA: Sage Publications.

Johnson, B., and S. S. Seshia. 1992. "Discriminant Analysis When All Variables Are Ordered." *Statistics in Medicine* 11:1023-1032.

Johnson, R. A., and D. W. Wichern. 1988. *Applied Multivariate Statistical Analysis.* 2d ed. Englewood Cliffs, NJ: Prentice Hall.

Jöreskog, K. G., and D. Sörbom. 1989. *LISREL 7: A Guide to the Program and Applications.* 2d ed. Chicago: SPSS Inc.

Knoke, J. D. 1982. "Discriminant Analysis with Discrete and Continuous Variables." *Biometrics* 38:191-200.

Lachenbruch, P. A. 1967. "An Almost Unbiased Method of Obtaining Confidence Intervals for the Probability of Misclassification in Discriminant Analysis." *Biometrics* 23:639-645.

Loehlin, J. C. 1992. *Latent Variable Models: An Introduction to Factor, Path, and Structural Analysis.* Hillsdale, NJ: Lawrence Erlbaum Associates.

McDonald, R. P. 1989. "An Index of Goodness-of-Fit Based on Noncentrality." *Journal of Classification* 6:97-103.

Meshbane, A., and J. D. Morris. "Predictive Discriminant Analysis versus Logistic Regression in Two-Group Classification Problems." Paper presented at the annual meeting of the American Educational Research Association, New York, April 1996 (ERIC Documentation Reproduction Services No. ED 400 280).

Mulaik, S. A., L. R. James, J. Van Alstine, N. Bennett, S. Lind, and C. D. Stillwell. 1989. "An Evaluation of Goodness of Fit Indices for Structural Equation Models." *Psychological Bulletin* 105:430-445.

Neter, J., W. Wasserman, and M. H. Kutner. 1989. *Applied Linear Regression Models.* 2d ed. Boston: Irwin.

Pedhazur, E. J., and L. P. Schmelkin. 1991. *Measurement, Design, and Analysis: An Integrated Approach.* Hillsdale, NJ: Lawrence Erlbaum Associates.

Press, S. J., and S. Wilson. 1978. "Choosing between Logistic Regression and Discriminant Analysis." *Journal of the American Statistical Association* 73:699-705.

SAS Institute Inc. 1997. SAS/STAT Software: Changes and Enhancements through Release 6.12. Cary, NC: SAS Institute Inc.

Steiger, J. H. 1990. "Structural Model Evaluation and Modification: An Interval Estimation Approach." *Multivariate Behavioral Research* 25:173-180.

Steiger, J. H., and J. C. Lind. 1980. "Statistically Based Tests for the Number of Common Factors." Paper presented at the annual meeting of the Psychometric Society, Iowa City, IA.

Stevens, J. 1996. *Applied Multivariate Statistics for the Social Sciences.* 3d ed. Mahwah, NJ: Lawrence Erlbaum Associates.

Tabachnick, B. G., and L. S. Fidell. 1996. *Using Multivariate Statistics.* 3d ed. New York: HarperCollins College Publishers.

Thompson, B., and L. G. Daniel. 1996. "Factor Analytic Evidence for the Construct Validity of Scores: An Historical Overview and Some Guidelines." *Educational and Psychological Measurement* 56: 213-224.

Wheaton, D. E., B. Muthén, D. F. Alwin, and G. F. Summers. 1977. "Assessing Reliability and Stability in Panel Models." In *Sociological Methodology,* ed. D. R. Heise, 84-136. San Francisco: Jossey-Bass.

Wilson, R. L., and B. C. Hardgrave. 1995. "Predicting Graduate Student Success in an MBA Program: Regression versus Classification." *Educational and Psychological Measurement* 55:186-195.

Yarnold, P. R., L. A. Hart, and R. C. Soltysik. 1994. "Optimizing the Classification Performance of Logistic Regression and Fisher's Discriminant Analyses." *Educational and Psychological Measurement* 54:73-85.

Chapter 8 Examples for Monte Carlo Simulation in Finance: Estimating Default Risk and Value-at-Risk

8.1 Introduction

Monte Carlo techniques are particularly useful when the function in question is the probability distribution of outcomes for a system whose properties make analytic or numeric solutions impractical. Such situations often arise in financial applications in which the distribution of interest is an aggregation of outcomes that may be correlated, that are characterized by empirical distributions with no functional representation, or both. They also arise in the pricing of options or other derivatives, whose current value depends on the distribution of future values for the underlying security. Monte Carlo methods provide a rich, computationally efficient framework for estimating the distribution of future values for an asset, yielding a simple options pricing formula.

In these probability applications, Monte Carlo methods involve setting up a mechanism that approximates the system in question and links the stochastic aspects of the system to random number generators whose properties can be controlled. Stimulating the system with the required number of random impulses produces a simulated outcome that should represent a plausible, feasible, potential realization of the system. By repeating this a large number of times, the set of simulated outcomes will trace out the true distribution of potential outcomes, and the frequency of these simulated outcomes will allow us to assign approximate probability measures to each potential outcome.

For example, the calculation of Value-at-Risk (VaR) centers around the simulation of losses over time for a portfolio of risky assets.[1] Simulation is key in this context, because the VaR concept relates to the *distribution* of potential future losses — a distribution which may or may not bear a very close resemblance to a known distribution function familiar to us from probability theory and statistics. Even when the loss distributions of portfolio components are known distributions such as the Gaussian (normal) distribution, correlations across portfolio components make analytic or numerical calculations of conditional probabilities virtually impossible. These conditional probabilities may be necessary for scenario analysis, or to determine how structural changes in the portfolio can affect VaR. By characterizing the distribution of portfolio returns through a Monte Carlo approach, we can obtain the values needed to calculate VaR, as well as the conditional probabilities necessary for scenario analysis.

The final step is straightforward, typically finding the appropriate quantile of the estimated distribution of losses. Therefore, most of our effort in VaR estimation, as with other Monte Carlo based applications, is absorbed in constructing an appropriate statistical model to approximate the system, and in creating an efficient procedure for generating the simulated responses.

Monte Carlo techniques are used in a wide variety of situations, giving rise to a wide range of approaches (Fisher, Nychka, & Zervos 1994; Frankfurter & Lamourex 1989; Gibson & Pritsker 2000; Jorion 1997; Picoult 1998). However, even with respect to a single well-specified situation, there is no accepted best way to conduct such simulations. Many subjective choices must be made. Usually, the analyst faces a tradeoff between computational efficiency, which recommends simplicity, and realism, which requires that the model contain every important aspect of the system under study. But simplicity can produce benefits beyond lowering the computer runtime. Understanding what the model is doing and not doing leads to greater confidence in the results. More complicated models may give the impression of greater "reality," but increased complexity may not change results appreciably, or worse, may simply add additional noise, either biasing the results, lowering our confidence in them, or both.

This chapter presents three examples of the use of Monte Carlo techniques in financial applications. In each case, we seek to obtain estimates of the distribution of an aggregate outcome deriving from a multivariate system. The first is a fairly simple case in which joint probabilities for correlated outcomes are estimated by simulation. Examples 2 and 3 consider VaR calculations for credit risk and market risk, respectively. These later introduce additional layers of complexity by including additional stochastic components and by decomposing asset price movements into correlated and uncorrelated components. The SAS programming code for these examples is presented, and some selected results are discussed.

---

[1] Such losses could be the result of changes in market conditions, credit events, or any set of events that can be characterized in probabilistic terms.

8.2 Example 1: Estimation of Default Risk

This section describes an approach to evaluating the default risk of holding companies for whom most, or all, of their income derives from the upstreaming of cash from subsidiaries in the form of dividends. We may need this default probability to price a loan to the holding company (holdco), or to assign a rating to its debt obligations.

In this example, the likelihood of a holdco default is defined as the likelihood that upstreamed cash will fall below the threshold necessary for the holdco to service its debts. Again, the holdco's assets consist entirely of a portfolio of cash flows coming from its subsidiaries. The likelihood of the total cash flow falling below the threshold can be decomposed into a set of conditional default probabilities associated with the complete set of outcomes for dividend payment/non-payment at the subsidiary level, multiplied by the likelihood of each specific outcome. Put another way, the likelihood that the holdco will default is the joint likelihood that a subset of subsidiaries will stop paying dividends, such that the combined value of dividends from still-paying subsidiaries falls below the above-mentioned threshold. The problem is complicated by the fact that the outcomes at the subsidiary level are not likely to be independent, but will exhibit some level of correlation. Because of this, even if we assumed that the relevant probability distributions were of a convenient form, the complexities involved in calculating the joint likelihoods for all possible outcomes would become overwhelming as the number of subsidiaries grew past three. A Monte Carlo technique provides an efficient alternative and can easily handle a realistic number of correlated subsidiary cash flows.

Using Monte Carlo simulation, we can avoid an analytic or numerical solution, and estimate the required joint probability using only a small set of information about the subsidiaries, and essentially one parameter describing the holdco. To make the example more concrete, consider the case of a utility holding company with seven subsidiaries. Six are power-producing operating companies (opcos) located in several states but in the same general region of the U.S., all with corporate bond ratings assigned by a public rating agency. Another subsidiary is an unregulated, unrated energy trading company. We will use numbers that are reasonable for the details of the example, but which are not intended to correspond to any specific company.

In spite of the computational complexity of the problem, it is fairly easy to write down an algebraic expression of what we want to calculate. The unconditional probability that the holdco defaults, $P(H^d)$, consists of the sum of conditional probabilities, $P(H^d_j)$, that the holdco defaults given that outcome j has occurred, times the probability that outcome j will occur, $P(O_j)$, where outcome j is a certain set of subsidiaries defaulting.

$$P(H^d) = \sum_j P(H^d_j)P(O_j) =$$

$$\sum_{i=1}^{7} P(H^d|O^d_i)P(O^d_i) + \sum_{i_1=1}^{7} \sum_{\substack{i_2=1 \\ i_2 \neq i_1}}^{7} P(H^d|\{O^d_{i_1},O^d_{i_2}\})P(\{O^d_{i_1},O^d_{i_2}\}) + \ldots +$$

$$P(H^d|\{O^d_1,O^d_2,\ldots,O^d_7\})P(\{O^d_1,O^d_2,\cdots,O^d_7\})$$

In our example with seven subsidiaries, we would need to calculate and sum 127 terms corresponding to the set of all possible outcomes of at least one subsidiary defaulting. For example, there are seven possible outcomes in which one, and only one, subsidiary stops paying dividends (the single-summation term in the previous equation). Not all of these outcomes are equally likely, nor do they affect the holdco in the same way. Another outcome is that all seven subsidiaries stop paying dividends. There is only one such outcome (the last term in the equation), and the probability that the holdco will default should reach a maximum in this case. The 127 terms in this equation can be thought of in terms of their associated number of non-paying subsidiaries as:

Number of subs not paying dividends	1	2	3	4	5	6	7
Number of terms	7	21	35	35	21	7	1

The first input requirement is a set of unconditional probabilities for cash-flow stoppage of each subsidiary, and a magnitude measure for the current stream of dividends being paid out. The amount of the dividend flow from each subsidiary can be found in the holdco's financial statements. We can also estimate the default threshold from leverage measures derived from the holdco's balance sheet. For analytical convenience, we convert both of these into proportional measures, i.e., each subsidiary provides x% of the upstreamed cash flow, and the holdco will default if y% of this cash flow is cut off. Example values are presented under the DIVIDEND (%) heading in Table 8.1.

We can estimate the unconditional probability of cash-flow stoppage from each rated subsidiary from rating migration and default frequency information provided by the major rating agencies. Or, if internal risk scores are used, we will need comparable estimates of migration and default risk. In our example, we need migration rate estimates as well as default probabilities to obtain the likelihood of cash-flow stoppage, since for regulated utilities, dividend payout is likely to stop well before default on debt securities. In fact, regulators are likely to require that dividend payments stop if the opco's debt rating falls into the single-B range (or equivalent). We can use the opcos' current ratings and empirical transition frequencies to obtain estimates of the probability that each opco will be downgraded to B1 (or equivalent) or lower within the next twelve months. As this is the probability that no cash is upstreamed, we denote it as P(NC), and the appropriate values are shown in Table 8.1.

Table 8.1 *Subsidiary Input Information*

SUBSIDIARY	RATING	P(NC)	DIVIDEND (%)
1	Baa3	0.05	0.129630
2	Baa3	0.05	0.060847
3	Ba1	0.10	0.243386
4	Baa3	0.05	0.034392
5	Baa3	0.05	0.238095
6	Not Rated	0.20	0.026455
7	Ba1	0.01	0.267196

In this case, we assumed that once a regulated utility was downgraded to a B1 or lower, it would stop paying dividends, either voluntarily or at the insistence of regulators. Probabilities for downgrades to this level can be obtained for each rated subsidiary using a one-year rating-migration matrix. The values in Table 8.1 are reasonable approximations. For the unrated subsidiary in this example, we simply guessed at the probability that no dividends would be paid during any future one-year period.

The next required input is a correlation matrix, which describes the potential for correlated outcomes, e.g., more than one subsidiary stopping its dividend payments in the same year. An example is shown in Table 8.2. In this case, correlations were assumed to be a significant 10% across all electricity-producing operating companies (subs 1-5 & 7), since they were operating in the same general region of the country, and were assumed to zero between these operating companies and sub 6, the unrated energy trading company.

The only other required input is a threshold value for the proportion of the expected dividend flow to the holdco that can be cut off without precipitating a holdco default. This will be discussed in more detail below.

Table 8.2 *Subsidiary Default Correlation Matrix*

	Sub1	Sub2	Sub3	Sub4	Sub5	Sub6	Sub7
Sub1	**1.0**	0.1	0.1	0.1	0.1	**0.0**	0.1
Sub2	0.1	**1.0**	0.1	0.1	0.1	**0.0**	0.1
Sub3	0.1	0.1	**1.0**	0.1	0.1	**0.0**	0.1
Sub4	0.1	0.1	0.1	**1.0**	0.1	**0.0**	0.1
Sub5	0.1	0.1	0.1	0.1	**1.0**	**0.0**	0.1
Sub6	**0.0**	**0.0**	**0.0**	**0.0**	**0.0**	**1.0**	**0.0**
Sub7	0.1	0.1	0.1	0.1	0.1	**0.0**	**1.0**

The P(NC) information required as an input, combined with the correlation information, allows us to determine the likelihood of each of these 127 outcomes. The DIVIDEND values tell us the extent that the dividend flow will be impaired under each of the 127 possible outcomes, and finally, the holdco threshold value determines which outcomes will produce a holdco default and which will not. By simulating a very large number of outcomes that are consistent with our inputs, we can simply use the frequency that the holdco default threshold is exceeded as an estimate of the default likelihood of the holdco, and finally, we can map this into a risk rating.

Our Monte Carlo technique is a simple latent variable model. Program 8.1 (Macro %EX1) consists of two main parts. The first generates a large number of correlated random standard normal variables, with the correlation structure defined by our correlation input matrix. Embedded in %EX1 is a call to macro %RMNC described in Chapter 4, which produces a file (TEMP) with one variable for each sub and as many observations as the number of simulations. Each variable represents a "latent" credit quality variable for a sub, and the macro %RMNC ensures that the entire set of latent variable values conforms to the correlation structure contained in our pre-specified correlation matrix. For each sub, if the value of the latent variable exceeds its cutoff, it indicates a stoppage of dividend payment from that sub.

The second main part is a DATA step, which executes the simulation on each set of random numbers given in file TEMP. The DATA step first maps the P(NC) values for each sub onto the standard normal function (because the default–non-default outcome of a sub is simulated by standard normal values), and then performs the simulation by reading file TEMP one observation at a time, comparing the standard normal random numbers to the cutoff values and summarizing the stopped dividends from the defaulting subs (variable DIVLOSS). If the total exceeds the threshold (variable DEFPOINT), then the macro flags the observation as a default. The number of defaults divided by the number of simulations is what we want: an estimate of the default probability for the holdco. This value is provided as the MEAN statistic of variable DEFAULT in PROC MEANS.

Program 8.1 *Macro (%EX1) for Simulating Default Risk for a Diversified Holding Company*

```
/**************************************************************************/
/* Macro EX1 calculates the default probability of a holding company.   */
/*                                                                      */
/* Parameters                                                           */
/* PARM       the name of a special file of the default probabilities, the */
/*            dividend payments and the default correlation matrix of the */
/*            subsidiaries. It is similar to a _TYPE_=CORR file. The first */
/*            row corresponds to the default probabilities of the       */
/*            subsidiaries, the second to the dividend payments of the  */
/*            subsidiaries and the rest forms the lower half of the     */
/*            correlation matrix of the subsidiaries' default rates. See the */
/*            example below.                                            */
/* NSUBS      the number of subsidiaries.                               */
/* DEFPOINT   percent of dividend over which default happens.           */
/* NSIMS      number of simulations.                                    */
/* OUT        name of the output data set, which contains the default flag */
/*            and the lost dividend.                                    */
/*                                                                      */
/* Example for creating an input file                                   */
/*                                                                      */
/* DATA SIMPAR;                                                         */
/*      INPUT _NAME_ $ _TYPE_ $ SUB1-SUB7;                              */
/*      CARDS;                                                          */
/*      PNC   0.05     0.05     0.10     0.05     0.05     0.20     0.01 */
/* .    DIV   0.129630 0.060847 0.243386 0.034392 0.238095 0.026455 0.267196 */
/* SUB1 CORR  1.00     .        .        .        .        .        .    */
/* SUB2 CORR  0.10     1.00     .        .        .        .        .    */
/* SUB3 CORR  0.10     0.10     1.00     .        .        .        .    */
/* SUB4 CORR  0.10     0.10     0.10     1.00     .        .        .    */
/* SUB5 CORR  0.10     0.10     0.10     0.10     1.00     .        .    */
/* SUB6 CORR  0.00     0.00     0.00     0.00     0.00     1.00     .    */
/* SUB7 CORR  0.10     0.10     0.10     0.10     0.10     0.00     1.00 */
/* ;                                                                    */
/*      RUN;                                                            */
/**************************************************************************/

%MACRO EX1(PARM=,NSUBS=,DEFPOINT=,NSIMS=,OUT=,SEED=123);

   /* create a file for generating the normally distributed correlated   */
   /* random numbers for the probabilities of subsidiary defaults. This  */
   /* file will be input into macro %RMNC.                              */

   DATA TEMP(TYPE=CORR DROP=I);
        SET &PARM;
        ARRAY SUB(&NSUBS) SUB1-SUB&NSUBS;
        IF _N_=1 THEN DO;        * add mean of zero for each subsidiary;
                      DO I=1 TO &NSUBS;
                         SUB(I)=0;
                      END;
```

```
                            _TYPE_='MEAN'; OUTPUT;

                            /* add standard deviation of one for each subsidiary. */

                            DO I=1 TO &NSUBS;
                               SUB(I)=1;
                            END;
                            _TYPE_='STD'; OUTPUT;

                            /* add number of simulations for each subsidiary. */

                            DO I=1 TO &NSUBS;
                               SUB(I)=&NSIMS;
                            END;
                            _TYPE_='N'; OUTPUT;
                    END;
         IF _TYPE_='CORR' THEN OUTPUT;
      RUN;

/* call macro %RMNC to generate correlated, normally distributed */
/* random numbers to simulate the defaults of the subsidiaries.  */

   %RMNC(DATA=TEMP,OUT=PROBS,SEED=&SEED)

   /* data step of the simulation */

   DATA &OUT;
      ARRAY PNC(&NSUBS) PNC1-PNC&NSUBS;    * array of default probabilities ;
      ARRAY DIV(&NSUBS) DIV1-DIV&NSUBS;    * array of dividends ;
      ARRAY SUB(&NSUBS) SUB1-SUB&NSUBS;

      /* load the default probability thresholds and the dividend */
      /* payments of all subsidiaries into the arrays above.      */

      DO WHILE (NOT EOFPARM);
         SET &PARM END=EOFPARM;
         IF _TYPE_='PNC' THEN DO; DO I=1 TO &NSUBS;

                                  /* transform the probability into  */
                                  /* a standard normal distribution. */

                                  PNC(I)=PROBIT(SUB(I));
                            END;
                         END;
         IF _TYPE_='DIV' THEN DO; DO I=1 TO &NSUBS;
                                  DIV(I)=SUB(I);
                            END;
                         END;
      END;

      /* go through each set of default probabilities generated above. */

      DO WHILE (NOT EOFSIM);
         SET PROBS END=EOFSIM;
         DIVLOSS=0;
         DO I=1 TO &NSUBS;

            /* does a subsidiary default? If it does, add its forgone */
            /* dividend to the losses (variable DIVLOSS).             */

            IF SUB(I)<PNC(I) THEN DIVLOSS=DIVLOSS+DIV(I);
         END;

         /* does the dividend loss exceed the default point? */
         /* if yes, mark this draw as 'default'.             */

         IF DIVLOSS>&DEFPOINT THEN DEFAULT=1;
                              ELSE DEFAULT=0;
         OUTPUT;
      END;
      STOP;
```

```
    KEEP DEFAULT DIVLOSS;
    RUN;

/* the default rate (the mean statistic of variable DEFAULT) and the */
/* characteristics of the dividend losses (whether or not the draw    */
/* results a default) are calculated by PROC MEANS.                   */

PROC MEANS DATA=&OUT N MEAN STD MIN MAX;
    VAR DEFAULT DIVLOSS;
    RUN;
%MEND;
```

The threshold for the holdco is expressed as the proportion of upstreamed dividends that it can forgo without defaulting. The threshold may depend on the amount of cash it has on hand relative to its debt service burden, but may also depend on other factors. It is important to point out that there is a key relationship between this threshold value and the effect of correlation among the subsidiaries. The relationship is this: correlation will not affect the mean value of stopped dividends for a large sample of draws. Correlation will only increase or decrease the variance of the observed (simulated) values. Thus, if the threshold for holdco default is equal to the mean value of stopped dividends, the holdco default probability will be indifferent to changes in the assumed correlation structure. However, if the threshold is more extreme (i.e., far from the mean value)—say a 10% reduction in dividend payouts, or a 90% reduction in dividend payouts—then the correlation structure will affect the estimated holdco default probability more strongly.

Program 8.2 presents an example of using Program 8.1 (macro %EX1) to run a simulation of 20,000 draws using the correlation matrix presented in Table 8.2 and a cutoff threshold of 35%. That is, the holdco is assumed to default if more than 35% of its dividend income is cut off. This is well above the mean value of 5.5% that results from the ratings, and consequent downgrade probabilities of the subsidiaries; hence, the correlation structure is affecting the results. The distribution of dividend stoppage proportions is presented in Output 8.1. As is evident from the plot, the most likely outcome is no dividend stoppage. However, given our threshold of 35%, there is a 1.8% chance that the dividend stoppage will be sufficiently large to precipitate a holdco default. We can translate this back into a debt rating using Moody's historical one-year default frequencies. Applying some smoothing to Moody's reported average one-year default rates, we can associate the 1.8% default likelihood with a Ba2 corporate bond rating.

Program 8.2 Using Program 8.1 (Macro %EX1)

```
DATA SIMPAR;
    INPUT _NAME_ $ _TYPE_ $ SUB1-SUB7;
    CARDS;
    PNC  0.05     0.05     0.10     0.05     0.05     0.20     0.01
.   DIV  0.129630 0.060847 0.243386 0.034392 0.238095 0.026455 0.267196
SUB1 CORR 1.00     .        .        .        .        .        .
SUB2 CORR 0.10     1.00     .        .        .        .        .
SUB3 CORR 0.10     0.10     1.00     .        .        .        .
SUB4 CORR 0.10     0.10     0.10     1.00     .        .        .
SUB5 CORR 0.10     0.10     0.10     0.10     1.00     .        .
SUB6 CORR 0.00     0.00     0.00     0.00     0.00     1.00     .
SUB7 CORR 0.10     0.10     0.10     0.10     0.10     0.00     1.00
;
    RUN;
%EX1(PARM=SIMPAR,NSUBS=7,DEFPOINT=0.035,NSIMS=20000,OUT=A,SEED=123)
```

Output 8.1
Average
and
Distribution
of Dividend
Stoppage
Proportions

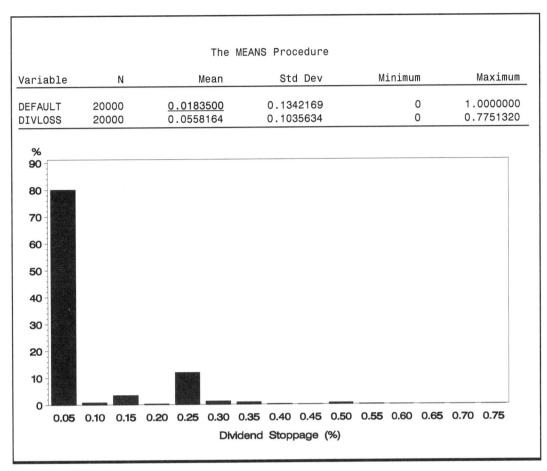

The MEANS Procedure

Variable	N	Mean	Std Dev	Minimum	Maximum
DEFAULT	20000	<u>0.0183500</u>	0.1342169	0	1.0000000
DIVLOSS	20000	0.0558164	0.1035634	0	0.7751320

In this example, we needed to characterize the distribution of potential dividend losses to the holdco to calculate the probability that these losses would exceed a certain threshold. This type of calculation, and the Monte Carlo techniques used to obtain solutions, arise in a wide range of similar situations in finance, broadly known as Value-at-Risk (VaR) problems. The next two sections treat two types of VaR problems, using methods closely resembling those applied in this example.

8.3 Example 2: VaR Estimation for Credit Risk

VaR refers to the calculation of the distribution of future losses (gains) on a portfolio of assets. It is always calculated with respect to a specific time horizon. That is, losses are accumulated over the period $t_0 \rightarrow T$, where T is the horizon and t_0 is usually the present. This leads to a methodological division; each simulation of portfolio losses may involve a single draw at the time horizon specified, or may be composed of a sequence of draws in which losses are accumulated over intermediate time horizons. VaR calculations for market risk are frequently directed to relatively short time horizons, which suggests that the single-draw approach may be appropriate. Such an example is presented in section 8.4. For longer horizons, where there is more overall uncertainty, a multi-period approach, which allows losses to accumulate in different ways, may be able to provide a richer description of the underlying dynamics. This is more common for credit risk VaR applications.

In a credit risk VaR context, we use Monte Carlo methods to model losses from a set of pure credit events—e.g., defaults on bonds, loans, or other contractual exposures to risky obligors. Such calculations are important for banks with loan portfolios, as well as for financial institutions with bond, swap, and other derivative exposures, where expected losses are a function of the counterparty's future creditworthiness, and for managed fixed income funds such as CLOs and CBOs whose own credit ratings are closely tied to the VaR from credit events. Because such portfolios are typically held and managed over relatively long periods of time, VaR calculations may be directed toward longer time horizons than is usually the case for market-risk VaR; often, multi-year time horizons are relevant. In this example, we focus on a multi-year loss distribution, generated by a series of simulated annual portfolio changes.

For this type of Monte Carlo simulation, credit movements are generally defined with respect to a manageable number of subsets of the portfolio as opposed to each individual exposure. The most common subsetting scheme is by credit quality—e.g., agency or internal ratings (Carey & Hrcay 2001). Losses are driven by default rates and recovery rates (or loss-in-the-event-of-default: LIED), which are themselves driven by the distribution of ratings in the portfolio. Thus, the simulation needs to incorporate both the stochastic nature of default rates year-to-year, and the stochastic rating migrations that affect the evolution of the distribution of ratings within the portfolio. In the simplest approach, default rates and migration rates are applied on a rating-by-rating basis, while LIED probabilities are applied to all defaulting credits. One benefit of this type of approach is that, if detailed data are not available from internal sources, we can use historical statistics published by rating agencies for default frequencies, LIED rates, and migration rates to characterize the portfolio dynamics on which we base our Monte Carlo procedure.

As is typical in VaR applications, we seek to characterize the distribution of future losses to obtain a cutoff loss value that is unlikely to be exceeded, with a specified confidence level, say 95%. To obtain an estimate of the future distribution of losses, our VaR calculations will consist of a set of multi-year portfolio simulations. Each simulation will consist of a set of iterations on a vector (set) of exposures, with each iteration corresponding to a one-year evolution of the portfolio.

We identify exposures by rating and default/non-default status only. Initially, and for each iteration, this vector of exposures will define the portfolio. Each iteration will itself consist of three steps. First, we obtain a default component of the obligor pool by applying the one-year default probability for each rating category. Secondly, we apply a set of LIED rates to the default component to obtain a loss amount/loss rate for this iteration. Finally, we allow non-defaulting obligors to experience stochastic rating changes based on a set of historical migration frequencies. This completes one iteration and produces a new distribution of ratings for the obligors that have not exited the portfolio through default. This basic portfolio evolution scheme is diagrammed in Figure 8.1.

Figure 8.1 *Calculation of One Portfolio Iteration*

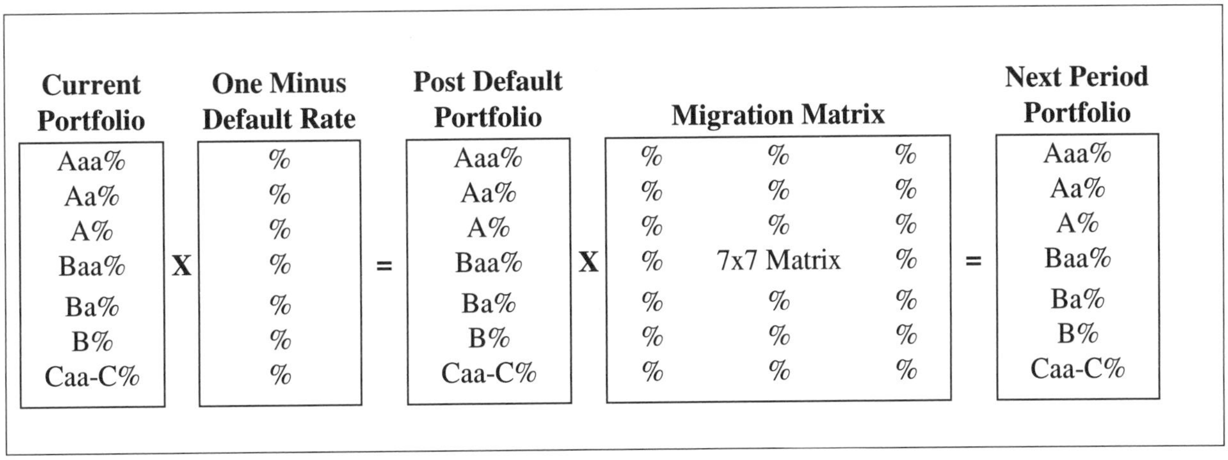

Current Portfolio		One Minus Default Rate		Post Default Portfolio		Migration Matrix				Next Period Portfolio
Aaa%		%		Aaa%		%	%	%		Aaa%
Aa%		%		Aa%		%	%	%		Aa%
A%		%		A%		%	%	%		A%
Baa%	X	%	=	Baa%	X	%	7x7 Matrix	%	=	Baa%
Ba%		%		Ba%		%	%	%		Ba%
B%		%		B%		%	%	%		B%
Caa-C%		%		Caa-C%		%	%	%		Caa-C%

Importantly, using this approach we can calculate expected losses directly for any forward time horizon without employing any Monte Carlo simulations. All we need are the default, loss, and migration frequencies, and we can obtain the expected value of losses by straight multiplication and subtraction. However, as noted above, for VaR calculations we need to estimate the entire distribution of loss rates for the portfolio, not just the expected value. To do this we will need more than the average default, loss, and migration frequencies, which are after all, just expected values.

We would also like to endow the system with a macroeconomic component to reflect changes in the general credit cycle. One approach involves the inclusion in our simulation of a single random variable that defines the state of the credit cycle, or "default intensity." Many variations on this theme have been used by academics and practitioners (Duffie & Singleton 1998). Here we consider a two-state macroeconomic environment with stochastic regime switching. Figure 8.2 shows Moody's speculative-grade corporate bond default rates (Keenan, Hamilton, & Bethault 2000), monthly from 1970 to 2000, which characterizes the type of credit cycle variation we would like to embed in our Monte Carlo simulation. The mean default rate for this period is 3.49%, with three distinct high-default episodes that drove the rate above 6.0% over this 30-year period. More remotely, the Great Depression produced another such high-default episode, extending this pattern back as far as data permit.

Figure 8.2 *Moody's Speculative-Grade Default Rate, 1970-2000*

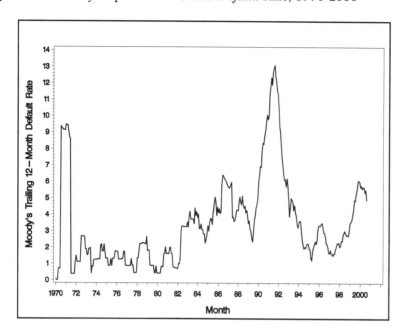

In our simple regime-switching model, we seek to distinguish between "normal" periods and "high-default" periods, and apply default probabilities and migration frequencies consistent with the observed frequencies in those periods. For expository purposes, we calculated migration frequencies and default rates for two periods, 1972-1996 (normal period), and 1989-1992 (high-default period). By cutting off the 1970-71 "railroad default" episode and the 1997-98 "Asia crisis" episode, our normal period is a continuous period that averages the low-default 1970s with the high-default late 1980s and early 1990s. The high-default period pulls out just the "junk-bond collapse" episode, which is also continuous. These choices, while arbitrary, seem reasonable from a broad historical perspective and prevent us from having to splice together data from disjoint periods. The default and migration frequencies associated with these two "regimes" are presented in Table 8.3. The main benefit of using discrete regimes is that we *can* calculate the default and migration frequencies from historical data, for any criterion we use to define the regimes. A more continuous approach would require us to continually adjust our default and migration rates based on the macroeconomic conditioning variable. However, this would require an additional modeling step and would introduce a number of complexities and forced assumptions.

Table 8.3 *Migration Frequencies for Normal vs. High-Default Periods*

From/To		Normal Conditions (Avg. 1972-1996)							
		Aaa (1)	Aa (2)	A (3)	Baa (4)	Ba (5)	B (6)	Caa-C (7)	Default (8)
Aaa	(1)	91.68%	7.61%	0.69%	0.00%	0.02%	0.00%	0.00%	0.00%
Aa	(2)	1.43%	90.70%	7.46%	0.29%	0.09%	0.01%	0.00%	0.02%
A	(3)	0.07%	2.35%	91.87%	5.02%	0.55%	0.12%	0.01%	0.01%
Baa	(4)	0.04%	0.26%	5.68%	87.86%	5.15%	0.77%	0.08%	0.14%
Ba	(5)	0.02%	0.05%	0.49%	5.47%	85.81%	6.55%	0.42%	1.19%
B	(6)	0.01%	0.03%	0.13%	0.46%	6.93%	83.98%	2.09%	6.37%
Caa-C	(7)	0.00%	0.00%	0.00%	0.71%	2.18%	4.50%	67.40%	25.20%

From/To		High Default (Avg. 1989-1992 Smoothed)							
		Aaa (1)	Aa (2)	A (3)	Baa (4)	Ba (5)	B (6)	Caa-C (7)	Default (8)
Aaa	(1)	91.00%	6.00%	2.75%	0.25%	0.00%	0.00%	0.00%	0.00%
Aa	(2)	0.45%	84.53%	12.06%	1.32%	0.82%	0.32%	0.30%	0.20%
A	(3)	0.00%	0.51%	88.92%	7.36%	0.94%	0.57%	1.20%	0.50%
Baa	(4)	0.00%	0.61%	3.77%	84.39%	5.12%	1.61%	3.50%	1.00%
Ba	(5)	0.00%	0.00%	0.66%	3.51%	83.87%	8.55%	0.66%	2.75%
B	(6)	0.00%	0.00%	0.00%	0.10%	4.00%	84.00%	1.33%	10.57%
Caa-C	(7)	0.00%	0.00%	0.00%	1.00%	2.00%	12.50%	47.00%	37.50%

The default rate itself is essentially the number of failures per unit of the borrowing population. This suggests a binomial distribution for the default rate itself. Program 8.3 presents a SAS macro (%EX2) for simulating portfolio credit risk. By setting the success/failure rate for the binomial distribution to the historical mean of 3.5% (see variable HISTDEFRATE in Program 8.3), we can generate random values for the overall default rate which can be used to determine the regime that applies for each iteration in our simulation. The cutoff value for a switch to the high-default regime is a parameter for the overall simulation and will have a dramatic affect on the results. In the following results, we set the cutoff at 6%. That is, a binomial draw of greater than 6 per hundred trials indicates a high-default episode (see variable THRESHOLD in Program 8.3). Since we will need to simulate the behavior of the portfolio repeatedly to estimate the distribution of potential future losses, we will need to run a large number of multi-year simulations. For each portfolio run of say twenty years, we need only generate 20 random binomial values, with lambda set to the mean, or 3.5% in this case.

Program 8.3 *Monte Carlo Simulation for Portfolio Credit Risk (Macro %EX2)*

```
/**********************************************************************/
/* Macro EX2 performs VaR-calculation from a set of pure credit events.  */
/*                                                                    */
/* Parameters                                                         */
/* PORTFOLIO the name of a file defining a credit portfolio of seven risk */
/*           categories. The file has one variable: EXPOSURE, which is   */
/*           numeric and defines the exposure in whole dollars for each risk */
/*           category. The number of risk categories, i.e., the number of */
/*           observations, must be seven, and they must be listed in   */
/*           increasing order of risk. See example below.             */
/* NYEARS    the number of years, which determines the time horizon of the */
/*           simulation.                                              */
/* NSIMS     number of simulations.                                   */
/* OUT       name of the output data set, which contains the loss for each */
/*           simulation and the number of high-default years.         */
/* SEED      Seed of the random number generator functions.          */
/*                                                                    */
/* Example for creating the input file for the portfolio:            */
/*                                                                    */
/* DATA PORTF(KEEP=EXPOSURE);                                         */
/*     INPUT RATING $ EXPOSURE;                                       */
/*     CARDS;                                                         */
/*     Aaa    10000    - Risk category 'Aaa' has the lowest level of risk. */
/*     Aa     10000                                                   */
/*     A      10000                                                   */
/*     Baa    10000                                                   */
/*     Ba     0                                                       */
/*     B      0                                                       */
/*     C      0        - Risk category 'C' has the highest level of risk. */
/*     ;                                                              */
/*     RUN;                                                           */
/**********************************************************************/

%MACRO EX2(PORTFOLIO=,NYEARS=,NSIMS=,OUT=,SEED=123);

 DATA &OUT(KEEP=LOSS HIGHDEFYEAR);

        /* supply the parameters of the simulation. */

        RETAIN HISTDEFRATE 0.035    * historical average default rate;
               THRESHOLD   0.06;    * threshold for 'high-default' year;

        ARRAY MIGR(2,7,8) MIGR1-MIGR112 (

            /* Migration matrix of "normal" years */
            /* From To:     Aaa    Aa     A      Baa    Ba     B      C      Default */
            /*              (1)    (2)    (3)    (4)    (5)    (6)    (7)    (8)    */

            /* Aaa (1) */  0.9168 0.0761 0.0069 0.0000 0.0002 0.0000 0.0000 0.0000
            /* Aa  (2) */  0.0143 0.9070 0.0746 0.0029 0.0009 0.0001 0.0000 0.0002
            /* A   (3) */  0.0007 0.0235 0.9187 0.0502 0.0055 0.0012 0.0001 0.0001
            /* Baa (4) */  0.0004 0.0026 0.0568 0.8786 0.0515 0.0077 0.0008 0.0014
            /* Ba  (5) */  0.0002 0.0005 0.0049 0.0547 0.8581 0.0655 0.0042 0.0119
            /* B   (6) */  0.0001 0.0003 0.0013 0.0046 0.0693 0.8398 0.0209 0.0637
            /* C   (7) */  0.0000 0.0000 0.0000 0.0071 0.0218 0.0450 0.6740 0.2520

            /* Migration matrix of "high-default" years */
            /* From To:     Aaa    Aa     A      Baa    Ba     B      C      Default */
            /*              (1)    (2)    (3)    (4)    (5)    (6)    (7)    (8)    */
```

```
       /* Aaa  (1)  */    0.9100 0.0600 0.0275 0.0025 0.0000 0.0000 0.0000 0.0000
       /* Aa   (2)  */    0.0045 0.8453 0.1206 0.0132 0.0082 0.0032 0.0030 0.0020
       /* A    (3)  */    0.0000 0.0051 0.8892 0.0736 0.0094 0.0057 0.0120 0.0050
       /* Baa  (4)  */    0.0000 0.0061 0.0377 0.8439 0.0512 0.0161 0.0350 0.0100
       /* Ba   (5)  */    0.0000 0.0000 0.0066 0.0351 0.8387 0.0855 0.0066 0.0275
       /* B    (6)  */    0.0000 0.0000 0.0000 0.0010 0.0400 0.8400 0.0133 0.1057
       /* C    (7)  */    0.0000 0.0000 0.0000 0.0100 0.0200 0.1250 0.4700 0.3750
       );

/* Define the distribution of loss in the event of default (LIED) as a    */
/* stepwise function. Array 'LIED' contains the discrete loss values from  */
/* 1.25% to 98.75%, and array 'LIEDPROB' provides the probabilities, by    */
/* which those losses happen. See Asarnow and Edwards (1995).              */

ARRAY LIED(21)       (0.0125 0.05    0.10    0.15    0.20    0.25    0.30    0.35
                      0.40    0.45    0.50    0.55    0.60    0.65    0.70    0.75
                      0.80    0.85    0.90    0.95    0.9875);
ARRAY LIEDPROB(20)   (0.1237 0.1410 0.1069 0.0708 0.0450 0.0394 0.0427 0.0405
                      0.0450 0.0247 0.0225 0.0337 0.0259 0.0326 0.0281 0.0225
                      0.0247 0.0236 0.0225 0.0236      );

ARRAY PROB(7) PROB1-PROB7;                    /* temporary array   */
ARRAY INITPORTF(7) INITPORTF1-INITPORTF7;     /* initial portfolio */
ARRAY CURPORTF(7)  CURPORTF1 -CURPORTF7;      /* current portfolio */
ARRAY NEWPORTF(7)  NEWPORTF1 -NEWPORTF7;      /* new portfolio after a migration */

/* load the input portfolio into array 'INITPORTF'. */

DO RATING=1 TO 7;
   SET &PORTFOLIO POINT=RATING;
   INITPORTF(RATING)=EXPOSURE;
END;

/* main loop of the simulations */

DO SIM=1 TO &NSIMS;

   /* start with the input portfolio, move */
   /* it into the current portfolio.       */

   DO RATING=1 TO 7;
      CURPORTF(RATING)=INITPORTF(RATING);
   END;

   /* variable 'LOSS' summarizes the losses, set it to zero initially. */

   LOSS=0;

   /* variable 'HIGHDEFYEAR' keeps track of the */
   /* number of years with high default rate.   */

   HIGHDEFYEAR=0;

   /* migrate the portfolio through &NYEARS. */

   DO YEAR=1 TO &NYEARS;

      /* array 'NEWPORT' has the current portfolio after each annual */
      /* migration. Set it to zero before each yearly migration, and */
      /* then collect the exposures by the risk categories to which  */
      /* they migrate.                                               */

      DO RATING=1 TO 7;
         NEWPORTF(RATING)=0;
      END;

      /* determine the type of year, i.e. 'Normal' (REGIME=1) */
      /* or 'High-default' (REGIME=2).                        */
```

```
        MACROECO=RANBIN(&SEED,100,HISTDEFRATE)/100;
        IF MACROECO>THRESHOLD THEN REGIME=2;    * high-default year;
                            ELSE REGIME=1;    * normal year;
        IF REGIME=2 THEN HIGHDEFYEAR=HIGHDEFYEAR+1;

        /* take one risk category of the portfolio. */

        DO RATING=1 TO 7;

            /* load the migration percentages of the given year-type and */
            /* rating into a temporary array to be used for each dollar   */
            /* of the current rating category.                            */

            DO I=1 TO 7;
                PROB(I)=MIGR(REGIME,RATING,I);
            END;

            /* go through every exposure of a given rating category. */

            DO P=1 TO CURPORTF(RATING);

                /* take a random draw from the migration probabilities */
                /* to determine the new risk category of the exposure. */

                NEWRATING=RANTBL(&SEED,OF PROB(*));

                /* if the exposure migrates to risk category '8', it goes */
                /* into default. Draw a random loss-value from the        */
                /* empirical loss distribution. If the migration does     */
                /* not result in default, assign the exposure to the new  */
                /* risk category.                                         */

                IF NEWRATING=8 THEN LOSS=LOSS+LIED(RANTBL(&SEED,OF LIEDPROB(*)));
                            ELSE NEWPORTF(NEWRATING)=NEWPORTF(NEWRATING)+1;
            END;

        END;

        /* make the new portfolio the current one, so the */
        /* next annual migration can be performed.        */

        DO RATING=1 TO 7;
            CURPORTF(RATING)=NEWPORTF(RATING);
        END;
    END;
    OUTPUT;
END;
STOP;
RUN;

/* check the distribution of the number of years with high-default rate. */

PROC FREQ DATA=&OUT;
    TABLE HIGHDEFYEAR;
    TITLE 'Distribution of the Number of High-Default Years';
    RUN;

/* describe the loss distribution and determine certain percentiles of it. */

PROC UNIVARIATE DATA=&OUT NOPRINT;
    VAR LOSS;
    OUTPUT OUT=RES N=N MEAN=MEAN STD=STD MAX=MAX MIN=MIN MEDIAN=MEDIAN
                Q1=Q1 Q3=Q3 P90=P90 P95=P95 P99=P99;
    TITLE F=SWISS H=1.5
        "Distribution of Losses (Number of Years=&NYEARS., Number of
Simulations=&NSIMS.)";
    run;
```

```
/* print the results in a comprehensive vertical layout. */

PROC TRANSPOSE DATA=RES OUT=TRES;
     RUN;
PROC PRINT DATA=TRES LABEL NOOBS;
     VAR _LABEL_ COL1;
     LABEL _LABEL_='STATISTIC' COL1='LOSS ($)';
     FORMAT COL1 10.0;
     RUN;

/* draw the graph of the ordered losses. Set up the labels */
/* for the two reference lines at 95 and 99 percentiles.   */

DATA ANNO;
     SET RES;
     FUNCTION='LABEL';  STYLE='DUPLEX'; SIZE=1.2;
     XSYS='2'; YSYS='2';
     Y=P95; X=10; TEXT='95% - '||COMPRESS(PUT(P95,10.0));
     POSITION='F'; OUTPUT;
     Y=P99; X=50; TEXT='99% - '||COMPRESS(PUT(P99,10.0));
     POSITION='C'; OUTPUT;
     CALL SYMPUT('VREF95',PUT(P95,BEST10.));
     CALL SYMPUT('VREF99',PUT(P99,BEST10.));
     RUN;
PROC SORT DATA=&OUT OUT=TEMP;
     BY LOSS;
DATA TEMP;
     SET TEMP;
     PERCENT=100*(_N_/&NSIMS);
     RUN;
PROC GPLOT DATA=TEMP ANNOTATE=ANNO;
     PLOT LOSS*PERCENT / VAXIS=AXIS1 HAXIS=AXIS2 VREF=&VREF95 &VREF99;
     SYMBOL1 I=JOIN V=NONE W=1;
     AXIS1 LABEL=(A=90 R=0 F=SWISS H=1.5 'Portfolio Loss ($)')
           VALUE=(H=1.2 F=SWISS) MINOR=(N=1) OFFSET=(0,0);
     AXIS2 LABEL=(F=SWISS H=1.5 'Percentile')
           VALUE=(H=1.2 F=SWISS) ORDER=0 TO 100 BY 10 MINOR=(N=1) OFFSET=(0,0);
     RUN;
     QUIT;
        %MEND;
```

To simulate the migration of non-defaulting credits to and from different rating categories over time, we use the RANTBL function by inputting the row of the migration matrix corresponding to the rating category in question:

```
NEWRATING=RANTBL(&SEED,OF PROB(*));.
```

Naturally, array PROB will contain the migration probabilities of either normal or high-default regimes chosen randomly before. If NEWRATING is 8, the exposure goes into default, and we register a randomly chosen loss value, utilizing the RANTBL function again with the empirical distribution of loss-in-the-event-of-default. If NEWRATING is not 8, we "migrate" the exposure and assign it to this new rating. After migrating all exposures in the portfolio, we obtain the losses from the defaults and the new portfolio of the remaining assets with their new rating categories. We are then ready to perform another annual migration of the portfolio over the specified time horizon (20 years).

Under this scheme, correlation of credit events is summarized by the common macroeconomic variable and by the common set of expected migration rates faced by obligors with common ratings. This means that all credit events are correlated, but that the correlation is higher for obligors within a given credit rating than for obligors with different ratings. Note also that, in spite of the fact that the macro regime shifts are independent and identically distributed (i.i.d.), this simulation scheme will generate serially correlated default rates, since the distribution of ratings in the portfolio will be strongly autocorrelated. Of course, an explicit serial dependence in the macro variable could be introduced as an additional feature.

Program 8.4 presents an example of using Program 8.3 (macro %EX2) for a portfolio of 40,000 investment-grade exposures, evenly distributed with 10,000 exposures in the rating categories Aaa through Baa. Suppose further that the exposures are of equal size, say $1.[2] The distribution of losses from a set of 10,000 20-year simulations using the approach described above is presented in Output 8.2. The chart in Output 8.2 simply plots the losses from each simulation run, ordered from lowest to highest, which traces out the distribution of potential losses. From this distribution of losses we can calculate the quantiles that answer the basic VaR question by reading the Y-axis loss level corresponding to a proportion of the simulated observations on the X-axis. That is, at an x% confidence level, we can predict that portfolio losses due to credit events will be no more than $y. Note that, in the credit risk context, we are accumulating losses only — no gains. Therefore, the extreme values we are interested are in are the upper tail of the distribution. In this case, assuming each exposure equals $1, at the 95% confidence level we can expect losses of no more than $1,633, or 4.08%. At the 99% confidence level we can expect losses of no more than $1,870, or 4.68%. The mean loss level is 1,190, or just 2.975% on this investment-grade portfolio, as given in Output 8.2.

Program 8.4 *Investment-Grade Portfolio Example (Using Program 8.3 – Macro %EX2)*

```
DATA PORTF1(KEEP=EXPOSURE);
     INPUT RATING $ EXPOSURE;
     CARDS;
     Aaa    10000    * Risk category 'Aaa' has the lowest level of risk.;
     Aa     10000
     A      10000
     Baa    10000
     Ba     0
     B      0
     C      0        * Risk category 'C' has the highest level of risk.;
     ;
     RUN;
%EX2(PORTFOLIO=PORTF1,NYEARS=20,NSIMS=10000,OUT=A,SEED=123);
```

---

[2] This last simplification is left to the reader to relax—for exposures of different sizes, we will need to keep track of each exposure individually, i.e., maintain an array containing the size and current rating for each exposure after each iteration.

Output 8.2
Output of Investment-Grade Portfolio Example

```
            Distribution of the Number of High-Default Years

                      The FREQ Procedure

                                           Cumulative    Cumulative
    HIGHDEFYEAR    Frequency      Percent    Frequency      Percent

          0          2749        27.49         2749        27.49
          1          3653        36.53         6402        64.02
          2          2368        23.68         8770        87.70
          3           906         9.06         9676        96.76
          4           264         2.64         9940        99.40
          5            44         0.44         9984        99.84
          6            14         0.14         9998        99.98
          7             2         0.02        10000       100.00

Distribution of Losses (Number of Years=20, Number of Simulations=10000)

         STATISTIC                               LOSS ($)

         number of nonmissing values, LOSS        10000
         the mean, LOSS                             1190
         the standard deviation, LOSS                242
         the largest value, LOSS                    2481
         the 99th percentile, LOSS                  1870
         the 95th percentile, LOSS                  1633
         the 90th percentile, LOSS                  1532
         the upper quartile, LOSS                   1361
         the median, LOSS                           1156
         the lower quartile, LOSS                    947
         the smallest value, LOSS                    834
```

Ordered Losses

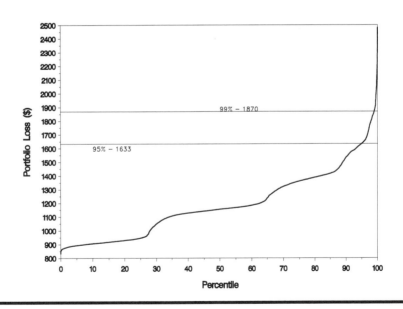

The distribution of losses exhibits some interesting and unusual features. Obviously, the distribution cannot be normal since it is bounded by zero and by the total amount of the portfolio. In fact, it is strongly non-normal, with an extremely fat lower tail (low losses), a relatively fat upper tail, and step-like increases over a few specific loss ranges. These unusual step-like features are a direct result of our assumption about potential macroeconomic disturbances. Specifically, losses over a 20-year period are dramatically affected by whether or not there are zero, one, two, or more aggregate credit cycles over that period. Bad draws from the binomial distribution, which governs the macro credit cycle, lead to multiple periods of weak aggregate credit conditions in our simulations. These, in turn, lead to a segmentation in the distribution of losses over the full 20-year period. In addition, the timing of high-default episodes has also affected the distribution, since early periods of credit weakness result in the lower rating grades being populated for longer periods of time — a recipe for higher default totals per simulation.

To see how well our cutoff threshold matched our beliefs about the likely frequency of aggregate credit problems, we can examine the distribution of high-default episodes per 20-year period. Figure 8.3 shows the frequency distribution of high-default episodes for our 10,000 runs, utilizing the variable HIGHDEFYEAR in the output data set of the macro.

Figure 8.3 Simulation Frequencies for High-Default Episodes (10,000 Simulations)

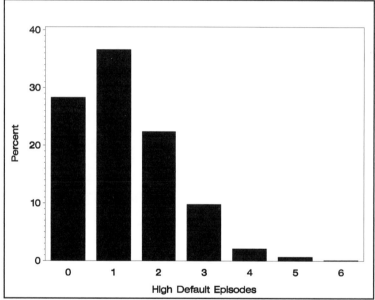

Given our cutoff of 6%, we can see by grouping the bars in Figure 8.3 that 64% of the time, a 20-year period will see 1 or less aggregate credit shocks. A significant 12.3% of the time, we will see 3 or more aggregate credit shocks. The applicability of these frequencies is subjective. We can use history, as in Figure 8.2, as our guide, but as the main goal of Monte Carlo methods is to quantify the distribution of potential future outcomes, we do not want to tie ourselves too closely to historical experiences. After all, the future can certainly produce new, different, and unexpected events, not just repetitions of past events. Highlighting such features and their effect on the potential distribution of losses is one of the reasons Monte Carlo simulations are so appealing.

Because our initial portfolio is defined as a vector of exposures by rating, we can easily explore the relationship between portfolio quality and potential loss, which can be useful in developing and setting investment strategy. For example, suppose we extended ourselves down the credit quality scale in forming our initial portfolio. Market spreads would tell us how much additional yield we would enjoy, but how would our credit risk exposure be effected? As an illustration, we consider an alternative $40,000 exposure portfolio, equally weighted across all rating categories (Program 8.5).[3] The distribution of losses for 10,000 simulations for this initial portfolio is presented in Output 8.3. In contrast to the investment-grade portfolio, this simulation shows higher loss levels. Our VaR values are 4,867, or 12.17%, and 5,082, or 12.7%, at the 95% and 99% confidence levels, respectively. The mean loss level is 4,456, or 11.14%, on this lower quality portfolio.

Program 8.5 *Uniform Portfolio Example*

```
DATA PORTF2(KEEP=EXPOSURE);
     INPUT RATING $ EXPOSURE;
     CARDS;
     Aaa   5714
     Aa    5714
     A     5715
     Baa   5715
     Ba    5714
     B     5714
     C     5714
     ;
     RUN;
%EX2(PORTFOLIO=PORTF2,NYEARS=20,NSIMS=10000,OUT=A,SEED=123);
```

---

[3] Here we have 5,714 in each, with A and Baa getting one additional exposure for rounding.

Output 8.3
Uniform
Portfolio
Example

Distribution of the Number of High-Default Years

The FREQ Procedure

HIGHDEFYEAR	Frequency	Percent	Cumulative Frequency	Cumulative Percent
0	2796	27.96	2796	27.96
1	3637	36.37	6433	64.33
2	2317	23.17	8750	87.50
3	906	9.06	9656	96.56
4	276	2.76	9932	99.32
5	57	0.57	9989	99.89
6	11	0.11	10000	100.00

Distribution of Losses (Number of Years=20, Number of Simulations=10000)

STATISTIC	LOSS ($)
number of nonmissing values, LOSS	10000
the mean, LOSS	4456
the standard deviation, LOSS	223
the largest value, LOSS	5548
the 99th percentile, LOSS	5082
the 95th percentile, LOSS	4867
the 90th percentile, LOSS	4764
the upper quartile, LOSS	4607
the median, LOSS	4427
the lower quartile, LOSS	4259
the smallest value, LOSS	4077

Ordered Losses

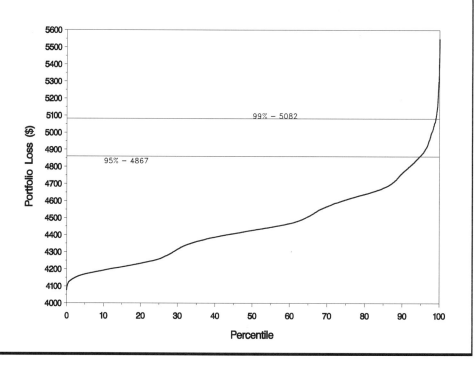

Note that the hump-shaped increases in losses due to discrete increases in the number of "bad" credit episodes are less pronounced for the lower quality portfolio. This reflects the fact that lower-rated credits are relatively more likely to default in good times than are investment-grade credits. This is typical of the type of intuitive fact that is extremely difficult to quantify analytically, but which can be evaluated and quantified quite easily using Monte Carlo simulation.

8.4 Example 3: VaR Estimation for Portfolio Market Risk

Our previous example uses a Monte Carlo approach to evaluate the risk associated with the change in the market value of a portfolio due to changes in market conditions, i.e., price fluctuations. In a market risk VaR application, we seek to be able to find the value x that satisfies the statement: for a given confidence level C, portfolio losses over a specific time horizon are likely to be no greater than x. For a diversified portfolio, i.e, a portfolio that consists of different *types* of assets, we need to generate estimates of future losses that are consistent with the joint distribution of returns for all relevant asset classes. Once we have established a mechanism for generating these "realistic" loss estimates, we can use the Monte Carlo approach to trace out the distribution of potential future losses on the portfolio and obtain our VaR result.

Market risk VaR calculations are typically directed toward measuring the potential losses from price movements over the very short term—often a single day. This type of high-frequency analysis creates some computational complexities, but also allows us to make use of a number of important simplifications. The calculations for market risk VaR may vary in a number of ways, but the critical issues relate to the two underlying dynamics associated with a portfolio of risky assets:

❑ the distribution of future returns for each asset or asset class in the portfolio

❑ the correlation of price movements across assets or asset classes.

To estimate the distribution of future returns for a portfolio of assets, we have two choices. One approach is to model each security's movement independently, given a complete set of volatilities and correlations for each asset and asset pair. That is, for n assets we would need n volatilities and $n(n-1)/2$ correlations. We can use the information in the variance-covariance matrix to transform a set of i.i.d. innovations into a set of innovations for each security with the appropriate volatilities and correlations. Under most circumstances,[4] we could do this by applying the Cholesky decomposition to the variance-covariance matrix, which is discussed in greater detail below. However, because the calculation of so large a variance-covariance matrix will present significant data processing and other computational problems, the matrix will generally need to be estimated once, and treated as a set of fixed parameters for each Monte Carlo simulation. This will severely limit the range of outcomes that such simulations can produce.

---

[4] The correlation matrix must be positive definite.

A second approach is the so-called factor approach, in which individual asset movements are modeled as a combination of response movements to a set of correlated factors and to a set of independent idiosyncratic movements. To derive the former, the so-called systematic component of asset price movements, one needs to identify the factors that are relevant for the specific portfolio, from macroeconomic and financial data. This is not a straightforward task and will require tradeoffs between increased completeness and increased complexity. The idiosyncratic components are assumed to be normally distributed and uncorrelated across assets. Hence, all correlation in asset prices then derives from their dependence on the correlated factors, which reduces the dimension of the required variance-covariance matrix to the number of factors included.

While this approach gives a simpler way to embed correlation in the simulated movements of multiple asset prices, it forces us to specify the relationship between changes in the factors and changes in each asset's price. In most cases, the relationship is assumed to be linear, and the issue then becomes one of specifying the weights, or "factor loadings," that will be used to translate factor movements into the systematic price movements for each specific asset. This can be done by regression analysis, although for equity prices one can obtain "betas" (the correlation coefficients between individual equities and major market indices) from published sources. A by-product of this analysis will be variance estimates for each asset or asset group in the portfolio under consideration.

In our example, we will assume that factors have been identified and that the factor loadings have been estimated. For simplicity, we consider a model with three factors, the S&P 500 Index, the yield to maturity on the 90-Day Treasury Bill, and the Japanese Yen/US Dollar exchange rate. Time series for the daily market values for these values from 1/1/1980 through 12/31/2000 are presented in Figure 8.4. We can imagine a portfolio of stocks, loans, and swaps for which the systematic changes in value are driven primarily by these three factors. We need to convert these data into stationary time series, i.e., percent changes, or log differences, for trending factors, since we are modeling the change in the portfolio's overall value, not the value itself.

Figure 8.4 *Historical Time Series of Key Factors*

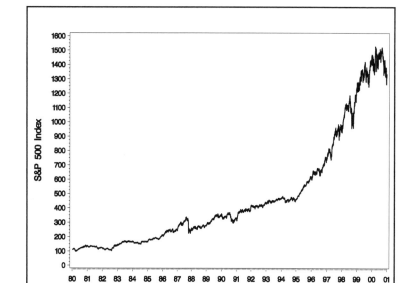

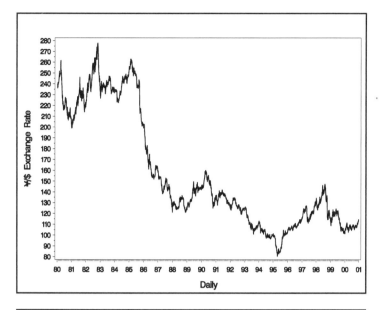

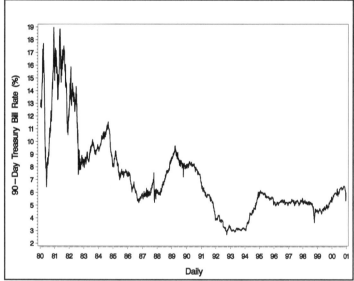

The variance of these factors and the correlation among factors are the key components that remain to be identified. These values can be straightforwardly calculated from a specified length of historical time series data, leading to one fixed set of variance and correlation parameters. While the tractability of this fixed-parameter variance-covariance approach lends it a great deal of appeal, it is not clear that it will accomplish the job for which it has been designed: to measure the risk on the portfolio by characterizing the distribution of potential future returns. The assumption of fixed variance-covariance parameters is itself heroic. Because empirical evidence suggests that variance-covariance relationships change over time, fixing them at average values means we will be excluding from our simulations whole categories of potential future outcomes for the portfolio. Obviously, if we are mischaracterizing the distribution of potential losses, our VaR calculations will be wrong.

Consider, for example, the sign of the correlation between interest rates and stock prices. Lower interest rates mean lower cost of capital for corporate borrowers, with positive implications for balance sheets and with potentially expanded opportunity sets for corporate investment. Moreover, lower yields on fixed income instruments lowers the opportunity cost of holding stocks, which makes stocks relatively more attractive investment vehicles. Thus, we would often expect to see a negative short-run correlation between interest rates and stock returns. However, during inflationary or recessionary periods, interest rate cuts can be viewed as exacerbating inflationary pressures, or as remedial treatments to prop up a flagging economy. Under these conditions, the contemporaneous correlation could well be positive. If the sign of the correlation may switch, the use of average values is definitely going to prevent a range of plausible scenarios from being manifested in our Monte Carlo procedure.

An alternative to the fixed correlation approach that is not too computationally demanding involves random sampling from historical factor data, to allow for a wider range of factor co-movements in our simulations. Because the variance-covariance matrix is relatively small, and because our short time horizon suggests using a small time-window for deriving the variance-covariance structure, we can re-estimate it for each portfolio iteration in the simulation. By randomly selecting the starting point for our window, we will allow the estimated variance-covariance matrix to drift stochastically over its historical range. When we apply random innovations to the set of factors governed by this stochastic correlation scheme, we obtain a richer set of potential outcomes, centered around, but not restricted to their recent or historical range of co-movement. Program 8.6 presents a SAS macro program for this approach.

Program 8.6 *VaR Estimation for Portfolio Market Risk (Macro %EX3)*

```
/**************************************************************************/
/* Macro EX3 evaluates the risk associated with the change in the market  */
/* value of a portfolio due to changes in market conditions.              */
/*                                                                        */
/* Parameters                                                             */
/* FACTORS    a SAS file containing the historical time series of the key */
/*            factors. (For example S&P 500 Index, Yield to Maturity on the */
/*            90-Day Treasury Bill and US Dollar/Japanese Yen Exchange Rate.) */
/*            The factors must be named FACTOR1, FACTOR2,... The file can  */
/*            have any number of factors, but it must not contain any other */
/*            variables.                                                   */
/* PORT       a SAS file describing the portfolio. Every observation is an */
/*            asset and the variables are VAR (the variance of the security), */
/*            and LOAD1, LOAD2,... (the loadings of the securities along the */
/*            factors given in the file defined by parameter FACTORS).     */
/* WINDOW     the length of the window to estimate a variance matrix of the */
/*            factors. The macro will take WINDOW number of consecutive    */
/*            observations, starting at a randomly selected observation, from */
/*            the historical time series of factors to determine a variance */
/*            matrix.                                                      */
/* NSIMS      number of simulations.                                      */
/* OUT        name of the output data set, which contains the loss of the  */
/*            portfolio (variable LOSS) for each simulation.              */
/* SEED       Seed of the random number generator functions.             */
/*                                                                        */
/* Example for creating the files of factors and portfolio and calling the */
/* macro to perform a simulation:                                         */
/*                                                                        */
/* DATA FACT;                                                             */
/*     INPUT FACTOR1-FACTOR3;                                             */
/*     CARDS;                                                             */
/*  0.002980003    0.014606266    0.003610108                            */
/* -0.000351830   -0.006259128   -0.006255865                            */
/* -0.001370942    0.007348310    0.021561221                            */
/*  0.001449151   -0.001042101    0.002619011                            */
```

```
/*   0.004008841    0.005633215    0.013214505                                      */
/*  -0.002291797   -0.005394191   -0.004322111                                      */
/*   0.007452402   -0.010221110   -0.013022618                                      */
/*   0.000994247    0.008851423    0.014969136                                      */
/*  -0.000343905    0.001044496    0.008742588                                      */
/*    . . .      more data lines                                                    */
/*  ;                                                                               */
/*  RUN;                                                                            */
/*  DATA PORT;                                                                      */
/*       INPUT VAR LOAD1 LOAD2 LOAD3;                                               */
/*       CARDS;                                                                     */
/*  0.785011716    0.352891914    0.373870389    0.273237697                        */
/*  0.811390100    0.294478292    0.384795108    0.320726600                        */
/*  0.873502876    0.118961592    0.375286443    0.505751965                        */
/*  0.883075376    0.628817260    0.016169149    0.355013591                        */
/*  0.894593499    0.221131166    0.356409292    0.422459543                        */
/*  0.014082599    0.135102802    0.429376615    0.435520583                        */
/*  0.516532135    0.293662375    0.420554950    0.285782675                        */
/*  0.073421956    0.616759924    0.051255603    0.331984474                        */
/*  0.288352860    0.093046026    0.525914520    0.381039454                        */
/*  0.124769632    0.315012854    0.132633282    0.552353864                        */
/*    . . .      more data lines                                                    */
/*  ;                                                                               */
/*  RUN;                                                                            */
/*  %EX3(FACTORS=FACT,PORT=PORT,WINDOW=45,NSIMS=10000,OUT=LOSSES,SEED=123)          */
/*                                                                                  */
/*********************************************************************************/

%MACRO EX3(FACTORS=,PORT=,WINDOW=,NSIMS=,OUT=,SEED=);

 /* Create a new file that has a randomly chosen window */
 /* of market factors for each simulation.              */

 DATA TEMP(DROP=START);
      IF _N_=1 THEN DO;
         SET &FACTORS NOBS=NPERIODS;
         ARRAY FACTORS(*) _NUMERIC_;

         /* Determine the number of factors in the model, and store it in */
         /* macro variable 'NFACT'. It will be utilized at other parts of */
         /* the macro.                                                    */

         CALL SYMPUT('NFACT',LEFT(PUT(DIM(FACTORS),BEST10.)));
         CALL SYMPUT('NFACT2',LEFT(PUT(DIM(FACTORS)*DIM(FACTORS),BEST10.)));

         /* Create as many random windows as the number of simulations. */

         DO SIM=1 TO &NSIMS;

            /* Variable START is the starting observation of the window. */

            START=1+INT((NPERIODS+1-&WINDOW)*RANUNI(&SEED));
            DO I=START TO START+&WINDOW-1;
               SET &FACTORS POINT=I;
               OUTPUT;
            END;
         END;
      END;
      RUN;

 /* Determine the covariance matrix for each window. */

 PROC CORR DATA=TEMP COV NOPRINT OUT=TEMP(WHERE=(_TYPE_='COV') DROP=_NAME_);
      BY SIM;

 /* Calculate the Cholesky decomposition of each covariance matrix, */
 /* and create factor innovations with the desired correlation.     */

 DATA TEMP(KEEP=FACTOR1-FACTOR&NFACT);
      ARRAY COV(&NFACT) FACTOR1-FACTOR&NFACT;
      ARRAY COVSQ(&NFACT,&NFACT) COVSQ1-COVSQ&NFACT2;
```

```
      ARRAY CHOL(&NFACT,&NFACT) CHOL1-CHOL&NFACT2;
      ARRAY RANNUM(&NFACT) R1-R&NFACT;

   /* Perform the calculation for each window separately. */

   DO SIM=1 TO &NSIMS;

      /* Read the current covariance matrix and store it in array 'COVSQ'.*/

      START=&NFACT*(SIM-1);
      DO I=1 TO &NFACT;
         POINT=START+I;
         SET TEMP(DROP=SIM _TYPE_) POINT=POINT;
         DO J=1 TO &NFACT;
            COVSQ(I,J)=COV(J);
         END;
      END;

      /* Calculate the elements of the Cholesky matrix    */
      /* (lower triangle). It is stored in array 'CHOL'. */

      DO I=1 TO &NFACT;
         DO J=1 TO &NFACT;
            SELECT;
              WHEN(J>I)  CHOL(I,J)=0;
              WHEN(J=I)  DO; SUM=0;
                            DO K=1 TO I-1;
                               SUM=SUM+CHOL(I,K)**2;
                            END;
                            CHOL(I,I)=SQRT(COVSQ(I,I)-SUM);
                            END;
              OTHERWISE DO; SUM=0;
                            DO K=1 TO J-1;
                               SUM=SUM+CHOL(I,K)*CHOL(J,K);
                            END;
                            CHOL(I,J)=(COVSQ(I,J)-SUM)/CHOL(J,J);
                            END;
            END;
         END;
      END;

      /* Utilizing the Cholesky matrix, introduce random */
      /* factors with the desired correlation.           */

      DO I=1 TO &NFACT;
         RANNUM(I)=RANNOR(&SEED);
      END;
      DO J=1 TO &NFACT;
         SUM=0;
         DO I=1 TO &NFACT;
            SUM=SUM+CHOL(I,J)*RANNUM(I);
         END;
         COV(J)=SUM;
      END;

      /* Output the random factors, one observation for each simulation. */

      OUTPUT;
   END;
   STOP;
   RUN;

/* Determine the number of securities in the portfolio file. */
/* Store it in macro variable 'NSECS'.                       */

DATA _NULL_;
   IF 0 THEN SET &PORT NOBS=COUNT;
   CALL SYMPUT('NSECS',LEFT(PUT(COUNT,8.)));
   STOP;
   RUN;
%LET PORT2=%EVAL(&NSECS*&NFACT);
```

```
/* The main simulation section: Apply the random change to each security */
/* of the portfolio and calculate the losses for the entire portfolio.    */

DATA &OUT(KEEP=LOSS);

    /* Array VARS stores the variances of the securities                   */
    /* Array ALLFACTORS stores all loads of all securities along all factors */
    /*              as a two-dimension array                               */
    /* Array FACTORS stores the factor innovations with the desired        */
    /*              correlation                                            */
    /* Array LOADS stores the loads of one security along the factors      */

    ARRAY VARS(&NSECS) VAR1-VAR&NSECS;
    ARRAY ALLFACTORS(&NFACT,&NSECS) F1-F&PORT2;
    ARRAY FACTORS(&NFACT) FACTOR1-FACTOR&NFACT;
    ARRAY LOADS(&NFACT) LOAD1-LOAD&NFACT;
    RETAIN VAR1-VAR&NSECS F1-F&PORT2;

    /* Store the loads of the securities in the portfolio. */

    SET &PORT END=EOPORT;
    VARS(_N_)=VAR;
    DO J=1 TO &NFACT;
        ALLFACTORS(J,_N_)=LOADS(J);
    END;

    /* Main simulation loop. */

    IF EOPORT THEN DO;

        DO SIM=1 TO &NSIMS;

            /* Read the factor innovations for the current simulation. */

            SET TEMP POINT=SIM;
            LOSS=0;

            /* Go through each security in the portfolio. */

            DO SEC=1 TO &NSECS;

                /* Calculate the sum of changes in the factors (variable  */
                /* DELTA) and the idiosyncratic variation (variable IDIO) */
                /* for the security in question.                          */

                IDIO=0;
                DELTA=0;
                DO J=1 TO &NFACT;
                    IDIO=IDIO+ALLFACTORS(J,SEC)**2;
                    DELTA=DELTA+VARS(SEC)*ALLFACTORS(J,SEC)*FACTORS(J);
                END;
                IDIO=VARS(SEC)*SQRT(1-IDIO)*RANNOR(&SEED);
                CHANGE=DELTA+IDIO;

                /* Summarize the loss (change) throughout the portfolio. */

                LOSS=LOSS+CHANGE;
            END;
            OUTPUT;
        END;
    END;
    RUN;

/* Describe the loss distribution and determine certain percentiles of it. */

PROC UNIVARIATE DATA=&OUT NOPRINT;
    VAR LOSS;
    OUTPUT OUT=RES N=N MEAN=MEAN STD=STD MAX=MAX MIN=MIN MEDIAN=MEDIAN
                Q1=Q1 Q3=Q3 P10=P10 P5=P5 P1=P1;
    TITLE F=SWISS H=1.5
```

```
                "Distribution of Losses (Length of Window=&WINDOW., Number of
Simulations=&NSIMS.)";
      RUN;

 /* Print the results in a comprehensive vertical layout. */

 PROC TRANSPOSE DATA=RES OUT=TRES;
      RUN;
 PROC PRINT DATA=TRES LABEL NOOBS;
      VAR _LABEL_ COL1;
      LABEL _LABEL_='Statistic' COL1='Loss ($)';
      FORMAT COL1 10.2;
      RUN;

 /* Draw the graph of the ordered losses. Set up the labels */
 /* for the two reference lines at 5 and 1 percentiles.     */

 DATA ANNO;
      SET RES;
      FUNCTION='LABEL';  STYLE='DUPLEX'; SIZE=1.2;
      XSYS='2'; YSYS='2';
      Y=P5; X=50; TEXT='5% '||COMPRESS(PUT(P5,10.0));
      POSITION='C'; OUTPUT;
      Y=P1; X=80; TEXT='1% '||COMPRESS(PUT(P1,10.0));
      POSITION='F'; OUTPUT;
      CALL SYMPUT('VREF5',PUT(P5,BEST10.));
      call symput('vref1',put(p1,best10.));
      run;
 PROC SORT DATA=&OUT OUT=TEMP;
      BY LOSS;
 DATA TEMP;
      SET TEMP;
      PERCENT=100*(_N_/&NSIMS);
      RUN;
 PROC GPLOT DATA=TEMP ANNOTATE=ANNO;
      PLOT LOSS*PERCENT / VAXIS=AXIS1 HAXIS=AXIS2 VREF=&VREF5 &VREF1;
      SYMBOL1 I=JOIN V=NONE W=1;
      AXIS1 LABEL=(A=90 R=0 F=SWISS H=1.5 'Portfolio loss ($)')
            VALUE=(H=1.2 F=SWISS) MINOR=(N=1) OFFSET=(0,0);
      AXIS2 LABEL=(F=SWISS H=1.5 'Percentile')
            VALUE=(H=1.2 F=SWISS) ORDER=0 TO 100 BY 10 MINOR=(N=1) OFFSET=(0,0);
      RUN;
      QUIT;
%MEND;
```

The first step in our simulation, then, is to calculate the variance-covariance matrix for our key factors, and use it to produce a set of random innovations to apply to the factors to get one simulated "state of the world." After drawing a random time window w from our historical time series, we obtain the variance-covariance matrix Σ_w for the three factors over that time interval:

$$\Sigma_w = \begin{bmatrix} \sigma_i^2 & \sigma_i\sigma_j\rho_{jk} & \sigma_i\sigma_k\rho_{ik} \\ \sigma_i\sigma_j\rho_{ij} & \sigma_j^2 & \sigma_j\sigma_k\rho_{jk} \\ \sigma_i\sigma_k\rho_{ik} & \sigma_j\sigma_k\rho_{jk} & \sigma_k^2 \end{bmatrix}$$

This is accomplished by creating the data set `TEMP` and running `PROC CORR` in Program 8.6 (macro `%EX3`).

In order to convert a set of independent normal draws into simulated factor innovations whose variance-covariance relationships are defined by Σ_w, we apply a Cholesky decomposition to Σ_w, to obtain the matrix **A**, where

$$A \times A^T = \Sigma_w = \begin{bmatrix} \sigma_i^2 & \sigma_i\sigma_j\rho_{jk} & \sigma_i\sigma_k\rho_{ik} \\ \sigma_i\sigma_j\rho_{ij} & \sigma_j^2 & \sigma_j\sigma_k\rho_{jk} \\ \sigma_i\sigma_k\rho_{ik} & \sigma_j\sigma_k\rho_{jk} & \sigma_k^2 \end{bmatrix}.$$

The matrix **A** is essentially the lower left square root of Σ_w. When we multiply the matrix **A** by independent random variables with unit variance, we obtain new variables whose variance-covariance structure is precisely Σ_w. Denote the changes in the three key factors as $X=\{X_i, X_j, X_k\}$. We combine **A** and a set of random, independent standard normal variables Z_i, Z_j, Z_k, to create factor innovations with the desired properties as

$$\begin{bmatrix} X_i \\ X_j \\ X_k \end{bmatrix} = A \times \begin{bmatrix} Z_i \\ Z_j \\ Z_k \end{bmatrix}.$$

The Cholesky decomposition and subsequent generation of the factor innovations are carried out in the second DATA step of the macro. With these factor innovations in hand, and our pre-calculated factor loadings for each security in the portfolio, we can simulate the changes in value for every security, and hence for the portfolio as a whole, using random, independent standard normal variables to simulate the idiosyncratic component of each security's value change.

Consider first an equity, S_i, whose value-changes consist of only two components: a component that is perfectly correlated with the S&P 500 index, and an idiosyncratic component z_i that has unit variance and is independent of other factors and other equities. Denoting the factor loading for the S&P 500 index as β_{1i}, we can describe the innovation to security i as

$$\Delta S_i = \sigma_i\beta_{1i}X_1 + \sigma_i\sqrt{1 - \beta_{1i}^2}\, z_i.$$

The second term contains the factor $\sqrt{1 - \beta_{1i}^2}$ to adjust the overall variance of security i to its appropriate value. That is, by including this adjustment, we ensure that

$$E(\Delta S_i^2) = \sigma_i.$$

For a security dependent on two factors plus idiosyncratic variation, we have

$$\Delta S_i = \sigma_i \beta_{1i} X_1 + \sigma_i \beta_{2i} X_2 + \sigma_i \sqrt{1 - \beta_{1i}^2 - \beta_{2i}^2} \, z_i,$$

etc.

Thus, each simulated outcome involves drawing one random number for each factor innovation, and one random number for the idiosyncratic innovation to each individual security's value. After having calculated the value changes for all of the securities in the portfolio, we simply sum them to obtain the simulated change in portfolio value.[5] This task is performed by the third DATA step of the macro. Note that in the market risk case, our simulations will produce losses as well as gains. Therefore, the extreme values we are interested in are in the lower tail, and the so-called 95% confidence level will correspond to the 5% quantile of our loss distribution.

Notice also the asymmetry of our assumption about factor variances vs. security variances. We treated the variance of the security as a fixed value σ_i, but allowed the variance-covariance matrix for the key factors to vary stochastically, based on the randomly selected historical window over which it was estimated. This was done for simplicity and in order to illustrate a less rigid approach to representing factor movements/co-movements. In order to apply the random window approach to each security, we would need historical time series for each. But the simplification in our example has an effect that we might wish to avoid, even at the computational expense of selecting random windows for hundreds, or even thousands, of individual securities.

The problematic effect comes from the requirement that the expectation of the simulated variance equals the fixed parameter

$$E(\Delta S_i^2) = \sigma_i.$$

This implies that the relationship between the innovations to each security and the volatility of the key factors will be offsetting — the variance of the security-specific innovation is scaled up when the factor window produces low variance factors. This is counterintuitive. We would normally expect volatile factors to be associated with more extreme values for losses, but our assumption ensures that volatile factors will be associated with less volatile idiosyncratic security price changes. Obviously, a security's volatility is not fixed but is variable, with a volatility of its own. The analyst can counter the effect of this assumption by adding an additional scaling factor that links the volatility of the factors with the variance of the idiosyncratic security-specific innovations. It is left to the reader to consider the possibilities for establishing such a link.

Using the formula presented above, we ran a sample of 10,000 draws on a hypothetical portfolio of 300 securities and estimated the 95% and 99% VaR levels with the following macro call:

```
%EX3(FACTORS=FACT,PORT=PORT,WINDOW=45,NSIMS=10000,OUT=A,SEED=123);
```

---

[5] As with Example 2, we are assuming equal weighted exposures. In general, security value changes need to be multiplied by portfolio concentration weights to obtain the change in portfolio value.

In our example, we included three types of securities, related in three different ways. One hundred securities were dependent on one factor only, one hundred depended on two factors, and one hundred depended on all three factors. The time window over which we estimated the factors' variance-covariance matrix was fixed at 45 days. Output 8.4 presents the distribution of losses from the 10,000 draws and shows the 95% and 99% VaR levels. Again, since the term "losses" is being used to describe market value changes, which may be negative or positive, we focus on the lower tail of the distribution, i.e., the 1% and 5% quantiles. From these simulations, we can say with 95% confidence that the portfolio is unlikely to lose more than 11.4% of its value, and can say with 99% confidence that it will lose no more than 16.33%.

Output 8.4
Ordered
Losses From
10,000
Simulations

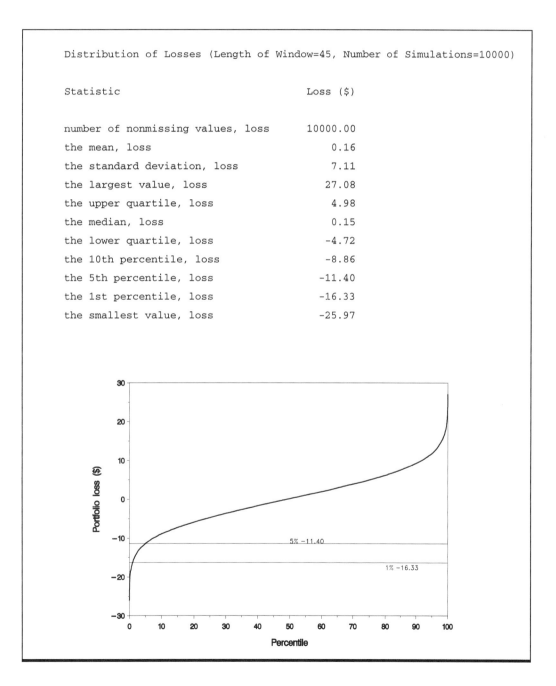

```
Distribution of Losses (Length of Window=45, Number of Simulations=10000)


Statistic                              Loss ($)


number of nonmissing values, loss      10000.00
the mean, loss                             0.16
the standard deviation, loss               7.11
the largest value, loss                   27.08
the upper quartile, loss                   4.98
the median, loss                           0.15
the lower quartile, loss                  -4.72
the 10th percentile, loss                 -8.86
the 5th percentile, loss                 -11.40
the 1st percentile, loss                 -16.33
the smallest value, loss                 -25.97
```

As is evident from Output 8.4, the simulated loss distribution is smooth, symmetric around zero, and approximately normal. A qq-plot comparing quantiles of the loss distribution with quantiles of the standard normal distribution is presented in Figure 8.5 and confirms the approximate normality of the simulated losses. This is not surprising, given that portfolio losses are linear functions of standard normal variables. However, the assumptions made in our example were extremely simple. Many relaxations or extensions of our example can be envisioned which could cause the loss distribution to deviate from normality. Because the complexities of numerical evaluation of the loss distribution are going to grow with model complexity, we would expect that evaluating these richer, more complex systems analytically, or numerically, will be infeasible. Hence, we will need to resort to Monte Carlo methods to evaluate the likely behavior, under extreme conditions, of portfolios with complex dynamics.

While our simple example has given us a way to approximate some of the key dynamics of market value changes, the simplicity of our assumptions is manifested in the regularity of the simulated outputs. It remains a challenge to VaR practitioners how best to embed irregularities such as price jumps and other non-normal behavior in VaR models without increasing the dependency of the results on a growing set of parameters that may have been poorly estimated. More generally, we would like to draw as much relevant information from history as we can, without becoming so tied to history that our simulations fail to produce a full description of possible future outcomes.

Figure 8.5 *QQ-Plot Testing the Normality of the Loss Distribution*

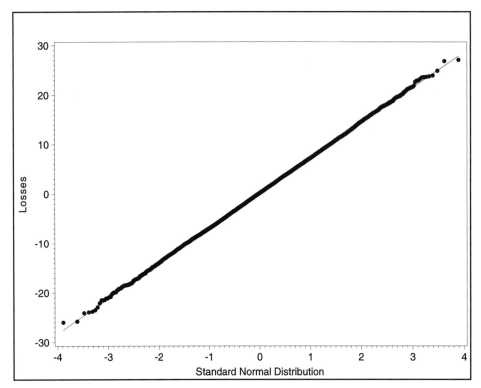

8.5 Summary

Monte Carlo techniques are particularly useful for characterizing the distribution of potential outcomes for a system whose properties make analytic or numeric solutions impractical. Such situations often arise in financial applications in which the distribution of interest is an aggregation of outcomes that may be correlated, that are characterized by empirical distributions with no functional representation, or both. They also arise in options pricing contexts, where the option value is a function of the distribution of future values of the underlying security.

We have presented three examples of the use of Monte Carlo techniques to solve problems that arise in finance. We chose problems in which correlated stochastic components with, in some cases, non-standard distributions, combined to generate an outcome. Our task was to trace out the probability distribution of future potential outcomes, and to locate various cutoff points defined in probabilistic terms. The Monte Carlo solutions involved setting up a model that characterized the stochastic components of the system, and specified their interrelationships. We showed how the SAS System provides us with convenient ways to characterize the stochastic components of the models we developed. We also described ways to apply random innovations drawn from known distributions to those stochastic components in order to simulate the response of the system overall. Repeated draws of these simulated responses gives us the observations needed to estimate the distribution function and the required cutoff values. The macro solutions presented here utilize only base SAS software; however, they can also be programmed, sometimes in an even simpler way, using SAS/IML software.

Furthermore, the SAS Solution for Risk Management (also known as Risk Dimensions) is a SAS software product specifically geared towards providing a robust framework for solving risk measurement problems such as VaR calculations. It encompasses all relevant aspects of the risk measurement problem, including data management, analytics, and reporting. In particular, the challenge alluded to in the previous section, regarding how to embed non-normal behavior in risk models without causing dependence on an unmanageable and unestimable number of parameters, is addressed by a copula approach for multivariate Monte Carlo simulation. A full treatment of the capabilities of the SAS Solution for Risk Management is beyond the scope of this chapter or this book.

It cannot be overemphasized that the results obtained from any Monte Carlo estimation are valid only insofar as the model captures the critical elements of the system under study, and that for any such system there will be a large number of modeling approaches that could be applied. One important consideration is computational efficiency, but it is far more important to ensure that the model's assumptions are consistent with reality and with each other.

8.6 References

Asarnow, E., and D. Edwards. 1995. "Measuring Loss on Defaulted Bank Loans: A 24-Year Study." *Journal of Commercial Lending* (March): 11-23.

Carey, M., and M. Hrcay. 2001. "Parameterizing Credit Risk Models with Rating Data." *Journal of Banking and Finance* 25(1).

Duffie, D., and K. Singleton. 1998. "Simulating Correlated Defaults." Palo Alto, CA: Stanford University, Graduate School of Business.

Fisher, M., D. Nychka, and D. Zervos. 1994. "Fitting the Term Structure of Interest Rates with Smoothing Splines." *Finance and Economics Discussion Series 95-1*. Washington: Board of Governors of the Federal Reserve System.

Frankfurter, G. M., and C. G. Lamourex. 1989. "Estimation and Selection Bias in Mean-Variance Portfolio Selection." *Journal of Financial Research* XII(2):173-181.

Gibson, M. S, and M. Pritsker. 2000. "Improving Grid-Based Methods for Estimating Value at Risk of Fixed-Income Portfolios." Washington: Board of Governors of the Federal Reserve System, Working Paper 2000-25.

Jorion, P. 1997. *Value at Risk: The New Benchmark for Controlling Derivatives Risk.* Burr Ridge, IL: McGraw Hill.

Keenan, S. C., D. T. Hamilton, and A. Bethault. 2000. *Historical Default Rates of Corporate Bond Issuers, 1920-1999.* New York: Moody's Investor Services.

Picoult, E. 1998. "Calculating Value-at-Risk with Monte Carlo Simulation." In *Monte Carlo Methodologies and Applications for Pricing and Risk Management*, ed. B. Dupire, 209-229. London: Risk Books.

Chapter 9 Modeling Time Series Processes with SAS/ETS Software

9.1 Introduction to Time Series Methodology

Time series methodology encompasses the collection of statistical procedures designed to empower quantitative researchers to handle issues particularly germane to temporal data. These statistical procedures are based upon assumptions that, theoretically, must be met so that inferences are accurate. Unfortunately, observations and measurements collected in the field do not always conform to the requirements, or the assumptions, of the statistics we intend to use. It is at this point that Monte Carlo research finds its place in applied research.

9.1.1 Box and Jenkins ARIMA Models

Data successively collected on the same person(s) or phenomenon (phenomena) over time notoriously evidence a nuisance condition known as autocorrelation. Autocorrelation in time data simply refers to a condition in which temporally adjacent or proximal observations evidence higher relationships than distally positioned observations. To clarify this point by way of an example, it is first important to define a lag.

Consider an unrealistically short series comprised of six observations taken on one person, say (20, 22, 24, 26, 28, 30). Essentially, this series will be correlated with itself, but in a special way—a way that does not necessarily give a 1.0 correlation. To estimate the degree of autocorrelation present, this series must first be lagged to some degree. With each lag, an observation is dropped, so the number of paired observations drops by one for each correlation between the original series and each series lagged to some order.

	Observations	First lag	Second lag
1	20	22	24
2	22	24	26
3	24	26	28
4	26	28	30
5	28	30	
6	30		

Autocorrelated observations are thought to be generated by probabilistic models called stochastic processes. By examining the features of the autocorrelation at hand, the stochastic process in question may be identified (Box & Jenkins 1976).

Stationary times series data may be modeled for two stochastic processes: Autoregressive (AR) and Moving Average (MA) (Box & Jenkins 1976). Autoregressive models represent the most recent observation in a series as a function of previous observations within the same series. The most general univariate case is represented by

$$y_t = \phi_1 \, y_{t-1} + \phi_2 \, y_{t-2} + \ldots + \phi_p \, y_{t-p} + \varepsilon_t$$

where t = 1 to T occasions, y_t denotes an observed score taken on some occasion (t) deviated from the original level y_0 of the series, ε denotes error associated with a given occasion (t), and ϕ $(-1 < \phi < 1)$ denotes a covariance among temporally ordered scores at some lag (e.g., t−1 = a lag of 1, t−2 = a lag of 2). The autocorrelation function of an AR process has the characteristic of tapering off exponentially following the lag of the process. The multivariate counterpart of this general case is

$$\mathbf{y}_t = \mathbf{\Phi}_1 \, \mathbf{y}_{t-1} + \mathbf{\Phi}_2 \, \mathbf{y}_{t-2} + \ldots + \mathbf{\Phi}_p \, \mathbf{y}_{t-p} + \mathbf{\varepsilon}_t$$

where the parameters are contained within the $\mathbf{\Phi}$ matrices. Following from the general univariate case, an AR model with a lag one relationship (i.e., AR1) is represented by

$$y_t = \phi_1 \, y_{t-1} + \varepsilon_t$$

and has the following multivariate counterpart

$$\mathbf{y}_t = \mathbf{\Phi}_1 \, \mathbf{y}_{t-1} + \mathbf{\varepsilon}_t$$

Unlike AR models, moving average (MA) models represent the most recent observation in a series as a function of autocorrelated errors among earlier observations. The most general univariate case is represented by

$$y_t = \varepsilon_t + \theta_1 \, \varepsilon_{t-1} + \theta_2 \, \varepsilon_{t-2} + \ldots + \theta_q \, \varepsilon_{t-q}$$

where t = 1 to T occasions, y_t denotes an observed score taken on some occasion (t) deviated from the original level y_0 of the series, ε denotes error associated with a given occasion (t), and θ $(-1 < \theta < 1)$ denotes a covariance among errors at some lag (e.g., t−1 = a lag of 1, t−2 = a lag of 2). By extension, the multivariate form of this model is

$$\mathbf{y}_t = \mathbf{\varepsilon}_t + \mathbf{\theta}_1 \, \mathbf{\varepsilon}_{t-1} + \mathbf{\theta}_2 \, \mathbf{\varepsilon}_{t-2} + \ldots + \mathbf{\theta}_q \, \mathbf{\varepsilon}_{t-q}$$

where the parameters are contained within the θ matrices. Following from the general univariate case, an MA model with a lag one relationship (i.e., MA1) is represented by

$$y_t = \varepsilon_t + \theta_1 \, \varepsilon_{t-1}$$

with the multivariate counterpart being

$$\mathbf{y}_t = \varepsilon_t + \theta_1 \varepsilon_{t-1}$$

An MA1 model would have the error for the first occasion correlate with the second occasion error, and would have the second occasion error correlate with the third occasion error. However, the first occasion error would not be correlated with the third occasion error. This is possible when a unique component is introduced on each occasion—a component that covaries with a subsequent error, but is independent of the previous error. Each unique component, jointly with the previous error, codetermines the following error in the series. The net effect of an MA1 process is that the autocorrelation function cuts off immediately after lag 1. Put simply, all error covariances beyond the first lag will be zero. Only the errors on temporally adjacent occasions possess a non-zero covariance and constitute the MA1 lag.

When both AR and MA processes are present in the same data, ARMA models may best represent the variation in the data. The univariate form of the most general case of the ARMA model is

$$y_t = \phi_1 y_{t-1} + \phi_2 y_{t-2} + \dots + \phi_p y_{t-p} + \theta_1 \varepsilon_{t-1} + \theta_2 \varepsilon_{t-2} + \dots + \theta_q \varepsilon_{t-q} + \varepsilon_t,$$

and the multivariate form is

$$\mathbf{y}_t = \Phi_1 \mathbf{y}_{t-1} + \Phi_2 \mathbf{y}_{t-2} + \dots + \Phi_p \mathbf{y}_{t-p} + \theta_1 \varepsilon_{t-1} + \theta_2 \varepsilon_{t-2} + \dots + \theta_q \varepsilon_{t-q} + \varepsilon_t,$$

The ARMA model with a lag one relationship for both its AR and MA processes is represented by

$$y_t = \phi_1 y_{t-1} + \varepsilon_t + \theta_1 \varepsilon_{t-1}$$

and its multivariate form is

$$\mathbf{y}_t = \Phi_1 \mathbf{y}_{t-1} + \varepsilon_t + \theta_1 \varepsilon_{t-1}$$

If growth or a trend is expected in the observed time series (i.e., the data is nonstationary), an ARMA model is tested against the data only after a differencing procedure is applied to the data to remove the trend. Thus, an ARMA model is applied to residualized data. When an ARMA model is applied to differenced data, the model is properly called an autoregressive integrated moving-average (ARIMA) model. In other words, ARMA and ARIMA models differ only in that the latter are applied to residualized data originally possessing a trend. Most often a trend is removed from the data through a differencing procedure. The differencing procedure involves systematically obtaining the numerical difference between paired values of different temporal occasions. First differences are calculated by subtracting temporally earlier values from later adjacent values. Using the unrealistically short series of six observations [20, 22, 21, 26, 30, 28], the initial value obtained for the first difference is 2 (or 22-20); the fifth value, -2 (or 28-30).

	Observations	First Difference	Second Difference
1	20		
2	22	2	
3	21	- 1	- 3
4	26	5	6
5	30	4	-1
6	28	- 2	- 6

Note that an observation is lost as a result of this manner of de-trending. The impact of this loss, of course, is far less severe for series with a more realistic number of observations (e.g., 50 or more; see Box & Jenkins 1976). If the trend is not removed by obtaining first differences, second differences may be obtained to further stabilize the series. Higher order differences are possible so long as the series is large enough to withstand the loss of an observation for each difference. Several of the SAS/ETS procedures include an option that automatically differences a series to whatever extent is necessary when a trend is present. Statistical routines are automatically invoked by these procedures to test whether a given series is still nonstationary. Differencing ends when a stationary solution has been attained.

9.1.2 Akaike's State Space Models for Multivariate Times Series

When multiple series of observations are collected over time, the researcher becomes concerned not just with modeling the individual series, but also with the cross-lagged relationships that may occur between the series and/or the weighted aggregate of the multiple series. Several approaches for modeling multivariate time series exist. A very common approach involves using state space modeling, an approach Akaike (1976) advocated and introduced clearly. Representing a multivariate time series in what is known as a state vector, the state space modeling approach invokes canonical analysis in the analysis of the data (Moryson 1998).

State space procedures identify the multivariate times series models that best fit the data according to the value of an Akaike information criterion (AIC), with smaller AIC values signaling the better fitting models. The SAS/ETS STATESPACE procedure (PROC STATESPACE) can report the AIC values for each lag considered so that the researcher may rank differently lagged models according to their degree of fit. By default, PROC STATESPACE eliminates variables not sufficiently contributive to the model, according to their degree of statistical significance. An important feature of PROC STATESPACE to note is its ability to treat data requiring differencing.

9.1.3 Modeling Multiple Regression Data with Serially Correlated Disturbances

Harvey (1981) defines dynamic regression models as regression models designed to accommodate criterion variables in which an autoregressive process is present. They are so called because the models handle situations in which the relationships between the variables under investigation are non-contemporaneous. In other words, the observations of the criterion variable may have been collected over time. Of course, all standard time series statistical procedures assume that the observations are equidistant from one another in time. For example, data for the dependent variable may be collected daily, once a week on Saturdays, every three days, every four months, etc. Harvey (1981) stresses that maximum likelihood estimation, as opposed to ordinary least squares, must be used when a lagged dependent variable is introduced into the model. Indeed, the SAS/ETS AUTOREG procedure (PROC AUTOREG) uses maximum likelihood estimation for its solutions.

9.2 Introduction to SAS/ETS Software

SAS/ETS software, a component of the SAS System, provides SAS procedures for econometric analysis, time series analysis, forecasting time series, systems modeling and simulation, seasonal adjustment, financial analysis and reporting, access to economic and financial databases, and time series data management.

SAS/ETS Software: Applications Guide 1 discusses features of SAS/ETS software for time series modeling and forecasting, financial reporting, and loan analysis. The second volume, *SAS/ETS Software: Applications Guide 2*, discusses features of SAS/ETS software for econometric modeling and simulation. Table 9.1 provides an overview of the SAS/ETS procedures that are available.

Table 9.1 *Overview of SAS/ETS Procedures*

PROCEDURE	DESCRIPTION
PROC ARIMA	ARIMA (Box-Jenkins) and ARIMAX (Box-Tiao) modeling and forecasting
PROC AUTOREG	regression analysis with autocorrelated errors and ARCH and GARCH modeling
PROC CITIBASE	access to DRI/McGraw-Hill Basic Economic database files
PROC COMPUTAB	spreadsheet calculations and financial report generation
PROC DATASOURCE	access to financial and economic databases
PROC EXPAND	time series interpolation and frequency conversion, and transformation of time series
PROC FORECAST	automatic forecasting
PROC LOAN	loan analysis and comparison
PROC MODEL	nonlinear simultaneous equations regression and nonlinear systems modeling and simulation
PROC MORTGAGE	fixed-rate mortgage amortization tables
PROC PDLREG	polynomial distributed lag regression (Almon lags)
PROC SIMLIN	linear systems simulation
PROC SPECTRA	spectral and cross-spectral analysis
PROC STATESPACE	state space modeling and automated forecasting of multivariate time series
PROC SYSLIN	linear simultaneous equations models
PROC TSCSREG	time series cross-sectional regression analysis
PROC X11	seasonal adjustment (Census X-11 and X-11-ARIMA)

9.3 Example 1: Generating Univariate Time Series Processes

Recall that the lag one autoregressive (AR1) process may be modeled by

$$y_t = \phi_1 \, y_{t-1} + \varepsilon_t \tag{9.1}$$

When generating a univariate time series to have an AR1 process, the generating equation will bear a similar form. The SAS RANNOR function is used to generate a random normal deviate (scaled to have a mean of zero and a standard deviation of one) for each term in the equation (y_{t-1}, ε_t). Because the expected standard deviation of the RANNOR function is 1.0, the random variable component may be modified with whatever autoregressive coefficient parameter is desired.

Consider the case of generating a 50-observation series with an AR1 process in which the squared parameter value is .50. Equation (9.1) indicates that the most recent observation in the series (y_t) is determined by the previous observation (y_{t-1}) plus some amount of error (ε_t). The degree of relationship between temporally adjacent observations is denoted by ϕ_1. By definition,

$$y_1 = \varepsilon_1$$

$$y_2 = \phi_1 \, y_1 + \varepsilon_2$$

$$y_3 = \phi_1 \, y_2 + \varepsilon_3$$

Because $y_1 = \varepsilon_1$, begin by specifying

```
SERIES (1) = RANNOR(-1);
```

The remainder of the series is generated as

```
do j = 2 to 50;
SERIES (j) = SQRT(.50) *SERIES(j-1) + SQRT(.50)*RANNOR(-1);
end;
```

Notice that the squared coefficients of both terms sum to 1.0. Because the expected SERIES(2) observation is constrained to 1.0, the expected value for SQRT(.50) *SERIES(j-1) when defining the SERIES(3) observation will be .50. Moreover, the SERIES(3) observation is thereby constrained to an expected value of 1.0.

These commands are now placed within the context of a SAS program. In the following program, PROC ARIMA is used to estimate the value of the generated AR process.

Program 9.1 *Generating AR1 Data for PROC ARIMA*

```
/**************************************************************************/
/* This program generates a series of 50 observations with an AR1 process.  The  */
/* expected AR1 value will be .8367, the square of which is .70.  The error      */
/* variance component is made to account for 30% of each total observation variance */
/*(with the exception of the most recent observation in the series).             */
/*                                                                               */
/**************************************************************************/

DATA AR;
      ARRAY OBS OBS1-OBS50;    *** Room is made for 50 observations;

  OBS (1) = RANNOR (-1);    *** The most recent observation in the series;
    DO J = 2 TO 50;
        OBS (J) = SQRT(.70) * OBS (J-1) + SQRT(.30) * RANNOR(-1);
    END; OUTPUT;
        KEEP OBS1-OBS50;
  PROC TRANSPOSE OUT=AR1;    *** The series is transposed into a column for PROC ARIMA;

DATA AR1; SET AR1;

PROC ARIMA DATA = AR1; IDENTIFY VAR=COL1 NLAG=1;   *** The AR1 lag value is estimated;
        ESTIMATE P = 1;
RUN;
```

An adaptation of this program now may be incorporated into the following macro so that the results of 200 replications could be accumulated. This program was written to consider only six different research situations, though in a true Monte Carlo study many more situations would most likely be considered, depending upon the number of theoretically relevant conditions.

Program 9.2 *PROC ARIMA Macro Example for a Monte Carlo Study*

```
/**************************************************************************/
/* Macro AR1 generates a lag one autoregressive process 200 times for each of six   */
/* research conditions.  In a true Monte Carlo study more than six conditions       */
/* ordinarily will be planned.  For each additional AR1 process desired, add        */
/* another AR1 statement with the parameters of interest. If so many AR1 statements */
/* are added that the program lacks sufficient memory to run, the research plan may */
/* be accomplished with more than one run, each run responsible for some set of     */
/* conditions.                                                                      */
/*                                                                                  */
/* Parameters:                                                                      */
/* N          The number of observations in the series.                            */
/* ARLAG      The squared value of the lag relationship desired.                    */
/* VARIANCE   The squared value of the error variance desired.                      */
/* SCENARI    The designated number id of a given condition.                        */
/*                                                                                  */
/**************************************************************************/

OPTIONS LINESIZE=100 NOSOURCE NOSOURCE2 NONOTES; *** Log file will report errors only;

LIBNAME AUTOREG 'C:\MY DOCUMENTS\MY SAS FILES\RESULTS';

PROC FORMAT;VALUE SCENE                          *** Labels six conditions;
             1 = 'ARLAG**2 = .40, N = 100'
             2 = 'ARLAG**2 = .60, N = 100'
             3 = 'ARLAG**2 = .80, N = 100'
             4 = 'ARLAG**2 = .40, N = 500'
```

```
                5 = 'ARLAG**2 = .60, N = 500'
                6 = 'ARLAG**2 = .80, N = 500';
%MACRO AR1(N,ARLAG,VARIANCE,SCENARI);                  *** Macro begins;
  %DO J=1 %TO 200;                                     *** 200 replications;

    DATA SEM&J;
      ARRAY SERIE SERIE1-SERIE&N;

   SERIE(1)=RANNOR(-1);                                *** Generates AR1 data;
      DO J=2 TO &N;
        SERIE(J)= SQRT(&ARLAG)*SERIE(J-1) + SQRT(&VARIANCE)*RANNOR(-1);

END;OUTPUT;
                                             *** Transposes series to a column;
      KEEP SERIE1-SERIE&N; PROC TRANSPOSE OUT=D2;

DATA D2;SET D2;

PROC ARIMA DATA=D2;IDENTIFY VAR=COL1 NLAG=1 NOPRINT; *** Output is suppressed;
               ESTIMATE P=1 OUTSTAT=ARIMA1 OUTMODEL=ARIMA2 NOPRINT MAXIT=5000;
                                     *** Select statistics are outputted;
DATA ARIMA1;SET ARIMA1;KEEP _VALUE_ _STAT_;IF 1<=_N_<= 2;
          PROC TRANSPOSE OUT=ARIMA1;
DATA ARIMA1;SET ARIMA1; AIC=COL1; SBC=COL2;OUTPUT;
          KEEP AIC SBC;
DATA ARIMA2;SET ARIMA2;IF _N_= 6;ARLAG=_VALUE_;ARLAGSTD=_STD_;
          TTEST=ARLAG/ARLAGSTD;OUTPUT;KEEP ARLAG TTEST;
DATA COMBINE;MERGE ARIMA1 ARIMA2;SCENARIO=&SCENARI;OUTPUT;
                          *** OUTMODEL and OUTSTAT results are merged;

   PROC APPEND BASE=AUTOREG.RESULT1 (CNTLLEV=MEMBER); *** Results compiled in library;

  %END;
%MEND COMPUTE;                                 *** End of Macro;

%AR1 (100,.40,.60,1);            *** Each AR1 presents one research situation;
%AR1 (100,.60,.40,2);
%AR1 (100,.80,.20,3);
%AR1 (500,.40,.60,4);
%AR1 (500,.60,.40,5);
%AR1 (500,.80,.20,6);

FORMAT SCENARIO SCENE.;

PROC SORT;BY SCENARIO;
PROC SUMMARY PRINT VARDEF=N MAXDEC=2 FW=8;CLASS SCENARIO;  *** Summarizes Results;
          VAR AIC SBC ARLAG TTEST;
RUN;
```

PROC SUMMARY presents the overall findings which are shown in Output 9.2. Of course, a full Monte Carlo study was not intended for this example, but a couple of findings nonetheless may be drawn from these results. Given that scenarios 1-3 were generated to have 100 observations, and scenarios 4-6 were generated to have 500 observations, it can be seen that the true AR1 lag value is overall modestly underestimated when N = 100. Note that the squared AR1 parameter values were .40, .60, and.80. The expected AR1 parameter values were therefore .6325, .7746, and .8944. The expected AR1 lag values for scenarios 4-6 were accurately estimated. Observe also that the magnitudes of the AIC and the SBC were much higher for the larger sample size (N = 500). Furthermore, their magnitudes were, overall, greater when the AR1 lag parameters were lower in value.

Output 9.2 *Summary of 200 PROC ARIMA Results (Program 9.2)*

```
                           The SUMMARY Procedure

scenario    Obs    Variable      N       Mean    Std Dev    Minimum    Maximum
-----------------------------------------------------------------------------
      1     200    AIC         200     234.13      14.07     200.72     268.38
                   SBC         200     239.34      14.07     205.93     273.59
                   ARlag       200       0.61       0.08       0.34       0.82
                   ttest       200       7.76       1.56       3.59      13.91

      2     200    AIC         200     194.09      13.58     160.19     227.27
                   SBC         200     199.30      13.58     165.40     232.48
                   ARlag       200       0.76       0.08       0.48       0.99
                   ttest       200      12.20       5.06       5.45      53.94

      3     200    AIC         200     124.06      14.28      83.62     156.56
                   SBC         200     129.27      14.28      88.83     161.77
                   ARlag       200       0.88       0.07       0.63       1.00
                   ttest       200      22.08      12.16       8.01      82.33

      4     200    AIC         200    1160.56      30.92    1071.40    1245.79
                   SBC         200    1168.99      30.92    1079.83    1254.22
                   ARlag       200       0.63       0.03       0.55       0.72
                   ttest       200      18.04       1.49      14.70      22.98

      5     200    AIC         200     961.55      32.80     860.55    1054.47
                   SBC         200     969.98      32.80     868.98    1062.90
                   ARlag       200       0.77       0.03       0.68       0.84
                   ttest       200      26.96       2.54      20.70      34.76

      6     200    AIC         200     619.06      30.32     520.87     696.78
                   SBC         200     627.49      30.32     529.30     705.21
                   ARlag       200       0.89       0.02       0.82       0.99
                   ttest       200      44.13       9.09      31.46     128.96
```

9.4 Example 2: Generating Multivariate Time Series Processes

Recall that the multivariate AR model is defined by

$$\mathbf{y}_t = \Phi_1\,\mathbf{y}_{t-1} + \Phi_2\,\mathbf{y}_{t-2} + \ldots + \Phi_p\,\mathbf{y}_{t-p} + \varepsilon_t$$

where parameters for more than one series are contained within the Φ matrices. What may not be obvious is that a Φ matrix holds not only the AR coefficients for each process, but also cross-lag coefficients existing between the multiple series collected. So, both autoregressive correlations and cross-lagged correlations are calculated when multivariate autoregressive time series procedures are used. Cross-lag coefficients allow the researcher to specify causal relationships between the lags, an important feature of any multivariate time series model. Cross-lag coefficients represent lagged relationships between two or more series. Suppose that two series have 15 observations. Cross-lagging Series A with Series B would give 14 paired observations.

Occasion	Series A	Series B	Paired Observations	Series A	Lagged Series B
1	3	53	1	3	54
2	4	54	2	4	55
3	7	55	3	7	56
4	8	56	4	8	57
5	2	57	5	2	55
6	4	55	6	4	58
7	6	58	7	6	59
8	14	59	8	14	56
9	15	56	9	15	60
10	14	60	10	14	62
11	16	62	11	16	64
12	17	64	12	17	65
13	17	65	13	17	66
14	18	66	14	18	67
15	19	67			

To correlate the paired cross-lagged observations, a cross-lagged correlation is calculated. Cross-lagged correlations, like autocorrelations, may be lagged beyond the first order. Of course, both of these 15-occasion series are far shorter than what is recommended in practice. Box and Jenkins (1976) advise that at least 50 observations be collected to ensure positive identification of the time series processes under study. Employing power analysis to determine the needed sample size in a particular scenario would be much more precise.

The lag one multivariate autoregressive model (i.e., Multivariate AR1) appropriate for the data presented would be:

$$\mathbf{y}_t = \Phi_1 \, \mathbf{y}_{t-1} + \varepsilon_t$$

When generating a univariate time series to have a Multivariate AR1 process, more than one generating equation, of course, is needed. Not only are the random variable components modified with whatever autoregressive coefficient parameter is desired, but cross-lagged relationships will participate in the sequence of occasions. Consider the case in which a researcher wants to model three 200-observation series holding cross-lagged relationships. Again, because the first observation in each series equals the first error, we begin by specifying

```
SerieA(1)=rannor(-1);
SerieB(1)=rannor(-11);
SerieC(1)=rannor(-111);

    do j=2 to 200;

        VAR_A(j) =rannor(-1111);
        VAR_B(j) =rannor(-11111);
        VAR_C(j) =rannor(-111111);

SerieA(j)=VAR_A(j)*SQRT(.20) + SerieA(j-1)*SQRT(.80);
SerieB(j)=VAR_B(j)*SQRT(.20) + SerieB(j-1)*SQRT(.60) + SerieA(j-1)*(.20);
SerieC(j)=VAR_C(j)*SQRT(.15) + SerieC(j-1)*SQRT(.45) + SerieA(j-1)*(.10) +
          SerieB(j-1)*(.30);
```

These commands are now placed within the context of a SAS program. In the following program, PROC STATESPACE is used to estimate the value of the generated Multivariate AR process, with cross-lagged relationships. Moryson (1998) demonstrates how the state space statistical procedure accommodates multivariate time series data. Indeed, more than one analytical approach to analyzing multivariate time series exists.

Program 9.3 *Generating Multivariate AR1 Data for PROC STATESPACE*

```
/*********************************************************************************/
/* This program generates three series (Series A, B, and C) of 200 observations   */
/* each with a Multivariate AR1 process with cross-lagged relationships.  The      */
/* autoregressive coefficients for each series are .80, .60, and .45, respectively,*/
/* and the error variance components are .20, .20 and .15, respectively.  The cross-*/
/* lagged relationship between Series A and B is .20; between Series A and C, .10;  */
/* and between Series B and C, .30.                                               */
/*                                                                               */
/*********************************************************************************/
DATA GENERATE;
  ARRAY SERIEA SERIEA1-SERIEA200;           *** each creates room for 200 observations;
  ARRAY SERIEB SERIEB1-SERIEB200;
  ARRAY SERIEC SERIEC1-SERIEC200;
  ARRAY VAR_A  VAR_A1 -VAR_A200;
  ARRAY VAR_B  VAR_B1 -VAR_B200;
  ARRAY VAR_C  VAR_C1 -VAR_C200;

  SERIEA(1)=RANNOR(-1);                      *** generates the first occasion;
  SERIEB(1)=RANNOR(-11);
  SERIEC(1)=RANNOR(-111);

      VAR_A(1) =0;
      VAR_B(1) =0;
      VAR_C(1) =0;

   DO J=2 TO 200;

      VAR_A(J) =RANNOR(-1111);  *** random normal deviates are generated;
      VAR_B(J) =RANNOR(-11111);
      VAR_C(J) =RANNOR(-111111);

                             *** the equations which generate the process follow;
SERIEA(J)=VAR_A(J)*SQRT(.20) + SERIEA(J-1)*SQRT(.80);
SERIEB(J)=VAR_B(J)*SQRT(.20) + SERIEB(J-1)*SQRT(.60) + SERIEA(J-1)*(.20);
SERIEC(J)=VAR_C(J)*SQRT(.15) + SERIEC(J-1)*SQRT(.45) + SERIEA(J-1)*(.10) +
          SERIEB(J-1)*(.30);

   END;KEEP SERIEA1-SERIEA200
           SERIEB1-SERIEB200
           SERIEC1-SERIEC200;  *** retains only the series generated;
OUTPUT;
```

This program may be inserted into the following macro so that the results of 200 replications can be accumulated. This program was written to consider only three different research situations (far fewer than necessary in a true Monte Carlo study).

Program 9.4   *Macro for Multivariate AR1 Data Using PROC STATESPACE*

```
/***************************************************************************/
/* This macro generates 200 replications and aggregates the results. As before,  */
/* three series (Series A, B, and C) of 200 observations each with a Multivariate  */
/* AR1 process with cross-lagged relationships.  The autoregressive coefficients  */
/* for each series are .80, .60, and .45, respectively, and the error variance  */
/* components are .20, .20 and .15, respectively.  The cross-lagged relationship  */
/* between Series A and B is .20; between Series A and C, .10; and between Series  */
/* B and C, .30.                                                            */
/*                                                                          */
/***************************************************************************/

OPTIONS LINESIZE=100 NOSOURCE NOSOURCE2 NONOTES;

LIBNAME MULTITS 'C:\MY DOCUMENTS\MY SAS FILES\RESULTS';

%MACRO MULTITS (REPS,N,VARA,AR_AA,
                       VARB,AR_BB,AR_BA,
                       VARC,AR_CC,AR_CA,AR_CB,SCENARI);

    %DO J=1 %TO &REPS;                     *** 200 replications are undertaken;

DATA GENERATE&J;
   ARRAY SERIEA SERIEA1-SERIEA&N;          *** creates space for the observations;
   ARRAY SERIEB SERIEB1-SERIEB&N;
   ARRAY SERIEC SERIEC1-SERIEC&N;
   ARRAY VAR_A  VAR_A1 -VAR_A&N ;
   ARRAY VAR_B  VAR_B1 -VAR_B&N ;
   ARRAY VAR_C  VAR_C1 -VAR_C&N ;

   SERIEA(1)=RANNOR(-1);
   SERIEB(1)=RANNOR(-11);
   SERIEC(1)=RANNOR(-111);

       VAR_A(1) =0;
       VAR_B(1) =0;
       VAR_C(1) =0;

     DO J=2 TO &N;

       VAR_A(J) =RANNOR(-1111);
       VAR_B(J) =RANNOR(-11111);
       VAR_C(J) =RANNOR(-111111);

*** generates the multivariate processes with cross-lagged relationships;

SERIEA(J)=VAR_A(J)*SQRT(&VARA) + SERIEA(J-1)*SQRT(&AR_AA);
SERIEB(J)=VAR_B(J)*SQRT(&VARB) + SERIEB(J-1)*SQRT(&AR_BB) + SERIEA(J-1)*(&AR_BA);
SERIEC(J)=VAR_C(J)*SQRT(&VARC) + SERIEC(J-1)*SQRT(&AR_CC) + SERIEA(J-1)*(&AR_CA) +
            SERIEB(J-1)*(&AR_CB);

   END; KEEP SERIEA1-SERIEA&N
          SERIEB1-SERIEB&N
          SERIEC1-SERIEC&N;
OUTPUT;


                              *** transposes series a to prepare it for analysis;
DATA GENERAT1;SET GENERATE&J;
   KEEP SERIEA1-SERIEA&N;PROC TRANSPOSE OUT=GENERAT1;
   DATA GENERAT1;SET GENERAT1;ID=_N_;SERIESA=COL1;OUTPUT;DROP COL1;

                              *** transposes series b to prepare it for analysis;
DATA GENERAT2;SET GENERATE&J;
   KEEP SERIEB1-SERIEB&N;PROC TRANSPOSE OUT=GENERAT2;
   DATA GENERAT2;SET GENERAT2;ID=_N_;SERIESB=COL1;OUTPUT;DROP COL1;

                              *** transposes series c to prepare it for analysis;
DATA GENERAT3;SET GENERATE&J;
```

```
        KEEP SERIEC1-SERIEC&N;PROC TRANSPOSE OUT=GENERAT3;
        DATA GENERAT3;SET GENERAT3;ID=_N_;SERIESC=COL1;OUTPUT;DROP COL1;

                              *** merges the three series by observation;

DATA GENERATE&J;MERGE GENERAT1 GENERAT2 GENERAT3;BY ID;
            KEEP ID SERIESA SERIESB SERIESC ;

                              *** fits the multivariate model to the series data;

PROC STATESPACE INTERVAL=DAY MAXIT=200 ARMAX=1 LAGMAX=1
      NOPRINT    OUTMODEL=ARCOEFFS;

                  *** outputs the collected statistics var seriesa seriesb seriesc;

        TITLE 'MULTIVARIATE ARIMA (1,0,0) CROSSLAGGED RESULTS';

                        *** plucks parameter estimates for series a out of statespace output;

DATA GENERAT1;SET ARCOEFFS;IF _N_ = 1;
        KEEP F_1 F_2 F_3 SIG_1 SIG_2 SIG_3;
        AR_AA=F_1**2;    AR_AB=F_2;    AR_AC=F_3;
        RESCOVAA=SIG_1; RESCOVAB=SIG_2; RESCOVAC=SIG_3;
        KEEP AR_AA AR_AB AR_AC RESCOVAA RESCOVAB RESCOVAC;
        OUTPUT;

                        *** plucks parameter estimates for series b out of statespace output;

DATA GENERAT2;SET ARCOEFFS;IF _N_ = 3;
        KEEP F_1 F_2 F_3 SIG_1 SIG_2 SIG_3;
        AR_BA=F_1;    AR_BB=F_2**2;    AR_BC=F_3;
        RESCOVBA=SIG_1; RESCOVBB=SIG_2; RESCOVBC=SIG_3;
        KEEP AR_BA AR_BB AR_BC RESCOVBA RESCOVBB RESCOVBC;
        OUTPUT;

                        *** plucks parameter estimates for series c out of statespace output;

DATA GENERAT3;SET ARCOEFFS;IF _N_ = 5;
        KEEP F_1 F_2 F_3 SIG_1 SIG_2 SIG_3;
        AR_CA=F_1;    AR_CB=F_2;    AR_CC=F_3**2;
        RESCOVCA=SIG_1; RESCOVCB=SIG_2; RESCOVCC=SIG_3;
        KEEP AR_CA AR_CB AR_CC RESCOVCA RESCOVCB RESCOVCC;
        OUTPUT;

                        *** merges the parameter estimates for each of the three series;

DATA ARCOEFFS; MERGE GENERAT1 GENERAT2 GENERAT3 GENERATE&J;
            SCENARIO=&SCENARI;OUTPUT;

        KEEP AR_AA AR_AB AR_AC RESCOVAA RESCOVAB RESCOVAC
            AR_BA AR_BB AR_BC RESCOVBA RESCOVBB RESCOVBC
            AR_CA AR_CB AR_CC RESCOVCA RESCOVCB RESCOVCC
            SCENARIO M_A M_B M_C VAR_A VAR_B VAR_C;

  PROC DELETE DATA=GENERATE&J;    *** frees some of the memory space for SAS;
  PROC DELETE DATA=GENERAT1;
  PROC DELETE DATA=GENERAT2;
  PROC DELETE DATA=GENERAT3;
```

```
      *** adds the parameter information to an output file for one of 200 iterations;

   PROC APPEND BASE=MULTITS.RESULT (CNTLLEV=MEMBER);

 %END;
%MEND COMPUTE;

*** the following macro statements feed the macro above the parameters for each
    condition under study;

%MULTITS (200, 100,   .20, .80,
                      .20, .60, .20,
                      .15, .45, .10, .30, 1);

%MULTITS (200, 500,   .20, .80,
                      .20, .60, .20,
                      .15, .45, .10, .30, 2);

%MULTITS (200, 1000,  .20, .80,
                      .20, .60, .20,
                      .15, .45, .10, .30, 3);

PROC SORT;BY SCENARIO;

                        *** proc summary summarizes the results for each condition;

PROC SUMMARY PRINT VARDEF=N MAXDEC=2 FW=8;
       CLASS SCENARIO;   *** summarizes results;
            VAR   AR_AA AR_AB AR_AC
                  AR_BA AR_BB AR_BC
                  AR_CA AR_CB AR_CC
                  RESCOVAA RESCOVAB RESCOVAC
                  RESCOVBA RESCOVBB RESCOVBC
                  RESCOVCA RESCOVCB RESCOVCC;

            TITLE1   '*****   SCENARIO 1 (N=100)   *****';
            TITLE2   '*****   SCENARIO 2 (N=500)   *****';
            TITLE3   '*****   SCENARIO 3 (N=1000)  *****';

            TITLE5   'AR_AA=.80 AR_BB=.60 AR_CC=.45';
            TITLE6   'AR_BA=.20 AR_CA=.10 AR_CB=.30';
            TITLE7   ' ';
RUN;
```

PROC SUMMARY presents the estimates derived from the data replications (see Output 9.4). The results confirm that the autoregressive coefficients, cross-lagged coefficients, and errors are very accurate. Often, in a Monte Carlo simulation study, the researcher is concerned with studying accuracy of estimates under particular conditions, perhaps conditions in which assumptions of the statistical procedure are violated to varying extents so that the robustness of the statistic to violations may be evaluated. PROC STATESPACE outputs a number of statistical estimates that may be subjected to study under whatever conditions specified. Any of these output options may be incorporated into the macro and thereby collected for each replication.

Output 9.4 *Summary of 200 PROC STATESPACE Results (Program 9.4)*

```
***** Scenario 1 (n=100)   *****  Scenario 2 (n=500)  *****  Scenario 3 (n=1000)  ****
                                  The SUMMARY Procedure
              N
SCENARIO     Obs    Variable      N      Mean      Std Dev    Minimum    Maximum
--------------------------------------------------------------------------------------
    1        200    AR_AA        200      0.70       0.12       0.40       1.00
                    AR_AB        200     -0.00       0.08      -0.26       0.23
                    AR_AC        200     -0.02       0.07      -0.25       0.18
                    AR_BA        200      0.21       0.07       0.04       0.39
                    AR_BB        200      0.54       0.10       0.26       0.77
                    AR_BC        200      0.00       0.06      -0.17       0.16
                    AR_CA        200      0.11       0.06      -0.05       0.28
                    AR_CB        200      0.30       0.07       0.17       0.48
                    AR_CC        200      0.41       0.07       0.17       0.60
                    ResCovAA     200      0.20       0.03       0.13       0.31
                    ResCovAB     200      0.01       0.02      -0.06       0.07
                    ResCovAC     200      0.00       0.02      -0.07       0.09
                    ResCovBA     200      0.01       0.02      -0.06       0.07
                    ResCovBB     200      0.21       0.03       0.12       0.32
                    ResCovBC     200      0.01       0.02      -0.05       0.09
                    ResCovCA     200      0.00       0.02      -0.07       0.09
                    ResCovCB     200      0.01       0.02      -0.05       0.09
                    ResCovCC     200      0.17       0.03       0.11       0.28

    2        200    AR_AA        200      0.79       0.04       0.67       0.91
                    AR_AB        200      0.00       0.03      -0.09       0.09
                    AR_AC        200     -0.00       0.03      -0.08       0.07
                    AR_BA        200      0.20       0.03       0.13       0.26
                    AR_BB        200      0.59       0.05       0.45       0.75
                    AR_BC        200      0.00       0.03      -0.07       0.07
                    AR_CA        200      0.10       0.02       0.04       0.16
                    AR_CB        200      0.30       0.03       0.21       0.37
                    AR_CC        200      0.44       0.04       0.35       0.54
                    ResCovAA     200      0.20       0.01       0.17       0.24
                    ResCovAB     200      0.00       0.01      -0.02       0.03
                    ResCovAC     200      0.00       0.01      -0.02       0.02
                    ResCovBA     200      0.00       0.01      -0.02       0.03
                    ResCovBB     200      0.20       0.01       0.17       0.23
                    ResCovBC     200      0.00       0.01      -0.02       0.02
                    ResCovCA     200      0.00       0.01      -0.02       0.02
                    ResCovCB     200      0.00       0.01      -0.02       0.02
                    ResCovCC     200      0.15       0.01       0.13       0.19

    3        200    AR_AA        200      0.80       0.03       0.70       0.86
                    AR_AB        200     -0.00       0.02      -0.07       0.07
                    AR_AC        200     -0.00       0.02      -0.05       0.06
                    AR_BA        200      0.20       0.02       0.14       0.25
                    AR_BB        200      0.59       0.03       0.49       0.67
                    AR_BC        200     -0.00       0.02      -0.04       0.05
                    AR_CA        200      0.10       0.02       0.05       0.14
                    AR_CB        200      0.30       0.02       0.24       0.37
                    AR_CC        200      0.45       0.02       0.39       0.50
                    ResCovAA     200      0.20       0.01       0.18       0.23
                    ResCovAB     200      0.00       0.01      -0.02       0.02
                    ResCovAC     200      0.00       0.01      -0.01       0.02
                    ResCovBA     200      0.00       0.01      -0.02       0.02
                    ResCovBB     200      0.20       0.01       0.18       0.22
                    ResCovBC     200      0.00       0.01      -0.01       0.02
                    ResCovCA     200      0.00       0.01      -0.01       0.02
                    ResCovCB     200      0.00       0.01      -0.01       0.02
                    ResCovCC     200      0.15       0.01       0.13       0.17
--------------------------------------------------------------------------------------
```

9.5 Example 3: Generating Correlated Variables with Autocorrelated Errors

Autocorrelation is a nuisance condition that, when left uncontrolled, biases the outcome of ordinary least squares procedures. Neter, Wasserman, and Kutner (1989) identify several problems this condition causes, including the inefficiency of estimated regression coefficients, and an underestimation of the error variances and the standard deviation of the estimated regression coefficients. A common approach to modeling autocorrelation is to identify and directly model the process present in the data as a form of control. The residuals of the analysis, purified of the process, may then be analyzed by the statistical procedure of choice.

PROC AUTOREG permits the researcher to conduct a regression analysis when autocorrelated errors are present in the dependent variable data. The general case for a multiple regression model with a first order autoregressive process running through the dependent variable takes the form

$$Y_t = \alpha + \beta_1 X_{t1} + \beta_2 X_{t2} + \dots + \beta_i X_{ti} + \phi_1 \varepsilon_{t-1} + u_t$$

where $\phi_1 \varepsilon_{t-1} + u_t$ is the AR1 process.

To understand how to generate data for PROC AUTOREG, it may be useful first to generate data for multiple regression. Consider Program 9.5. This program generates data comprised of one criterion variable and two predictor variables. Beta weights for each of the predictor variables on the criterion variable are aggregated for 200 replications, and the results—the distributions of both statistics—are summarized using PROC UNIVARIATE.

Program 9.5 Macro for Multiple Regression Data

```
/**********************************************************************************/
/* This macro generates 200 replications of data comprised of two predictors and  */
/* one criterion variable and aggregates the results.  The squared Beta weight for */
/* predictor A is.35; for predictor B, .25.  PROC UNIVARIATE is used to display the */
/* sampling distribution of each statistic.  Match the squared Beta weights used to */
/* generate the data with the estimated Beta weights.                              */
/*                                                                                 */
/**********************************************************************************/
OPTIONS LINESIZE=100 NONUMBER NODATE SPOOL ERASE NOSOURCE NOSOURCE2 NONOTES;

LIBNAME REG 'C:\MY DOCUMENTS\MY SAS FILES\RESULTS';

%MACRO REG (REPS,N,ERR,BETA1,BETA2);
   %DO J=1 %TO &REPS;

DATA GENERATE&J;

   DO I=1 TO &N;

      A=RANNOR(-2);            *** predictor a generated to have unit variance;
      B=RANNOR(-3);            *** predictor b generated to have unit variance;
                              *** weighted predictors a and b plus random error give y;
      Y=RANNOR(-6)*SQRT(&ERR) + A*SQRT(&BETA1) + B*SQRT(&BETA2);
      OUTPUT;
   END;
```

```
DATA GENERATE&J;SET GENERATE&J;

PROC REG NOPRINT OUTEST=GENERATE&J;     *** proc reg outputs the beta coefficients;
  MODEL Y = A B/OUTSTB;
 RUN;

DATA GENERATE&J;SET GENERATE&J;KEEP A B A_SQ B_SQ;
A_SQ=A**2; B_SQ=B**2;OUTPUT;

DATA GENERATE&J;SET GENERATE&J;KEEP A_SQ B_SQ;

   PROC APPEND BASE=REG.RESULT1 (CNTLLEV=MEMBER);
   PROC DELETE DATA=GENERATE&J;

  %END;
%MEND REG;

   *** 200 reps, n= 500, .45= squared error, .35= beta a squared, .25= beta b squared;

%REG (200,500,.45,.30,.25);

DATA REG;SET REG.RESULT1;

PROC UNIVARIATE PLOT; VAR A_SQ B_SQ;   *** proc univariate displays the distributions;

QUIT;
```

Output 9.5a *Summary of 200 PROC REG Results for the Squared A Weight (Program 9.5)*

```
                      The UNIVARIATE Procedure
                         Variable:  A_SQ

                             Moments

N                           204    Sum Weights            204
Mean                  0.29888145    Sum Observations  60.9718165
Std Deviation         0.03284431    Variance          0.00107875
Skewness              0.24515997    Kurtosis          0.64665644
Uncorrected SS        18.4423311    Corrected SS      0.21898593
Coeff Variation       10.9890745    Std Error Mean    0.00229956

    Stem Leaf                                 #          Boxplot
      42 8                                    1             0
      41
      40
      39
      38
      37 6                                    1             |
      36 449                                  3             |
      35 02344689                             8             |
      34 12223333445668                      14             |
      33 000345888                            9             |
      32 011122233335567899                  18          +-----+
      31 1112333455788999                    16          |     |
      30 0111111122333444455778899           25          |     |
      29 0012222333344466678899999           25          *--+--*
      28 0011233444455566678888888888899     30          |     |
      27 00011333445555667                   17          +-----+
      26 0444555668888                       13             |
      25 333455556679999                     15             |
      24 2346                                 4             |
      23 17                                   2             |
      22 8                                    1             |
      21 3                                    1             |
      20 3                                    1             0
         ----+----+----+----+----+----+
       Multiply Stem.Leaf by 10**-2
```

Output 9.5b Summary of 200 PROC REG Results for the Squared B Weight (Program 9.5)

```
                        The UNIVARIATE Procedure
                           Variable:  B_SQ

                                Moments

N                           204      Sum Weights                  204
Mean                   0.24926106    Sum Observations       50.8492569
Std Deviation          0.03057254    Variance               0.00093468
Skewness              -0.0221854     Kurtosis              -0.0808511
Uncorrected SS          12.86448     Corrected SS           0.18974011
Coeff Variation        12.2652701    Std Error Mean         0.00214051


      Stem Leaf                                 #          Boxplot
        34 2                                    1             0
        33
        32 0                                    1             |
        31 4                                    1             |
        30 45677                                5             |
        29 0224446778889                       13             |
        28 01122334589                         11             |
        27 001222233334455557777889            24          +-----+
        26 0000222244456778888                 19             |
        25 0000111233334555557777799           25          |     |
        24 0000111122233334445566677999        28          *--+--*
        23 0111222333444667777899999           25          +-----+
        22 001122234455667888999               21             |
        21 0024566679                          10             |
        20 0223478                              7             |
        19 0334789                              7             |
        18 299                                  3             |
        17 347                                  3             |
           ----+----+----+----+----+---
         Multiply Stem.Leaf by 10**-2
```

Generating data in which the dependent variable is lagged involves using components of the regression program previously presented (see Program 9.5). The criterion variable is programmatically assembled by adding autoregressive data as the error component to the data for each of the predictor variables, of course both having been modified by the respective Beta weights. The autoregressive process is generated first; then the predictors and criterion variables are generated. When the criterion variable is assembled using the predictor variables, the error component is omitted (unlike Program 9.5). Instead, later in the program, the AR1 process data are added to the incomplete criterion data. Program 9.6 shows how this is accomplished.

Program 9.6 *Macro for Regression Data with AR1 Process in the Criterion Variable*

```
/*****************************************************************************/
/* THIS MACRO GENERATES 200 REPLICATIONS OF DATA COMPRISED OF TWO PREDICTORS AND    */
/* ONE CRITERION VARIABLE.  THE CRITERION VARIABLE HAS A LAG 1 AUTOREGRESSIVE       */
/* PROCESS RUNNING THROUGH IT.  THIS EXAMPLE DIRECTLY BUILDS UPON THE REGRESSION    */
/* PROGRAM PRESENTED IN PROGRAM 9.5.  THE SQUARED BETA WEIGHT FOR PREDICTOR A IS.35;*/
/* FOR PREDICTOR B, '.25. THE AR1 COEFFICIENT IS EITHER .80 OR .20, DEPENDING UPON  */
/* WHICH OF THE SIX CONDITIONS ARE EXAMINED.                                        */
/*                                                                                  */
/*****************************************************************************/
OPTIONS LINESIZE=100 NOSOURCE NOSOURCE2 NONOTES;

LIBNAME AUTOREG 'C:\MY DOCUMENTS\MY SAS FILES\RESULTS';

%MACRO AUTOREG (REPS,N,RES,AR,ERR,BETA1,BETA2,SCENARI);
   %DO J=1 %TO &REPS;

DATA GENERATE&J;

  ARRAY SERIEA SERIEA1-SERIEA&N;

  SERIEA(1)=RANNOR(-1);

    DO J=2 TO &N;

       SERIEA(J)=RANNOR(-11)*SQRT(&RES) + SERIEA(J-1)*SQRT(&AR);   *** ar1 process;

    END; KEEP SERIEA1-SERIEA&N;OUTPUT;

DATA GENERATE&J; SET GENERATE&J;
   PROC TRANSPOSE OUT=GENERATE&J;   *** move the data from horizontal to vertical;

DATA GENERATE&J;SET GENERATE&J;ID=_N_;SERIESA=COL1;OUTPUT;DROP COL1 _NAME_;

DATA GENERATE;

    DO ID=1 TO &N;

       A=RANNOR(-2);          *** predictor a generated to have unit variance;
       B=RANNOR(-3);          *** predictor b generated to have unit variance;

                              *** weighted predictors a and b - no error yet;
       Y=A*SQRT(&BETA1) + B*SQRT(&BETA2);

OUTPUT;
    END;

DATA GENERATE&J;MERGE GENERATE GENERATE&J;BY ID;

Y = Y + SERIESA*SQRT(&ERR);OUTPUT;          *** add the ar1 process to the criterion;

DATA GENERATE&J;SET GENERATE&J;

PROC AUTOREG NOPRINT DATA=GENERATE&J OUTEST=GENERATE&J;  *** produces estimates;
MODEL Y = A B / ALL NLAG=1 LAGDEP DW=1 DWPROB ;
```

```
DATA GENERATE&J;SET GENERATE&J;KEEP A B A_SQ B_SQ _A_1 AR1_SQ;
A_SQ=A**2; B_SQ=B**2; AR1_SQ=_A_1**2;_A_1=ABS(_A_1); OUTPUT; *** obtain square values;

DATA GENERATE&J;SET GENERATE&J;SCENARIO=&SCENARI;OUTPUT;
     KEEP A_SQ B_SQ AR1_SQ _A_1 A B SCENARIO;

   PROC APPEND BASE=AUTOREG.RESULT1 (CNTLLEV=MEMBER);        *** accumulate the results;
   PROC DELETE DATA=GENERATE&J;

  %END;
%MEND AUTOREG;

%AUTOREG (200, 50,.80,.20,.45,.30,.25,1); *** parameters for six different conditions;
%AUTOREG (200,100,.80,.20,.45,.30,.25,2);
%AUTOREG (200,500,.80,.20,.45,.30,.25,3);
%AUTOREG (200, 50,.20,.80,.45,.30,.25,4);
%AUTOREG (200,100,.20,.80,.45,.30,.25,5);
%AUTOREG (200,500,.20,.80,.45,.30,.25,6);

DATA AUTOREG;SET AUTOREG.RESULT1;              *** accessing the output file;

PROC SUMMARY PRINT VARDEF=N MAXDEC=2 FW=8;    *** summarize results for six conditions;
         CLASS SCENARIO;   *** summarizes results;
              VAR  A_SQ B_SQ AR1_SQ _A_1 A B;
                         *****  Scenario 1 (n= 50; Squared AR1 = .20)  *****
                         *****  Scenario 2 (n=100; Squared AR1 = .20)  *****
                         *****  Scenario 3 (n=500; Squared AR1 = .20)  *****
                         *****  Scenario 4 (n= 50; Squared AR1 = .80)  *****
                         *****  Scenario 5 (n=100; Squared AR1 = .80)  *****
                         *****  Scenario 6 (n=500; Squared AR1 = .80)  *****
         QUIT;
```

A review of the output associated with Program 9.6 (shown in Output 9.6) reveals that PROC AUTOREG's ability to estimate the Beta weight parameters was very accurate for all sample sizes considered (50, 100, 500), though it must be noted that the squared Beta weight values were moderately large (.30 and .25, respectively). As would be expected, the standard errors for Beta weights estimated from the smaller samples were much wider than when N=500 (see Output 9.5a).

The results for the estimated lag 1 autoregressive coefficient, on the other hand, were not as invariant to sample size, particularly when the autoregressive parameter was larger (.80). The estimated autoregressive parameter of .80 was, on average, about .11 lower than the parameter value. Conversely, at N=500, the estimate was very accurate. So a tentative review of the results suggests that larger autoregressive coefficients are much more likely to be underestimated in practice when the overall sample size is around 50 or lower. Identifying just how much higher sample size must be for accurate autoregressive estimates under these conditions would require another study that intends to map the estimated parameter space more thoroughly.

Output 9.6 *Summary of 200 PROC AUTOREG Results (Program 9.6)*

```
                    *****  Scenario 1 (n= 50; Squared AR1 = .20)  *****
                    *****  Scenario 2 (n=100; Squared AR1 = .20)  *****
                    *****  Scenario 3 (n=500; Squared AR1 = .20)  *****
                    *****  Scenario 4 (n= 50; Squared AR1 = .80)  *****
                    *****  Scenario 5 (n=100; Squared AR1 = .80)  *****
                    *****  Scenario 6 (n=500; Squared AR1 = .80)  *****

                         The SUMMARY Procedure
```

SCENARIO	N Obs	Variable	N	Mean	Std Dev	Minimum	Maximum
1	200	A_SQ	200	0.30	0.10	0.08	0.63
		B_SQ	200	0.26	0.09	0.06	0.56
		AR1_SQ	200	0.18	0.10	0.00	0.47
		_A_1	200	0.40	0.13	0.07	0.68
		A	200	0.54	0.09	0.28	0.79
		B	200	0.50	0.09	0.25	0.75
2	200	A_SQ	200	0.31	0.06	0.14	0.49
		B_SQ	200	0.25	0.05	0.13	0.43
		AR1_SQ	200	0.19	0.08	0.03	0.44
		_A_1	200	0.43	0.09	0.17	0.66
		A	200	0.55	0.06	0.38	0.70
		B	200	0.50	0.05	0.36	0.66
3	200	A_SQ	200	0.30	0.03	0.23	0.37
		B_SQ	200	0.25	0.03	0.19	0.34
		AR1_SQ	200	0.20	0.03	0.09	0.30
		_A_1	200	0.44	0.04	0.29	0.54
		A	200	0.55	0.02	0.48	0.61
		B	200	0.50	0.03	0.44	0.58
4	200	A_SQ	200	0.30	0.04	0.22	0.42
		B_SQ	200	0.25	0.03	0.16	0.36
		AR1_SQ	200	0.69	0.15	0.15	0.95
		_A_1	200	0.83	0.09	0.38	0.97
		A	200	0.55	0.03	0.47	0.65
		B	200	0.50	0.03	0.40	0.60
5	200	A_SQ	200	0.30	0.03	0.24	0.38
		B_SQ	200	0.25	0.02	0.19	0.35
		AR1_SQ	200	0.75	0.09	0.47	0.92
		_A_1	200	0.86	0.05	0.68	0.96
		A	200	0.55	0.02	0.49	0.61
		B	200	0.50	0.02	0.44	0.59
6	200	A_SQ	200	0.30	0.01	0.27	0.33
		B_SQ	200	0.25	0.01	0.23	0.28
		AR1_SQ	200	0.79	0.03	0.70	0.87
		_A_1	200	0.89	0.02	0.84	0.93
		A	200	0.55	0.01	0.52	0.58
		B	200	0.50	0.01	0.48	0.53

9.6 Example 4: Monte Carlo Study of How Autocorrelation Affects Regression Results

One very common motive for a Monte Carlo study concerns answering the question, "To what extent or under what conditions is it OK to assume that the violation of a statistical assumption is, in all likelihood, inconsequential with respect to accurate parameter estimation?" Some Monte Carlo studies are designed to explore whether modest violations of a statistical assumption make a noteworthy difference with regard to the trust one may place in the accuracy of the statistical results. Although ostensibly lofty at the outset, this motive is often very practical in nature, perhaps centering on an applied problem.

In applied research, data seldom behave well enough to completely satisfy statistical assumptions. Very often assumptions are violated to a modest degree, and without access to the population data, the researcher is only positioned to guess whether the violation is severe enough to make parameter estimation untrustworthy. The conclusions of Monte Carlo simulation studies offer very practical insights regarding just how pronounced a violation may be before threatening the accuracy of parameter estimation.

Consider, for example, the case in which a researcher desires to use multiple linear regression to predict a dependent variable, the data for which was collected over time. When dependent variable scores are collected over time, there is a great chance that the scores will be autocorrelated. This possibility would concern a researcher intending to use ordinary linear regression, because this procedure assumes that dependent variable scores are independent. In fact, statistical procedures exist to forewarn the data analyst whether linear dependence in the serially collected scores is statistically significant.

When dependent variable scores are autocorrelated to a statistically significant extent, the researcher may still ask whether this will truly undermine an interpretation of the regression results. Neter, Wasserman, and Kutner (1989) indicate that when dependent variable scores are autocorrelated, the regression coefficients are still unbiased; however, they are inefficient and no longer have the minimum variance property. The mean square error (MSE) may seriously misrepresent the variance of the error terms. Moreover, the estimated standard error of the regression coefficients may be inaccurate relative to the true standard deviation. This, in turn, diminishes the applicability of confidence intervals and tests using t and F distributions.

Suppose a researcher is concerned about whether estimates are biased by the autocorrelation detected in temporal data. Suppose further that the researcher plans a simulation study in which the autoregressive parameter is systematically varied, while sample size and the Beta coefficients are held constant. The researcher would want to choose a reasonably large sample size (for this analysis, an N of 500 would be suitable) and reasonably large Beta coefficients (say, .30 and .25).

To sufficiently map the parameter space, the researcher would want to vary the size of the autoregressive coefficient widely enough in this study to sufficiently accommodate research situations encountered in practice. Suppose the researcher chose the values ranging from .00 to .75, incrementing by .05 for a total of sixteen values. Starting with a value of .00 is very important because this situation specifies that no autocorrelation exists, a condition by which other results may be compared when judging the impact of the autoregression of the dependent variable scores. A value of .75 is thought to be a pronounced degree of autoregression. More than likely, autocorrelation this severe will make other regression results not interpretable, so no evident need exists to consider any higher value.

Using the Monte Carlo Program 9.6, the researcher would have to modify the program to calculate the mean square error before the correction for autocorrelation and after. The researcher would also want to collect the standard errors for each Beta coefficient since, it too, is directly affected by the violation of the assumption of independent scores. The program modified for this investigation is Program 9.7.

Program 9.7 *Monte Carlo Example of How Autocorrelation Affects Regression Results*

```
/******************************************************************************/
/* This macro generates 200 replications of data comprised of two predictors and   */
/* one criterion variable.  The criterion variable has a lag 1 autoregressive       */
/* process running through it.  This example directly builds upon the regression    */
/* program presented in Program 9.6.  The squared Beta weight for predictor A is.35;*/
/* for predictor B, .25. The AR1 coefficient ranges from .00 to .75, depending upon */
/* which of the sixteen conditions are examined.                                    */
/*                                                                                  */
/******************************************************************************/
OPTIONS LINESIZE=100 NOSOURCE NOSOURCE2 NONOTES;

LIBNAME AUTOREG 'C:\MY DOCUMENTS\MY SAS FILES\RESULTS';

%MACRO AUTOREG (REPS,N,RES,AR,ERR,BETA1,BETA2,SCENARI);
   %DO J=1 %TO &REPS;

DATA GENERATE&J;

  ARRAY SERIEA SERIEA1-SERIEA&N;

  SERIEA(1)=RANNOR(-1);

    DO J=2 TO &N;

       SERIEA(J)=RANNOR(-11)*SQRT(&RES) + SERIEA(J-1)*SQRT(&AR);   *** ar1 process;

    END; KEEP SERIEA1-SERIEA&N; OUTPUT;

DATA GENERATE&J; SET GENERATE&J;
   PROC TRANSPOSE OUT=GENERATE&J;   *** move the data from horizontal to vertical;

DATA GENERATE&J; SET GENERATE&J; ID=_N_; SERIESA=COL1;OUTPUT; DROP COL1 _NAME_;

DATA GENERATE;

   DO ID=1 TO &N;

      A=RANNOR(-2);          *** predictor a generated to have unit variance;
      B=RANNOR(-3);          *** predictor b generated to have unit variance;

                             *** weighted predictors a and b - no error yet;
      Y=A*SQRT(&BETA1) + B*SQRT(&BETA2);

OUTPUT;
   END;

DATA GENERATE&J; MERGE GENERATE GENERATE&J; BY ID;

AAR=A; BAR=B;
Y = Y + SERIESA*SQRT(&ERR); OUTPUT;          *** add the ar1 process to the criterion;

DATA GENERATE&J; SET GENERATE&J;

   *** proc reg outputs the beta coefficients;
```

```
PROC REG DATA=GENERATE&J NOPRINT OUTEST=GENERATE ;
  MODEL Y = A B/OUTSTB OUTSEB;
 RUN;

   *** produces estimates;

PROC AUTOREG DATA=GENERATE&J NOPRINT OUTEST=GENERATE&J COVOUT;
  MODEL Y = AAR BAR / ALL NLAG=1 LAGDEP DW=1 DWPROB;

DATA GENERATEA; SET GENERATE;IF _N_=1; KEEP _RMSE_ A B MSE;
    MSE = _RMSE_**2; OUTPUT;

DATA GENERATEB; SET GENERATE; IF _N_=2; KEEP A B STERR_A STERR_B;
    STERR_A = A; STERR_B = B; OUTPUT;

DATA GENERATEB; SET GENERATEB; DROP A B;
DATA GENERATEA1; SET GENERATE&J; IF _N_=1; KEEP AAR BAR _A_1 _MSE_ AR_MSE;
    AR_MSE = _MSE_;OUTPUT;
DATA GENERATEB1; SET GENERATE&J; IF _N_=3; KEEP _STDERR_ STERRAAR;
    STERRAAR = _STDERR_; OUTPUT;
DATA GENERATEC1; SET GENERATE&J; IF _N_=4; KEEP _STDERR_ STERRBAR;
    STERRBAR = _STDERR_;OUTPUT;

DATA GENERATE&J;
MERGE GENERATEA1 GENERATEB1 GENERATEC1 GENERATEA GENERATEB;
KEEP A B A_SQ B_SQ AAR BAR AAR_SQ BAR_SQ _A_1 AR1_SQ
    MSE STERR_A STERR_B AR_MSE STERRAAR STERRBAR;

A_SQ=A**2; B_SQ=B**2; AAR_SQ=AAR**2; BAR_SQ=BAR**2; AR1_SQ=_A_1**2;
_A_1=ABS(_A_1);

LABEL A_SQ     ='SQUARED BETA 1 WEIGHT WITH PROC REG';
LABEL B_SQ     ='SQUARED BETA 2 WEIGHT WITH PROC REG';
LABEL AAR_SQ   ='CORRECTED SQUARED BETA 1 WEIGHT WITH PROC AUTOREG';
LABEL BAR_SQ   ='CORRECTED SQUARED BETA 2 WEIGHT WITH PROC AUTOREG';
LABEL A        ='BETA WEIGHT 1 WITH PROC REG';
LABEL B        ='BETA WEIGHT 2 WITH PROC REG';
LABEL AAR      ='CORRECTED BETA WEIGHT 1 WITH PROC AUTOREG';
LABEL BAR      ='CORRECTED BETA WEIGHT 2 WITH PROC AUTOREG';
LABEL _A_1     ='AUTOREGRESSION WEIGHT';
LABEL AR1_SQ   ='SQUARED AUTOREGRESSION WEIGHT';
LABEL MSE      ='PROC REG MEAN SQUARE ERROR';
LABEL STERR_A  ='BETA 1 STANDARD ERROR';
LABEL STERR_B  ='BETA 2 STANDARD ERROR';
LABEL AR_MSE   ='PROC AUTOREG MEAN SQUARE ERROR';
LABEL STERRAAR ='CORRECTED BETA 1 STANDARD ERROR';
LABEL STERRBAR ='CORRECTED BETA 2 STANDARD ERROR';

      OUTPUT; *** obtain square values;

PROC DELETE DATA=GENERATEA1;
PROC DELETE DATA=GENERATEB1;
PROC DELETE DATA=GENERATEC1;
PROC DELETE DATA=GENERATEA;
PROC DELETE DATA=GENERATEB;

DATA GENERATE&J; SET GENERATE&J; SCENARIO=&SCENARI; OUTPUT;
      KEEP A    B    STERR_A STERR_B MSE A_SQ  B_SQ
           AAR BAR STERRAAR STERRBAR AR_MSE _A_1 AAR_SQ BAR_SQ AR1_SQ SCENARIO;

   PROC APPEND BASE=AUTOREG.RESULT1 (CNTLLEV=MEMBER);        *** accumulate the results;
   PROC DELETE DATA=GENERATE&J;

   %END;
%MEND AUTOREG;


%AUTOREG (200,500,1.0,.00,.45,.30,.25,01); *** parameters for sixteen conditions;
%AUTOREG (200,500,.95,.05,.45,.30,.25,02);
%AUTOREG (200,500,.90,.10,.45,.30,.25,03);
%AUTOREG (200,500,.85,.15,.45,.30,.25,04);
```

```
%AUTOREG (200,500,.80,.20,.45,.30,.25,05);
%AUTOREG (200,500,.75,.25,.45,.30,.25,06);
%AUTOREG (200,500,.70,.30,.45,.30,.25,07);
%AUTOREG (200,500,.65,.35,.45,.30,.25,08);
%AUTOREG (200,500,.60,.40,.45,.30,.25,09);
%AUTOREG (200,500,.55,.45,.45,.30,.25,10);
%AUTOREG (200,500,.50,.50,.45,.30,.25,11);
%AUTOREG (200,500,.45,.55,.45,.30,.25,12);
%AUTOREG (200,500,.40,.60,.45,.30,.25,13);
%AUTOREG (200,500,.35,.65,.45,.30,.25,14);
%AUTOREG (200,500,.30,.70,.45,.30,.25,15);
%AUTOREG (200,500,.25,.75,.45,.30,.25,16);


DATA AUTOREG; SET AUTOREG.RESULT1;          *** accessing the output file;

PROC SUMMARY PRINT VARDEF=N MAXDEC=3 FW=8;   *** summarize results for six conditions;
       CLASS SCENARIO;   *** summarizes results;
           VAR A   B    STERR_A  STERR_B  MSE       A_SQ   B_SQ
                   AAR BAR STERRAAR STERRBAR AR_MSE _A_1 AAR_SQ BAR_SQ AR1_SQ;
QUIT;
```

A review of the results displayed by the SUMMARY procedure (Output 9.7) reveals that no matter how large the autoregression coefficient, the estimated Beta weights accurately represented the Beta weight parameters used to generate the data, supporting what Neter, Wasserman and Kutner (1989) indicate. This becomes clearer when examining the Squared Beta weights (.30 and .25, respectively), also included in the summary. However, the standard errors for the regression parameters progressed to be nearly twice as large as those estimated by the autoregression procedure (PROC AUTOREG) as the autoregression coefficient increased. The results may be interpreted to suggest that so long as the autoregression parameter is no higher than .20, the standard errors for the Beta weight coefficients may be used, because in Scenario 5, AR1 = .20, and the corrected standard errors are but .025, which may be rounded to .03.

The discrepancy between the MSE for the regression procedure (PROC REG) and the autoregression procedure (PROC AUTOREG) is perhaps a bit wider for Scenario 5: the difference between 0.359 and 0.446. Still, the researcher may consider this discrepancy tolerable enough to yield acceptably accurate estimates. The validity of the logic upon which this cutoff is based is of little consequence. Ultimately, the researcher is responsible for deciding what cutoff is personally meaningful and therefore tenable given the practical problem under study.

Output 9.7 *Summary of Autoregression Simulation Study Results (Program 9.7)*

| | N | | | |
SCENARIO	Obs	Variable	Label	Mean
			The SUMMARY Procedure	
1	200	A	Beta Weight 1 with PROC REG	0.544
		B	Beta Weight 2 with PROC REG	0.503
		StErr_A	Beta 1 Standard Error	0.030
		StErr_B	Beta 2 Standard Error	0.030
		MSE	Proc REG Mean Square Error	0.451
		A_SQ	Squared Beta 1 Weight with PROC REG	0.297
		B_SQ	Squared Beta 2 Weight with PROC REG	0.254
		AAR	Corrected Beta Weight 1 with PROC AUTOREG	0.544
		BAR	Corrected Beta Weight 2 with PROC AUTOREG	0.503
		StErrAAR	Corrected Beta 1 Standard Error	0.030

Output 9.7 *Summary of Autoregression Simulation Study Results (Program 9.7) (continued)*

		StErrBAR	Corrected Beta 2 Standard Error	0.030
		AR_MSE	Proc AUTOREG Mean Square Error	0.451
		_A_1	Autoregression Weight	0.035
		AAR_SQ	Corrected Squared Beta 1 Weight with PROC AUTOREG	0.297
		BAR_SQ	Corrected Squared Beta 2 Weight with PROC AUTOREG	0.254
		AR1_SQ	Squared Autoregression Weight	0.002
2	200	A	Beta Weight 1 with PROC REG	0.544
		B	Beta Weight 2 with PROC REG	0.500
		StErr_A	Beta 1 Standard Error	0.030
		StErr_B	Beta 2 Standard Error	0.030
		MSE	Proc REG Mean Square Error	0.448
		A_SQ	Squared Beta 1 Weight with PROC REG	0.296
		B_SQ	Squared Beta 2 Weight with PROC REG	0.251
		AAR	Corrected Beta Weight 1 with PROC AUTOREG	0.542
		BAR	Corrected Beta Weight 2 with PROC AUTOREG	0.500
		StErrAAR	Corrected Beta 1 Standard Error	0.029
		StErrBAR	Corrected Beta 2 Standard Error	0.029
		AR_MSE	Proc AUTOREG Mean Square Error	0.427
		_A_1	Autoregression Weight	0.218
		AAR_SQ	Corrected Squared Beta 1 Weight with PROC AUTOREG	0.295
		BAR_SQ	Corrected Squared Beta 2 Weight with PROC AUTOREG	0.251
		AR1_SQ	Squared Autoregression Weight	0.049
3	200	A	Beta Weight 1 with PROC REG	0.550
		B	Beta Weight 2 with PROC REG	0.496
		StErr_A	Beta 1 Standard Error	0.030
		StErr_B	Beta 2 Standard Error	0.030
		MSE	Proc REG Mean Square Error	0.450
		A_SQ	Squared Beta 1 Weight with PROC REG	0.304
		B_SQ	Squared Beta 2 Weight with PROC REG	0.247
		AAR	Corrected Beta Weight 1 with PROC AUTOREG	0.549
		BAR	Corrected Beta Weight 2 with PROC AUTOREG	0.494
		StErrAAR	Corrected Beta 1 Standard Error	0.027
		StErrBAR	Corrected Beta 2 Standard Error	0.027
		AR_MSE	Proc AUTOREG Mean Square Error	0.405
		_A_1	Autoregression Weight	0.316
		AAR_SQ	Corrected Squared Beta 1 Weight with PROC AUTOREG	0.302
		BAR_SQ	Corrected Squared Beta 2 Weight with PROC AUTOREG	0.245
		AR1_SQ	Squared Autoregression Weight	0.102
4	200	A	Beta Weight 1 with PROC REG	0.545
		B	Beta Weight 2 with PROC REG	0.500
		StErr_A	Beta 1 Standard Error	0.030
		StErr_B	Beta 2 Standard Error	0.030
		MSE	Proc REG Mean Square Error	0.447
		A_SQ	Squared Beta 1 Weight with PROC REG	0.298
		B_SQ	Squared Beta 2 Weight with PROC REG	0.251
		AAR	Corrected Beta Weight 1 with PROC AUTOREG	0.546
		BAR	Corrected Beta Weight 2 with PROC AUTOREG	0.498
		StErrAAR	Corrected Beta 1 Standard Error	0.026
		StErrBAR	Corrected Beta 2 Standard Error	0.026
		AR_MSE	Proc AUTOREG Mean Square Error	0.382
		_A_1	Autoregression Weight	0.379
		AAR_SQ	Corrected Squared Beta 1 Weight with PROC AUTOREG	0.299
		BAR_SQ	Corrected Squared Beta 2 Weight with PROC AUTOREG	0.249
		AR1_SQ	Squared Autoregression Weight	0.146

Output 9.7 *Summary of Autoregression Simulation Study Results (Program 9.7) (continued)*

5	200	A	Beta Weight 1 with PROC REG	0.549
		B	Beta Weight 2 with PROC REG	0.498
		StErr_A	Beta 1 Standard Error	0.030
		StErr_B	Beta 2 Standard Error	0.030
		MSE	Proc REG Mean Square Error	0.446
		A_SQ	Squared Beta 1 Weight with PROC REG	0.302
		B_SQ	Squared Beta 2 Weight with PROC REG	0.249
		AAR	Corrected Beta Weight 1 with PROC AUTOREG	0.548
		BAR	Corrected Beta Weight 2 with PROC AUTOREG	0.498
		StErrAAR	Corrected Beta 1 Standard Error	0.025
		StErrBAR	Corrected Beta 2 Standard Error	0.025
		AR_MSE	Proc AUTOREG Mean Square Error	0.359
		_A_1	Autoregression Weight	0.440
		AAR_SQ	Corrected Squared Beta 1 Weight with PROC AUTOREG	0.301
		BAR_SQ	Corrected Squared Beta 2 Weight with PROC AUTOREG	0.248
		AR1_SQ	Squared Autoregression Weight	0.195
6	200	A	Beta Weight 1 with PROC REG	0.551
		B	Beta Weight 2 with PROC REG	0.497
		StErr_A	Beta 1 Standard Error	0.033
		StErr_B	Beta 2 Standard Error	0.030
		MSE	Proc REG Mean Square Error	0.451
		A_SQ	Squared Beta 1 Weight with PROC REG	0.309
		B_SQ	Squared Beta 2 Weight with PROC REG	0.251
		AAR	Corrected Beta Weight 1 with PROC AUTOREG	0.551
		BAR	Corrected Beta Weight 2 with PROC AUTOREG	0.497
		StErrAAR	Corrected Beta 1 Standard Error	0.023
		StErrBAR	Corrected Beta 2 Standard Error	0.023
		AR_MSE	Proc AUTOREG Mean Square Error	0.339
		_A_1	Autoregression Weight	0.497
		AAR_SQ	Corrected Squared Beta 1 Weight with PROC AUTOREG	0.308
		BAR_SQ	Corrected Squared Beta 2 Weight with PROC AUTOREG	0.250
		AR1_SQ	Squared Autoregression Weight	0.248
7	200	A	Beta Weight 1 with PROC REG	0.546
		B	Beta Weight 2 with PROC REG	0.503
		StErr_A	Beta 1 Standard Error	0.030
		StErr_B	Beta 2 Standard Error	0.030
		MSE	Proc REG Mean Square Error	0.451
		A_SQ	Squared Beta 1 Weight with PROC REG	0.299
		B_SQ	Squared Beta 2 Weight with PROC REG	0.254
		AAR	Corrected Beta Weight 1 with PROC AUTOREG	0.547
		BAR	Corrected Beta Weight 2 with PROC AUTOREG	0.500
		StErrAAR	Corrected Beta 1 Standard Error	0.022
		StErrBAR	Corrected Beta 2 Standard Error	0.022
		AR_MSE	Proc AUTOREG Mean Square Error	0.316
		_A_1	Autoregression Weight	0.546
		AAR_SQ	Corrected Squared Beta 1 Weight with PROC AUTOREG	0.299
		BAR_SQ	Corrected Squared Beta 2 Weight with PROC AUTOREG	0.251
		AR1_SQ	Squared Autoregression Weight	0.300
8	200	A	Beta Weight 1 with PROC REG	0.544
		B	Beta Weight 2 with PROC REG	0.498
		StErr_A	Beta 1 Standard Error	0.030

Output 9.7 *Summary of Autoregression Simulation Study Results (Program 9.7) (continued)*

		StErr_B	Beta 2 Standard Error	0.030
		MSE	Proc REG Mean Square Error	0.449
		A_SQ	Squared Beta 1 Weight with PROC REG	0.296
		B_SQ	Squared Beta 2 Weight with PROC REG	0.249
		AAR	Corrected Beta Weight 1 with PROC AUTOREG	0.545
		BAR	Corrected Beta Weight 2 with PROC AUTOREG	0.500
		StErrAAR	Corrected Beta 1 Standard Error	0.021
		StErrBAR	Corrected Beta 2 Standard Error	0.021
		AR_MSE	Proc AUTOREG Mean Square Error	0.292
		_A_1	Autoregression Weight	0.590
		AAR_SQ	Corrected Squared Beta 1 Weight with PROC AUTOREG	0.297
		BAR_SQ	Corrected Squared Beta 2 Weight with PROC AUTOREG	0.250
		AR1_SQ	Squared Autoregression Weight	0.349
9	200	A	Beta Weight 1 with PROC REG	0.549
		B	Beta Weight 2 with PROC REG	0.499
		StErr_A	Beta 1 Standard Error	0.030
		StErr_B	Beta 2 Standard Error	0.030
		MSE	Proc REG Mean Square Error	0.447
		A_SQ	Squared Beta 1 Weight with PROC REG	0.302
		B_SQ	Squared Beta 2 Weight with PROC REG	0.250
		AAR	Corrected Beta Weight 1 with PROC AUTOREG	0.547
		BAR	Corrected Beta Weight 2 with PROC AUTOREG	0.500
		StErrAAR	Corrected Beta 1 Standard Error	0.020
		StErrBAR	Corrected Beta 2 Standard Error	0.020
		AR_MSE	Proc AUTOREG Mean Square Error	0.269
		_A_1	Autoregression Weight	0.629
		AAR_SQ	Corrected Squared Beta 1 Weight with PROC AUTOREG	0.300
		BAR_SQ	Corrected Squared Beta 2 Weight with PROC AUTOREG	0.251
		AR1_SQ	Squared Autoregression Weight	0.397
10	200	A	Beta Weight 1 with PROC REG	0.545
		B	Beta Weight 2 with PROC REG	0.501
		StErr_A	Beta 1 Standard Error	0.030
		StErr_B	Beta 2 Standard Error	0.030
		MSE	Proc REG Mean Square Error	0.446
		A_SQ	Squared Beta 1 Weight with PROC REG	0.298
		B_SQ	Squared Beta 2 Weight with PROC REG	0.252
		AAR	Corrected Beta Weight 1 with PROC AUTOREG	0.546
		BAR	Corrected Beta Weight 2 with PROC AUTOREG	0.500
		StErrAAR	Corrected Beta 1 Standard Error	0.019
		StErrBAR	Corrected Beta 2 Standard Error	0.019
		AR_MSE	Proc AUTOREG Mean Square Error	0.247
		_A_1	Autoregression Weight	0.666
		AAR_SQ	Corrected Squared Beta 1 Weight with PROC AUTOREG	0.299
		BAR_SQ	Corrected Squared Beta 2 Weight with PROC AUTOREG	0.250
		AR1_SQ	Squared Autoregression Weight	0.445
11	200	A	Beta Weight 1 with PROC REG	0.544
		B	Beta Weight 2 with PROC REG	0.501
		StErr_A	Beta 1 Standard Error	0.030
		StErr_B	Beta 2 Standard Error	0.030
		MSE	Proc REG Mean Square Error	0.449

Output 9.7 *Summary of Autoregression Simulation Study Results (Program 9.7) (continued)*

```
            A_SQ        Squared Beta 1 Weight with PROC REG                    0.297
            B_SQ        Squared Beta 2 Weight with PROC REG                    0.252
            AAR         Corrected Beta Weight 1 with PROC AUTOREG              0.546
            BAR         Corrected Beta Weight 2 with PROC AUTOREG              0.500
            StErrAAR    Corrected Beta 1 Standard Error                       0.017
            StErrBAR    Corrected Beta 2 Standard Error                       0.017
            AR_MSE      Proc AUTOREG Mean Square Error                        0.226
            _A_1        Autoregression Weight                                 0.703
            AAR_SQ      Corrected Squared Beta 1 Weight with PROC AUTOREG     0.298
            BAR_SQ      Corrected Squared Beta 2 Weight with PROC AUTOREG     0.251
            AR1_SQ      Squared Autoregression Weight                         0.496

  12  200   A           Beta Weight 1 with PROC REG                           0.547
            B           Beta Weight 2 with PROC REG                           0.499
            StErr_A     Beta 1 Standard Error                                 0.030
            StErr_B     Beta 2 Standard Error                                 0.030
            MSE         Proc REG Mean Square Error                            0.441
            A_SQ        Squared Beta 1 Weight with PROC REG                   0.300
            B_SQ        Squared Beta 2 Weight with PROC REG                   0.250
            AAR         Corrected Beta Weight 1 with PROC AUTOREG             0.547
            BAR         Corrected Beta Weight 2 with PROC AUTOREG             0.500
            StErrAAR    Corrected Beta 1 Standard Error                       0.016
            StErrBAR    Corrected Beta 2 Standard Error                       0.016
            AR_MSE      Proc AUTOREG Mean Square Error                        0.202
            _A_1        Autoregression Weight                                 0.734
            AAR_SQ      Corrected Squared Beta 1 Weight with PROC AUTOREG     0.299
            BAR_SQ      Corrected Squared Beta 2 Weight with PROC AUTOREG     0.250
            AR1_SQ      Squared Autoregression Weight                         0.540

  13  200   A           Beta Weight 1 with PROC REG                           0.548
            B           Beta Weight 2 with PROC REG                           0.502
            StErr_A     Beta 1 Standard Error                                 0.030
            StErr_B     Beta 2 Standard Error                                 0.030
            MSE         Proc REG Mean Square Error                            0.444
            A_SQ        Squared Beta 1 Weight with PROC REG                   0.301
            B_SQ        Squared Beta 2 Weight with PROC REG                   0.253
            AAR         Corrected Beta Weight 1 with PROC AUTOREG             0.550
            BAR         Corrected Beta Weight 2 with PROC AUTOREG             0.501
            StErrAAR    Corrected Beta 1 Standard Error                       0.015
            StErrBAR    Corrected Beta 2 Standard Error                       0.015
            AR_MSE      Proc AUTOREG Mean Square Error                        0.181
            _A_1        Autoregression Weight                                 0.767
            AAR_SQ      Corrected Squared Beta 1 Weight with PROC AUTOREG     0.302
            BAR_SQ      Corrected Squared Beta 2 Weight with PROC AUTOREG     0.251
            AR1_SQ      Squared Autoregression Weight                         0.588

  14  200   A           Beta Weight 1 with PROC REG                           0.548
            B           Beta Weight 2 with PROC REG                           0.499
            StErr_A     Beta 1 Standard Error                                 0.030
            StErr_B     Beta 2 Standard Error                                 0.030
            MSE         Proc REG Mean Square Error                            0.442
            A_SQ        Squared Beta 1 Weight with PROC REG                   0.301
            B_SQ        Squared Beta 2 Weight with PROC REG                   0.250
```

Output 9.7 *Summary of Autoregression Simulation Study Results (Program 9.7) (continued)*

```
              AAR       Corrected Beta Weight 1 with PROC AUTOREG          0.547
              BAR       Corrected Beta Weight 2 with PROC AUTOREG          0.499
              StErrAAR  Corrected Beta 1 Standard Error                    0.014
              StErrBAR  Corrected Beta 2 Standard Error                    0.014
              AR_MSE    Proc AUTOREG Mean Square Error                     0.157
              _A_1      Autoregression Weight                              0.801
              AAR_SQ    Corrected Squared Beta 1 Weight with PROC AUTOREG  0.300
              BAR_SQ    Corrected Squared Beta 2 Weight with PROC AUTOREG  0.249
              AR1_SQ    Squared Autoregression Weight                      0.642

     15  200  A         Beta Weight 1 with PROC REG                        0.543
              B         Beta Weight 2 with PROC REG                        0.501
              StErr_A   Beta 1 Standard Error                              0.030
              StErr_B   Beta 2 Standard Error                              0.030
              MSE       Proc REG Mean Square Error                         0.442
              A_SQ      Squared Beta 1 Weight with PROC REG                0.296
              B_SQ      Squared Beta 2 Weight with PROC REG                0.252
              AAR       Corrected Beta Weight 1 with PROC AUTOREG          0.546
              BAR       Corrected Beta Weight 2 with PROC AUTOREG          0.500
              StErrAAR  Corrected Beta 1 Standard Error                    0.013
              StErrBAR  Corrected Beta 2 Standard Error                    0.013
              AR_MSE    Proc AUTOREG Mean Square Error                     0.135
              _A_1      Autoregression Weight                              0.831
              AAR_SQ    Corrected Squared Beta 1 Weight with PROC AUTOREG  0.298
              BAR_SQ    Corrected Squared Beta 2 Weight with PROC AUTOREG  0.250
              AR1_SQ    Squared Autoregression Weight                      0.691

     16  200  A         Beta Weight 1 with PROC REG                        0.547
              B         Beta Weight 2 with PROC REG                        0.497
              StErr_A   Beta 1 Standard Error                              0.029
              StErr_B   Beta 2 Standard Error                              0.029
              MSE       Proc REG Mean Square Error                         0.433
              A_SQ      Squared Beta 1 Weight with PROC REG                0.300
              B_SQ      Squared Beta 2 Weight with PROC REG                0.248
              AAR       Corrected Beta Weight 1 with PROC AUTOREG          0.547
              BAR       Corrected Beta Weight 2 with PROC AUTOREG          0.499
              StErrAAR  Corrected Beta 1 Standard Error                    0.011
              StErrBAR  Corrected Beta 2 Standard Error                    0.011
              AR_MSE    Proc AUTOREG Mean Square Error                     0.112
              _A_1      Autoregression Weight                              0.859
              AAR_SQ    Corrected Squared Beta 1 Weight with PROC AUTOREG  0.299
              BAR_SQ    Corrected Squared Beta 2 Weight with PROC AUTOREG  0.249
              AR1_SQ    Squared Autoregression Weight                      0.738
--------------------------------------------------------------------------------
```

9.7 Summary

In this chapter, the Monte Carlo simulation of time series data was considered, using SAS/ETS procedures and generating functions. To demonstrate how SAS may be used to investigate theoretical issues concerning time series statistical procedures, attention in this chapter was focused on univariate and multivariate time series problems, followed by modeling time series processes in the context of regression. These particular time series problems were discussed because they are three of the more common types of procedures used in practice. A mini-simulation study was finally presented to give researchers a sense of just how such a study would be implemented. The prevalent use of time series procedures in some disciplines (e.g., economics and business) is well known, but the application of these procedures could very well be extended to many other disciplines in which they are currently not as popular. It is our hope that these examples will provide some foundation and guidance for researchers interested in conducting Monte Carlo studies involving time series and SAS/ETS procedures.

9.8 References

Akaike, H. 1976. "Canonical Correlations Analysis of Time Series and the Use of an Information Criterion." In *Advances and Case Studies in System Identification*, ed. R. Mehra and D. Lainiotis, 27-96. New York: Academic Press.

Box, G. E. P., and G. M. Jenkins. 1976. *Time Series Analysis: Forecasting and Control.* Oakland, CA: Holden-Day.

Harvey, A. C. 1981. *The Econometric Analysis of Time Series.* New York: Halsted Press.

Moryson, M. 1998. *Testing for Random Walk Coefficients in Regression and State Space Models.* New York: Physica-Verlag.

Neter, J., W. Wasserman, and M. H. Kutner. 1989. *Applied Linear Regression Models.* 2d ed. Burr Ridge, IL: Irwin.

Index

Call your local SAS office to order these books from Books by Users Press

Advanced Log-Linear Models Using SAS®
by **Daniel Zelterman** ....Order No. A57496

Annotate: Simply the Basics
by **Art Carpenter** ....Order No. A57320

Applied Multivariate Statistics with SAS® Software,
Second Edition
by **Ravindra Khattree**
and **Dayanand N. Naik**.............................Order No. A56903

Applied Statistics and the SAS® Programming Language,
Fourth Edition
by **Ronald P. Cody**
and **Jeffrey K. Smith**................................Order No. A55984

An Array of Challenges — Test Your SAS® Skills
by **Robert Virgile**......................................Order No. A55625

Basic Statistics Using SAS®: Student Guide and Exercises
(books in the set also sold seperateley)
by **Larry Hatcher**......................................Order No. A57541

Beyond the Obvious with SAS® Screen Control Language
by **Don Stanley** ....Order No. A55073

Carpenter's Complete Guide to the SAS® Macro Language
by **Art Carpenter** ....Order No. A56100

The Cartoon Guide to Statistics
by **Larry Gonick**
and **Woollcott Smith**................................Order No. A55153

Categorical Data Analysis Using the SAS® System,
Second Edition
by **Maura E. Stokes, Charles S. Davis,**
and **Gary G. Koch** ....Order No. A57998

Client/Server Survival Guide, Third Edition
by **Robert Orfali, Dan Harkey,**
and **Jeri Edwards**......................................Order No. A58099

Cody's Data Cleaning Techniques Using SAS® Software
by **Ron Cody**...Order No. A57198

Common Statistical Methods for Clinical Research with
SAS® Examples, Second Edition
by **Glenn A. Walker**...................................Order No. A58086

Concepts and Case Studies in Data Management
by **William S. Calvert**
and **J. Meimei Ma**......................................Order No. A55220

Debugging SAS® Programs: A Handbook of Tools
and Techniques
by **Michele M. Burlew** ....Order No. A57743

Efficiency: Improving the Performance of Your SAS®
Applications
by **Robert Virgile**......................................Order No. A55960

A Handbook of Statistical Analyses Using SAS®,
Second Edition
by **B.S. Everitt**
and **G. Der** ....Order No. A58679

Health Care Data and the SAS® System
by **Marge Scerbo, Craig Dickstein,**
and **Alan Wilson** ....Order No. A57638

The How-To Book for SAS/GRAPH® Software
by **Thomas Miron** ....Order No. A55203

In the Know ... SAS® Tips and Techniques From
Around the Globe
by **Phil Mason** ....Order No. A55513

Integrating Results through Meta-Analytic Review Using
SAS® Software
by **Morgan C. Wang**
and **Brad J. Bushman** ....Order No. A55810

Learning SAS® in the Computer Lab, Second Edition
by **Rebecca J. Elliott** ....Order No. A57739

The Little SAS® Book: A Primer
by **Lora D. Delwiche**
and **Susan J. Slaughter** ....Order No. A55200

The Little SAS® Book: A Primer, Second Edition
by **Lora D. Delwiche**
and **Susan J. Slaughter** ....Order No. A56649
(updated to include Version 7 features)

Logistic Regression Using the SAS® System:
Theory and Application
by **Paul D. Allison** ....Order No. A55770

Longitudinal Data and SAS®: A Programmer's Guide
by **Ron Cody** ....Order No. A58176

Maps Made Easy Using SAS®
by **Mike Zdeb** ....Order No. A57495

Models for Discrete Data
by **Daniel Zelterman** ....Order No. A57521

Multiple Comparisons and Multiple Tests Text and
Workbook Set
(books in this set also sold separately)
by **Peter H. Westfall, Randall D. Tobias,**
Dror Rom, Russell D. Wolfinger,
and **Yosef Hochberg** ....Order No. A58274

www.sas.com/pubs

www.sas.com/pubs

www.sas.com/pubs

*Welcome * Bienvenue * Willkommen * Yohkoso * Bienvenido*

SAS Publishing Is Easy to Reach

Visit our Web site located at www.sas.com/pubs

You will find product and service details, including

- **companion Web sites**
- **sample chapters**
- **tables of contents**
- **author biographies**
- **book reviews**

Learn about

- **regional user-group conferences**
- **trade-show sites and dates**
- **authoring opportunities**
- **e-books**

Explore all the services that SAS Publishing has to offer!

Your Listserv Subscription Automatically Brings the News to You

Do you want to be among the first to learn about the latest books and services available from SAS Publishing? Subscribe to our listserv **newdocnews-l** and, once each month, you will automatically receive a description of the newest books and which environments or operating systems and SAS® release(s) each book addresses.

To subscribe,

1. Send an e-mail message to **listserv@vm.sas.com**.

2. Leave the "Subject" line blank.

3. Use the following text for your message:

   subscribe NEWDOCNEWS-L *your-first-name your-last-name*

   For example: subscribe NEWDOCNEWS-L John Doe

You're Invited to Publish with SAS Institute's Books by Users Press

If you enjoy writing about SAS software and how to use it, the Books by Users program at SAS Institute offers a variety of publishing options. We are actively recruiting authors to publish books and sample code.

If you find the idea of writing a book by yourself a little intimidating, consider writing with a co-author. Keep in mind that you will receive complete editorial and publishing support, access to our users, technical advice and assistance, and competitive royalties. Please ask us for an author packet at **sasbbu@sas.com** or call 919-531-7447. See the Books by Users Web page at **www.sas.com/bbu** for complete information.

Book Discount Offered at SAS Public Training Courses!

When you attend one of our SAS Public Training Courses at any of our regional Training Centers in the United States, you will receive a 20% discount on book orders that you place during the course. Take advantage of this offer at the next course you attend!

SAS Institute Inc.
SAS Campus Drive
Cary, NC 27513-2414
Fax 919-677-4444

E-mail: sasbook@sas.com
Web page: www.sas.com/pubs
To order books, call SAS Publishing Sales at 800-727-3228*
For other SAS business, call 919-677-8000*

* Note: Customers outside the United States should contact their local SAS office.